ENERGY SECURITY TO 2000

Papers in this series are as follows:

Energy Paper No 8: *International Gas Trade in Europe*, Jonathan P. Stern

Energy Paper No 9: *Coal's Contribution to UK Self -Sufficiency*, Louis Turner

Energy Paper No 12: *Oil's Contribution to UK Self -Sufficiency*, Colin Robinson and Eileen Marshall

Energy Paper No 13: *Conservation's Contribution to UK Self-Sufficiency*, Mayer Hillman

Energy Paper No 14: *The Economics of Energy Self-Sufficiency*, Eileen Marshall and Colin Robinson

Energy Paper No 15: *Natural Gas Trade in North America and Asia*, Jonathan P. Stern

Energy Paper No 16: *Energy Management: Can We Learn From Others?* George F. Ray

Energy Paper No 17: *European Interests and Gulf Oil*, Valerie Yorke and Louis Turner

Energy Paper No 18: *Natural Gas in the UK: Options to 2000*, Jonathan P. Stern

Energy Paper No 19: *Petroleum and Mining Taxation: Handbook on a Method for Equitable Sharing of Profits and Risk*, Christopher Goss

Energy Paper No 20: *Electricity Supply in the UK*, Richard Eden and Nigel Evans

Energy Paper No 21: *Soviet Oil and Gas Exports to the West*, Jonathan P. Stern

Energy Paper No 22: *Acid Deposition and Vehicle Emissions: European Environmental Pressures on Britain*, Peter Brackley

The editor for the series is Margaret Cornell.

ENERGY SECURITY TO 2000

Edited by

Robert Belgrave
Charles K. Ebinger and
Hideaki Okino

Routledge
Taylor & Francis Group
LONDON AND NEW YORK

First published 1987 by Westview Press, Inc.

Published 2018 by Routledge
52 Vanderbilt Avenue, New York, NY 10017
2 Park Square, Milton Park, Abingdon, Oxon OX14 4RN

Routledge is an imprint of the Taylor & Francis Group, an informa business

ISBN 13: 978-0-367-00566-5 (hbk)
ISBN 13: 978-0-367-15553-7 (pbk)

Contents

Tables and Figures

Table

Figure

Preface

This report is the product of a research project carried out during 1986 jointly by the National Institute for Research Advancement, Tokyo; the Centre for Strategic and International Studies, Washington; and the Royal Institute of International Affairs, London. The views expressed are those of the authors, and not necessarily those of any of the institutions mentioned above, or of the numerous officials and experts whose advice has been sought.

The study concentrates on three main issues, and considers the implications for energy decisions within the OECD group of countries, and the options open to their governments. These issues are:

i. the consequences of the Chernobyl nuclear power station accident in April 1986,
ii. the effect of low and fluctuating oil prices and
iii. the continuing instability of the Middle East region.

The effect of Chernobyl has varied widely from country to country. No OECD government has decided to halt the development of nuclear energy as a direct result of the accident, although some opposition parties have said they would do so. The main effect is likely to be increased costs and lead times in most countries where development continues, and greater difficulty in gaining approval for new stations in countries where new nuclear development had already halted for other reasons, for example in the United States.

The effect of low oil prices (below $15 a barrel) and uncertainty about future prices will be to reduce investment in energy sources and in conservation within the OECD area, unless governments take steps individually, or preferably collectively, to counter this, by fiscal incentives, guaranteed prices or tariff barriers. The various mechanisms to achieve this are examined.

The combined consequence of Chernobyl and of low prices will be to increase the share of oil in energy demand, and to increase the share of Middle East oil in OECD imports, particularly the share of the Gulf because that is where the low-cost, high-volume reserves are. The sources of tension in that area are reviewed and the scope for improving relations is discussed.

The probability remains of periodic crises in energy, especially oil supplies. International crisis management mechanisms, including arrangements for holding and releasing emergency stocks, need to be kept in good repair. The world has to learn to live with uncertainty in energy matters, but governments can act to reduce that uncertainty and consequent vulnerability.

This report begins with a general statement agreed by all participants, about the problems of energy security as seen from the OECD point of view. This is followed by more detailed studies by each institute of the situation in its own region.

The authors wish to thank their colleagues in the sponsoring organisations both for their contribution to the substance of the report and for the administrative effort involved in a tripartite research effort. They also wish to thank all those who have attended study groups and conferences in London, Washington and Tokyo or who have given their views in other ways. The authors alone are responsible for any remaining errors or inconsistencies.

R. Belgrave
C. Ebinger
H. Okino

April 1987

1 Introduction

There are those who say that concern over security of energy supplies was an aberration of the 1970s, and that in the 1980s the market has been allowed to work, simultaneously correcting excessive consumption and bringing forth additional supply. One good result, they add, is that the power of the oil cartel, OPEC[1], to hold the West to economic and even political ransom has been destroyed, as that organisation's continuing difficulties in propping up a declining oil price have demonstrated. The market has worked - and will continue to do so, provided governments do not interfere.

Others hold a different view. They observe that even those governments that believe most strongly in the doctrine of market forces do in practice interfere in the energy market - constantly through fiscal and regulatory agencies, and intermittently in response to domestic or foreign political pressures. Moreover, just as an absence of war for a decade does not absolve a government from responsibility for military defence, so a period of plentiful supply and low prices does not absolve a government from a duty to ensure energy supplies at reasonable cost in the future. For uninterrupted supply of energy at reasonably stable prices constitutes the jugular vein of the world economy and ultimately of the political and military security of the West.

A definition of security

Energy security is a state in which consumers and their governments believe, and have reason to believe, that there are adequate reserves and production and distribution facilities available to meet their requirements in the foreseeable future, from sources at home or abroad, at costs which do not put them at a competitive disadvantage or otherwise threaten their well-being. Insecurity arises when the welfare of citizens or the ability of governments to pursue their other normal objectives is threatened, either as a result of physical failure of supplies or as a result of sudden and major price changes.

If, in 1986: (i) the price of oil had stabilised at around $20 a barrel, instead of fluctuating in the market between $8.00 and $19.00, (ii) the Middle East had shown any signs of moving into a period of internal stability, and (iii) the Chernobyl disaster had not happened, then it would have been tempting to argue that there was no pressing need in 1987 to review the issues of energy security for the rest of the century.

Even in 1984, however, it was possible to discern sources of instability in the apparent equilibrium of the energy system. Over-supply would lead to collapsing prices. A decline in prices would lead to increasing demand and at the same time concern about price volatility would lead to under-investment in the high-cost OECD[2] sources. Costs of development were being further increased by environmental and regulatory concerns. A return to increased reliance on the unstable Gulf region as the oil supplier of last resort would inevitably follow, but the willingness or ability of the countries of the Gulf to meet demand at reasonable price would remain in doubt.

These were the considerations that led research institutes from the US, Japan and Europe to agree in 1985 to undertake this study. The events of 1986 underline its validity. They serve to focus the attention of those concerned and to ensure a degree of official and public interest that might not otherwise have been obtained.

This study therefore addresses three main sources of insecurity: a) unstable oil prices averaging below $15 a barrel[3]; b) increased dependence on an unstable Middle East; c) the problems of developing nuclear energy in the aftermath of the Chernobyl accident.

The study seeks to analyse their implications into the 1990s and to suggest the options open to governmental and industrial decision makers in the short term, that could improve energy security in the medium term. The study considers possible future stresses on the system, without attempting to predict the precise events that may trigger the effect of those stresses. It considers also the nature and cost of insurance policies against disaster, and the consequences of having no insurance.

Each of the three regional groups has produced its own analysis of the three main issues, as seen from its own region, and of certain other issues of particular importance to it. This introductory essay is an attempt to pull together the views of the three participating groups and to set them in the context of the OECD countries as a whole. However, the opinions expressed here do not necessarily represent the views of the institutes which undertook the study, still less the various governments and inter-governmental organisations whose activities are discussed.

Oil prices

The apparent equilibrium of 1984

In 1984 and into the first half of 1985 it was widely believed that the world's energy system had settled down after the shocks of the 1970s, and that in a sense the 'market' had worked in correcting over-demand and under-supply through high prices. In the short term this was true, although at a cost, borne by the poorest individuals and nations, of economic recession and unemployment.

Be that as it may, oil supplies were plentiful; prices had come down from over $39 a barrel in 1980 to around $28 in 1985. (The excessive value of the dollar to some extent offset this for non-American buyers; it was not until mid-1985 that the latter began to enjoy a price fall in their own currencies.) OECD oil consumption had declined from 40 million barrels per day (mbd) in 1978 to 34 mbd in 1984.

The fact remained that the objective of the OECD to reduce oil's share in total energy, and dependence on oil imports from the Middle East, had to a large extent been achieved. It was a matter for debate whether this marked the success of the positive policies laid down by successive summit meetings and International Energy Agency [4] and European Community [5] resolutions, or was simply the market reaction to the 1979/80 price rise. OECD dependence on OPEC oil had declined from 25% of Total Primary Energy Requirements (TPER) in 1973 to 13% in 1984. US imports, which (at 6.3 mbd in 1973) had first tempted the Arab states to use the 'oil weapon' (and had subsequently gone up to 8 mbd), had declined to under 5.1 mbd in 1985. Japanese imports declined from 5.6 mbd to 4.6 mbd. Within Europe combined Norwegian and UK oil production had risen to 3.3 mbd in 1984, thus making them both net oil exporters. At any expectation of price above $20 a barrel, existing and future North Sea developments looked profitable to oil companies and also looked likely to provide their governments with a handsome 'rent'.

Encouraged by these prices, and by the widespread belief that they were likely to double in real terms by the year 2000, the development and use of fuels other than oil was accelerating in the OECD countries. Coal requirements grew from 13.2 million barrels per day of oil equivalent (mbdoe) in 1973 to 16 mbdoe in 1984, thereby increasing coal's share of TPER from 18.6% to 21.6%. Gas requirements only grew from 14 mbdoe in 1973 to 14.3 mbdoe in 1984, its share of TPER in fact declining from 19.7% to 19.2%. However, the profile of gas demand was changing radically in the three main OECD areas; within North America, demand fell from 11.3 mbdoe (29% of TPER) in 1973 to 9.6 mbdoe (23.6%) in 1984, the comparable figure for OECD Europe being an increase from 2.5 mbdoe (10.3%) to 3.8 mbdoe (15.5%) and for OECD Pacific an increase, mainly in Japan, from 0.18 mbdoe (2.2%) to 0.9 mbdoe (10%). The percentage of electricity generated by nuclear power in the OECD area rose from 4.4% in 1973 to 17.9% in 1984 and was planned to rise to over 25% by 2000. The share of oil in electricity generation in the same period fell from 25.1% to 10.5%.

Ambitious plans for further development of OECD resources were accompanied by steady progress in energy conservation. In the 1970s, it was observed that a 1% increase in GDP required a 1% increase in energy consumption, and it was assumed that this was an absolute relationship. By the 1980s, belief in this conventional link had been undermined. The relationship in the OECD as a whole had declined to 0.56% of energy increase to 1% of GDP increase by 1985 and the two indices were thought to have been 'decoupled'. However, this decoupling may have resulted from structural changes in the economy. The initial drive for this development came from conservation in the sense of avoiding waste, but, with continuing expectations of high prices, investment in plant, control systems and research increased. Energy companies and governments were coming to the view that within OECD there might be little or no further increase in energy demand even if substantial economic growth was resumed.

On the supply side, oil production within OECD had risen from 13.3 mbd in 1974 to 16.5 mbd in 1984. The Soviet Union and China were seen as future net exporters of oil, if in small amounts. The only question mark seemed to hang over the developing countries, where increasing industrialisation and rapid population growth seemed to indicate an increase in energy demand limited only by ability to pay. Yet even in these countries, the high costs of oil imports had in many cases brought forth discoveries on a locally significant scale, while a few such as Mexico and Egypt had become net exporters, giving a total increase in supply as important as the savings made in the industrialised countries. In addition, the Soviet Union and Algeria were seen as important suppliers of gas to Europe, while sources of coal imports were being developed in a number of countries both within and outside the OECD.

These improvements in the OECD energy scene, once achieved, seemed unlikely to be reversed, whilst the existence of spare capacity especially of oil seemed to make any sudden increase in prices equally unlikely. Well into 1985, it was possible to view the repeated failure of OPEC to halt the downward slide of oil prices, either by limiting their own production or by persuading the UK and other non-OPEC producers to do likewise, as further proof that the problem of energy security had gone away, and that plentiful supplies of energy at stable or only gently rising prices were assured well into the next century.

The events of 1986

In contrast, by December 1986, it required heroic faith in the power of the market to work for the best of all possible worlds, or remarkable blindness to recent events, to believe that energy security, for the rest of the century, can be left to take care of itself - either for individual countries, however well endowed, or for the OECD as a whole. Fears of unstable or low prices will mean that purely commercial decisions will not maintain the present proportion of indigenous OECD energy production. Low oil prices will further reduce incentives for investment in end-use efficiency and high-cost energy sources. In a low oil price scenario dependence on oil from the Middle East will increase faster, while the internal stability of the region will continue to deteriorate.

A major reason for reduced OECD dependence on imported oil in recent years has been the switch to coal (5 mbdoe) and nuclear power (4 mbdoe) in electricity generation. For a variety of reasons, the share of electricity generated by natural gas fell in most OECD countries, exceptions being Japan and certain areas of the United States where environmental concern dictated the opposite trend. While the nuclear contribution to total OECD energy supply will continue to grow, as plants currently under construction come into operation, the Chernobyl accident has renewed the debate over the future role that nuclear power will play in reducing demand for oil.

Likewise, while almost all OECD energy forecasts continue to predict major increases in coal use, low oil prices, combined with environmental uncertainties concerning acid deposition and the 'greenhouse effect', and political problems in some producing nations, could curtail coal use, thus increasing demand for oil. IEA figures suggest that, despite the steady progress of energy conservation, and the introduction of certain technical efficiencies in recent years, low prices in 1985/86 have led to some increase in energy demand.

The collapse of the oil price

Throughout 1979 and 1980 the 'official government selling price' of the so-called 'marker' crude (Saudi light), as decreed by OPEC, followed the price panic triggered by the Iranian Revolution, up from $12.50 a barrel to a peak of $34 a barrel in February 1981. Spot prices led this rise, and peaked at $41 a barrel in November 1979 and again in November 1980. The second peak was provoked by the outbreak of the Iran-Iraq war, but it was significant that this war, which removed as much oil from the market as the Iranian Revolution had done, did not lead to a corresponding panic amongst OECD buyers (whether governmental or private) and the price effect was short-lived. This was due partly to the effective response by the International Energy Agency, and partly (though not appreciated at the time) to the fact that stocks had been run up in 1979, but $30 oil, and the recession that went with it, had also sharply reduced demand. From 1981 onwards the nature of the market began to change. Buyers, in all areas, increased the proportion of spot and short-term deals in their supply pattern, as distinct from long-term contracts at official OPEC prices.

Exporters competed for market share by barter deals, by discounts on products, by 'netback' formulas, and in some cases by integration downstream into refining and marketing. Official OPEC prices inevitably followed the market downwards; Table 1.1 shows the change in the Saudi light crude price from 1981 to 1985.

At the same time, many OPEC members, in an attempt to stem the fall in revenues, constantly exceeded the share of production allocated to them at successive OPEC meetings. Nor did the continual removal from the market of an average of 2 mbd each from Iran and Iraq as a result of the war or sporadic attacks on tankers in the Gulf affect the market. Political events elsewhere in the Middle East occurred which were potentially comparable in gravity to the 1973 Yom Kippur war, or the 1979 Iranian Revolution, without causing so much as a ripple in the oil markets. Examples are Iranian threats to close the Strait of Hormuz; the Israeli invasion and continued occupation of southern Lebanon; and the American attack on Tripoli in 1986. The psychology of the market has been quite different from the 1970s, owing to the belief that there are ample alternative supplies available.

It has been suggested that the oil market is now so altered from that which existed before 1980 that the activities of OPEC are irrelevant to policy. Oil, it is argued, is now a commodity like any other: futures markets in New York, Chicago and London permit buyers to hedge against price changes, and act as a stabilising agent; thus no intervention by OECD governments is either necessary or desirable. All this might be true if oil were in any sense a perfect market, and if other futures markets - copper, tin, coffee - had in fact created price stability. But the situation in the 1980s is that crude oil produced outside the OECD has production costs which are one tenth of the average within OECD. If governments choose to rely solely on market forces, this can only be at the expense of indigenous OECD production, and dependence on Middle Eastern oil will increase. Thus conventional economic prescriptions conflict with security interests.

Once Saudi Arabia abandoned its policy of restricting exports in the summer of 1985, there was nothing to stop prices falling to below $10. How far this change of Saudi policy was due to a desire to protect its long-term market, how far to the fact that the shoe of lower revenues was beginning to pinch, how far to exasperation with the failure of its OPEC partners and non-OPEC exporters to bear their share of the burden of cuts in volume, and how far to a desire to see both Iran and Iraq further impoverished, may never be known (unless Shaikh Yamani publishes his memoirs). What matters to those who want to understand the market of the last five years, as a basis for judgement on what may happen in the next five, is that the price of oil throughout the world will turn on the export volume levels decided by the rulers of the Gulf states. In the first eight months of 1986, the Middle East as a whole (Iran plus all the

Arab states plus North Africa) accounted for 46% of OECD oil imports and had 85% of existing spare productive capacity. Moreover, the Gulf states alone (that is to say, at present only the members of the Gulf Co-operation Council[6], but if and when fighting between Iran and Iraq ceases, then these two countries also) have the reserves of oil that make them the future suppliers of last resort for the world oil importers, as well as large reserves of gas. With the possible exception of Mexico, other exporters, whether members of OPEC or not, will be of little significance, because their share of exports can only decline as their internal demand rises and their reserves are depleted.

One further effect of the 1986 price collapse on the Gulf states' production needs to be noted. In 1980, installed productive capacity in Saudi Arabia and the other GCC countries amounted to over 15 mbd. Iran and Iraq could probably each have exported 5 mbd in 1980 with little new investment or time delay. With the GCC exports now down to one third of 1980 capacity, it is unlikely that spare capacity has been maintained at former levels, and investment is certainly not now being made to develop existing proved reserves, let alone to develop new areas. With Iran and Iraq impoverished by the war and low prices (and exporting under 2.5 mbd each), and with many of their production and export facilities damaged by the fighting, it will take years rather than months after any cessation of hostilities to restore their full potential. But when it is restored, each might be capable of exporting 4 or 5 mbd, with new Iraqi export facilities through both Saudi Arabia and Turkey due to be completed in 1987.

The collapse of prices has had its effect on importing countries also, and nowhere more so than in the United States where the market is most price-sensitive. Imports were already above 5.9 mbd by the end of 1986. It has been estimated that a continuation of prices below $15 could by the end of 1988 remove between 1.5 and 2 mbd of US production from January 1986 levels. The combined effect of reduced oil supply (to say nothing of the results of shutting in uneconomic natural gas) and increased energy demand would be to increase US oil imports to above the levels that in 1973 left the US vulnerable to the oil weapon and in 1979 led the US

Government and companies to join the panic bidding that forced up oil prices. US imports could be expected to rise to between 7.5 and 9 mbd by 1990, and up to 11.4 mbd by 1995.[7]

Similarly in the North Sea, production which has already been developed is not going to be shut in at prices above $10 a barrel, and a considerable proportion would still be produced at $5. However, in the UK North Sea, the average cost of producing oil from new fields not yet developed was $18 before payment of royalties and taxes (£14 at the 1985 exchange rate), according to the government's 1985 figures. Some sources suggest $15 for larger and lower-cost projects.[8] Failure to develop new fields because of lack of confidence that this price level will be maintained would lead to a sharper decline from the peak in production from both the UK and Norwegian sectors than would otherwise have been the case - with the UK becoming a net importer before 2000.

In 1980 it was widely believed in both government and industry circles in the OECD that prices would double again by the end of the century. But with prices halved since 1984 and continuing expectations of low prices, the economics of new investment in all primary energy sources, including oil-related technologies such as heavy crudes and tar sands, has become much less favourable and many projects have been shelved. The major exception to this trend was the decision (in December 1986) between the partners in the Norwegian Troll gas field and a number of West European buyers to proceed with the development of that field. Much marginal coal production is no longer economic; and in those European countries where continued production is regarded as indispensable for either security or social reasons, it will require large government subsidies if volume is to be maintained. The alternative primary fossil fuel, particularly for power generation, becomes imported coal, and will remain so unless gas prices are drastically reduced and their link to oil broken.

The future of oil prices

The critical investment decisions described above depend as much on investors' perception of the likely future oil price as on what it is today. The fact that nobody knows to within $15 what it will be in 12 months, let alone in 12 years, makes for delay in decision taking in board rooms and government departments. The most likely prospect for 1987 therefore is for continued uncertainty, with prices fluctuating unpredictably.

The pattern will then have been set for increasing dependence on OPEC, principally the Middle East. It is for this reason that the stability of the Middle East is going to be the key to the security of oil and therefore energy supplies in the 1990s. To the extent that OECD governments take steps to override conventional short-term market signals in favour of the development of indigenous sources, and of an intensified campaign for energy efficiency, they will reduce the dependence. If they fail to do so, there will inevitably be a return to higher prices, as spare capacity elsewhere than in the Gulf becomes used up (85% of present spare productive capacity is in any case in the Middle East). Large new discoveries of oil or gas within OECD, which optimistic forecasters predict, would, even if found, not be in production within the time scale of this study. Nor is there help in sight from the USSR or from China (whose exports of oil will fall from current levels).[9]

The Middle East

As noted above, imports from the Middle East (all Arab countries plus Iran) accounted for a significant proportion of total OECD oil imports in 1986. The US, which had virtually freed itself from dependence on Middle East sources by 1985, began to reverse this process in 1986, and head towards even higher levels of dependence than in the 1970s. This is owing mainly to increased energy demand and to decline in 'Lower 48' and Alaska oil and gas production. Japan and Europe have remained heavily dependent on these countries. Almost all of the additional oil required must come from the Gulf, irrespective of price, that is to say, from the members of the Gulf Co-operation Council and, if the fighting stops, from Iraq and Iran. No other Middle East state - indeed no other OPEC or non-OPEC oil exporter, with the possible exceptions of Venezuela and Mexico - has adequate reserves to support increases in exports above today's levels.

Taking account of the other trends described in this chapter, the return to a greater degree of dependence, which leaves energy supplies for OECD as a whole as insecure as in the 1970s, could come as early as 1989 or as late as 1995 - but come it will. Differences of immediate interest among OECD members, as well as differences of domestic politics and of views on how best to deal with perceived sources of instability, lead - as they led in 1973 and 1979 - to a failure to adopt a common attitude to the West's relationship with the Middle East, and could conceivably provoke a breach in the Western 'alliance'. One has only to review briefly the present and potential sources of instability to illustrate this.[10]

Sources of instability

a) Anti-imperialism. The drive to free themselves from European (and later American) domination has been a major political force for both Arabs and Iranians throughout this century. The rhetoric of nationalism still provides ammunition for the opposition to those regimes that maintain reasonable relations with the West and also for regimes such as Khomeini's Iran and Gadaffi's Libya that declare their hostility. No Middle East politician can afford not to be seen to be on the side of anti-colonialism, which incidentally is one reason why too fulsome expressions of friendship, especially those from Washington, often amount literally to the kiss of death.

b) Palestine. For the Arabs, the establishment of the State of Israel in their midst and on their territory is seen not only as an outrage in itself, but also as further evidence of Western imperialism. This is not the place to review yet again the pros and cons of the issue. But the fact that other sources of instability tend today to distract both local and international opinion from the Palestine problem, does not mean that the threat to security of oil supplies, which it represents, has fundamentally altered. Whatever his personal emotions or lack of them, no Arab ruler can afford to abandon the claims of the Palestine refugees, or to be seen to acquiesce in Israeli occupation of the West Bank or of the Holy City of Jerusalem. Those who do so risk the fate of Anwar Sadat. Nor can any Western state that adopts a better than even-handed attitude to Israel (whether for reasons of domestic politics or foreign strategy) hope to maintain other than intermittent and superficially correct relations with the Arab world. Such relations will not survive heightened tensions or an opportunity to exert pressure, as in 1973 and in 1979. The fact has to be faced therefore that the US leaning towards Israel is a source of energy insecurity to the US itself. Moreover, it confronts the rest of the OECD countries with the dilemma of either having to share the opprobrium which America attracts in Arab eyes, or of facing fundamental and far-reaching disagreements on policy with the US Government. There have been too many instances of this in recent years. As demand for Middle East oil increases, these tensions will become even more dangerous.

c) Islam. The resurgence of Islam has coincided with and to some extent fed on anti-imperialist as well as anti-Israeli sentiment. Appeals to the *Jihad*, the holy war against the infidel, have become almost routine. And they are not mere rhetoric; individuals and groups are ready to sacrifice their lives in its name. Internally, the rise of Islam has led to a reaction against Western and secular values, not only materialistic but also liberal, and to criticism of the old ruling élite for failure to adhere to the strict tenets of their religion. It is a mistake to think of this simply as a Shi'a phenomenon, as is shown by the fundamentalist pressures and continuing activity of the Muslim Brotherhood in mainly Sunni Saudi Arabia, Egypt and Sudan and by the existence of Islamic republics in Pakistan and until recently Sudan. But the Shi'a version, given new impetus by Khomeini, now threatens to engulf its Arab neighbours and to undermine the Sunni-dominated regimes of the Gulf states as well as of Iraq.

d) Iran-Iraq war. The Iran-Iraq war is now in its seventh year and has cost the two sides loss of blood and treasure on the scale of 1914-18 in Europe. As of early 1987, its outcome remains unpredictable and its long-term consequences even more so. It faces the US and the USSR with temptations and risks at the frontier between their respective spheres of influence which have been avoided only by skilful and sometimes equivocal diplomacy. The surprising fact that so far it has neither spread to neighbouring states nor interfered seriously with oil exports to the rest of the world does not mean that this will always be the case. It will leave a legacy of hatred and mistrust in the region, and weaken the ability of the combatants to develop their reserves to meet increasing world demand for both oil and gas.

e) Terrorism. Assassination as a political weapon has been a characteristic of the Middle East throughout history. Leaders who elsewhere would have been ousted by the ballot box have been felled instead by the bullet. But terrorism in its modern guise, whether directed against foreign leaders or innocent bystanders, both by disgruntled minorities and as a means of carrying on diplomacy, is a particular feature of the region. In part it stems from the frustration of the (mainly Sunni or Christian) Palestine refugees. Differences of view among the Western powers as to how best to deal with state terrorism threaten Western solidarity and co-ordinated policies towards these problems.

f) Loss of revenues. These long-established sources of instability in the Middle East are now compounded by loss of revenue, due to loss of volume, and the price fall, of oil exports. Iran and Iraq, even if the fighting between them can be brought to an end (a development possibly accelerated by shortage of funds), will be hard put to finance the restoration of their economies. They will need aid. Even the other Gulf states, which have hitherto been able to afford to meet every issue with money, are now faced with hard choices, as their revenue has been halved and foreign debt begins to mount. They will need credit.

g) The Soviet threat. It is not by chance that the Soviet threat has been put last in this list of sources of instability. For so it is generally perceived in Europe and Japan - not least, it must be admitted, because of the belief that the USSR knows that the US will not permit further Soviet expansion into the region beyond Afghanistan, allied to the belief that the Russians have no wish to repeat the Afghan experience. This is not to say that they will not exploit any opportunity to extend their influence. But their successive failures to exercise effective control over Egypt, Iraq or even Syria must reinforce their natural caution. Here again, however, there is a danger of discord between the US and the rest of the Alliance, the latter being unwilling to run the risk of increased local hostility which a military presence in the area would involve and which would cost money, in order to meet a threat which they believe to be largely hypothetical.

The Western response to Middle East problems

It is easier to catalogue the sources of insecurity in the Middle East than to suggest action by the OECD countries to counter these. There are no instant solutions. There is no alternative to the traditional techniques of foreign relations with countries whose goodwill is important: discreet assistance to the forces of stability that exist in the region, coupled with restraint in publicising such friends as we have for our own domestic political advantage; concentration and consultation on policy amongst OECD members; willingness to trade; financial assistance when required and military assistance if (and only if) requested. The question of whether OECD countries should take action to help stabilise the oil price itself will be discussed in a different section of this study. Enough has been said here to emphasise that long-term security of supplies from the region may be improved but can never be guaranteed. The one safe policy is to minimise dependence on Gulf oil supplies.

Over the last five years, in the period of slack oil demand and spare productive capacity, OECD governments and consumers could afford to attend to other priorities and let the Middle East take care of itself. As the oil market comes more nearly into balance, this will again become a dangerously negligent attitude. Since Japan and Europe have more at stake, it seems logical that they should bear a greater part of the burden. There are things that Japan could do, which are not inconsistent with its constitutional renunciation of offensive military capability, and indeed might go some way to recycle its present huge current account surplus. These include increased aid to the poorer countries of the Middle East, such as Jordan, Egypt, Sudan, which are no longer so well supported by their richer Arab brethren; a readiness to provide technical and financial aid (jointly with Europe) for the rehabilitation of Iran and Iraq when the fighting stops; the supply of loans and access to markets for the oil-producing states that are in temporary difficulties. The European Community can offer similar assistance, including a possible Free Trade Area, initially to the Gulf Co-operation Council, in due course perhaps to Iran and Iraq also. Individual European Governments could also do more to provide security and defence assistance designed to protect the integrity of the Arab states' frontiers against external aggression or internal subversion by their Middle Eastern neighbours. However, only the US can ensure that further adventures in the Middle East after Afghanistan are clearly seen by the Soviet Union as too dangerous and too costly. Nor would the US Government in practice wish to abandon its role vis-à-vis the Soviets, however inadequate the contribution of its partners may appear to American opinion.

Chernobyl - The response of the OECD nations

Since 1973 nuclear energy has been responsible for reducing OECD dependence on oil imports by more than 4 mbd. Consequently, the prospect of enhanced dependence on imports from the unstable region of the Middle East mandates the need for the continued development of nuclear energy. Yet it is precisely at this time that two recent events - the crash in world oil prices and the Soviet nuclear power plant accident at Chernobyl - have raised questions both about the basic economic justification for additional commercial nuclear expansion and about its inherent safety.

While it is, perhaps, too soon to judge the long-term effects of the Chernobyl nuclear tragedy, it is possible to see some of the consequences. Curiously enough, these consequences seem likely to be greater outside the Soviet Union than within that country.

In the aftermath of Chernobyl, there was widespread speculation that the accident had been the death-knell for further commercial nuclear power expansion. To date, however, no OECD member government has declared that it will abandon nuclear power because of the accident. This is not to argue that opposition to nuclear power has not increased. In the OECD large sections of the public no longer agree with 'expert opinion' that nuclear power is acceptably safe. In the aftermath of both Three Mile Island and now Chernobyl even professionals in the industry realise that the propensity for the 'technically impossible' to happen has to be taken seriously, and that the training and discipline of reactor operators, even in highly advanced societies, do not eliminate the risks of human error or on occasion of human recklessness. Nevertheless, in the current political and emotional climate since Chernobyl, it should not be forgotten that nuclear energy contributes nearly 9% of total OECD energy supply and that a political decision by any OECD nation to forgo this technology will have grave implications for OECD energy and financial security, as well as the economic prosperity of many nations around the globe.

Even before Chernobyl perceptions about nuclear energy varied widely in the OECD nations. For example, in France, Belgium, and Japan governments were firmly committed to nuclear power, while some of the smaller nations in Western Europe had as a result of public opposition decided not to build nuclear power stations or to abandon stations already started. In almost all the sizable European nations, nuclear power was a major source of electricity.

While no new nuclear stations have been ordered in the United States since 1979 owing to projections of reduced electricity demand and complex regulatory, safety and environmental concern, the US has over 100 reactors in operation and 18 under construction. While not all these reactors may be allowed to operate by the early 1990s, nuclear energy will contribute nearly 20% of US electricity supply. No new stations beyond those already under construction are likely to be ordered in time to be in operation by 2000.

In contrast to the negative attitudes towards nuclear power in many Western countries, several nations including France, Japan, and the CMEA countries[11] have reaffirmed the need for expanded commercial nuclear programmes. In the autumn of 1986, Japan's Nuclear Sub-Committee of the Advisory Committee for Energy projected a doubling of the nuclear share of electricity supply from 26% in 1985 to 60% by 2030. The central theme of a plan such as this is the growing perception that continued economic growth and increased demand for electricity may be closely linked.

While opposition parties in the UK and Germany support either the closing down of existing nuclear stations or a halt on further construction, their present governments still declare their commitment in principle to continue. Projections by the European Community's Nuclear Indicative Programme foresee that by 1995 nuclear power will supply more than 40% of electricity demand, up from 35% in 1985. If nuclear power does not grow as projected, other fuels - imported coal or oil or natural gas - will have to be used.

The OECD thus stands at a crossroads in nuclear energy development. While Japan and France seem determined to proceed with development, the future of nuclear energy is no longer assured in the US or in a number of Western European countries. This means that for many countries nuclear energy can no longer be relied upon to contribute to solving the problem of increased dependence on oil. The decline in reactor building threatens to reduce the nuclear engineering capability to a level below the 'critical mass' at which it can efficiently continue. Research and development of inherently safer designs will not bear fruit in terms of electricity supply to the public in this century. Still less will the fast breeder reactor. One more nuclear accident anywhere in any type of design which releases radiation or injures people outside the plant would lead to public demand that all reactors of that design or at least of that generation of plants be closed down until assured of their continued safety.

In the emotionally charged atmosphere prevailing since Chernobyl, there is need for sombre reflection about the dangers of abandoning the nuclear option, even in a handful of OECD countries. If economic growth and increase in electricity demand are not decoupled, losing the nuclear option will lead to a massive increase in coal use. If coal cannot be developed, demand will have to be met by increased use of oil and natural gas, much of it imported. Thus the OECD objective of a highly diversified energy economy would be frustrated.

OECD options

Faced with these threats to the security of energy supplies, what possible options are open to the OECD countries acting collectively or individually? Widely and fundamentally different forecasts bring confusion to energy policies and thereby present big problems for the discussion of energy security in the 1990s. Energy security is determined by anticipated danger (whose degree depends on its scale, how often it occurs and how long it lasts) and countermeasures to deal with it (two types of measures, one before and the other after the danger takes place). If this anticipated danger contains too big a factor of probability, countermeasures will have to widen in scope to deal with every possible situation, and this makes the task difficult. Another factor is that energy security is a matter of degree. In other words, what constitutes security is relative in concept depending on countries and times.

Governments can choose to do nothing. In a situation of long lead times such as characterises the energy world, this is always tempting for politicians. Plausible arguments can be advanced for inaction. It can be argued that we do not know what is going to happen: therefore any action now to influence events, especially by governments, is bound to be wrong. But on examination, this argument usually boils down to a forecast that everything will remain unchanged from this day forward. It can be argued that the market worked in the period from 1980 to 1985 and will do so again if prices go too high. But in the process, consumers, especially the poorest individuals and nations, suffer, while even the rich may find themselves being blackmailed. Refusal to insure now against major risks may prove very expensive in the 5-10 year long run; which in one sense is the very essence of the problem.

Alternatively, governments, industries and individuals within the OECD group can take steps to increase the level of energy security by internal and external action - expenditure whose justification is similar to that which applies to defence. Such action can bear on demand as well as on supply and comprises both medium-term measures and crisis management.

The best energy security is to be able to do without. The United States, in particular, with energy consumption per head more than twice that of Europe and Japan, is placing a heavy burden of insecurity on its OECD partners, by reason of its increasing appetite for oil imports.

Demand

On demand, the medium-term possibilities are well known:

a) Efficiency. Much progress has been made in efficiency of energy use since the crises of 1973 and 1980, without any lowering of the standard of living. But if investors believe that prices are going to stay low, the rate of investment in efficiency will decline unless governments provide alternative incentives.

b) Energy objectives. The expression of general objectives in energy consumption has advanced furthest in Japan and the European Community. It is true that such objectives do not have the force of law or the impulsion of the market, but they can encourage private investment and they provide a set of norms against which individual countries' performance can be judged. In this connection, the periodic reviews by the IEA and the European Commission of each member state's performance provide a useful spur to action. Despite price falls, the European Community publicly renewed in September 1986 its commitment to objectives.

c) Excise taxes. Where price signals fail because of low oil prices, excise taxes can be increased so as to offer sufficient disincentive to wasteful or inefficient consumption. In particular, an increase in US gasoline tax to equal that levied in Europe and Japan (between 4 and 10 times higher than the US rate) would presumably have a marked effect by reinforcing the present regulatory standards on consumption and thus on the level of US imports.

d) Legal standards. The specification by law of energy consumption standards in buildings, vehicles or equipment is uneven within the OECD, with Europe and the US lagging behind Japan. There is no reason why the worst performers should not come up to the best in this respect. Exhortation to greater efficiency is not enough.

Supply

On supply there is a broader choice of possibilities. It is important to distinguish between two types of measures: those which can be effective in advance to avert a crisis; and those which can only be used after the event to counter a crisis and which can only work if they are in place in advance.

a) Flexibility. The first principle of security is flexibility. This has two aspects: of source and of substitution (see (b) below). For example, after studies and lengthy discussions within the framework of the IEA in 1984, importing governments agreed to 'avoid undue dependence upon any one source of gas', which in effect meant that Soviet gas should constitute no more than 30% of total gas supplies in any major West European country (chiefly West Germany, France and Italy).[12] Without being specific as to the precise figure, this principle could well be extended to other sources and other fuels.

b) Substitution. If market signals are no longer adequate to push oil consumers into other fuels, or away from the Gulf, it is necessary to consider what governments can do, beyond mere exhortation, to maintain this momentum. The extension of the European gas pipeline network, including a link between the UK and the Continent, would improve security and might facilitate additional penetration of gas into the market, even at current oil prices. Increased trade in electricity within Europe would also enhance security. Dual firing (about 40% in the US industrial sector) and other means of switching between fuels can also make an important contribution - both in averting trouble and in responding to it - to the security not only of the firm that invests in the facility but also to the rest of the community. If current opposition can be overcome, nuclear power offers a continuing option to reduce dependence on fossil fuels at economic cost.

c) Fiscal measures. As for oil itself, rationing has been proved ineffective except in a severe crisis of limited duration. Import quotas were shown to be ineffective and cumbersome in the US in the period 1959-73. Excise taxes on energy consumption particularly in transport may encourage conservation and switching into other fuels, but do not encourage the development of domestic sources. If governments want to maintain levels of indigenous supplies in the face of low international prices, there remain three possibilities for direct fiscal action on the oil market. What governments have to decide is whether the ultimate costs of doing nothing are greater than the immediate costs (both political and financial) of taking steps in advance to head off an undesirable but uncertain situation.

i) The reduction of taxes and royalties on domestic production, if necessary to zero, or even subsidies. The UK Government's 1985 figure of $18 a barrel for profitable development of an average new North Sea oil field was on the basis of the then existing tax and royalty regime (already considerably more favourable as a result of the 1984 budget). At zero tax and royalty, this figure might come down to $15 or even in some cases to $10. A corresponding figure to the $18 above for the US has been given as $20. Of course, existing production which does not require new investment will continue at much lower price levels, $5-10 a barrel. The decision on new investment depends on the view taken of what the price will be when the project comes on stream, but the minds of boards of directors and bankers when considering capital programmes are powerfully influenced by current prices, and by current cash flows. If governments of producing countries want to hedge their bets on future prices, or make production-cutting gestures in the short term, the device of 'banking royalty', that is to say, leaving the government's royalty oil in the ground until the end of the life of the field, is always open to them.

ii) Fixed tariffs, whether flat rate or ad valorem, invite retaliation, and are contrary to a whole series of international agreements. Moreover, they tend to continue in operation even if the import price has risen to a level that no longer threatens internal supplies, thus distorting the economy in the opposite direction and imposing a regressive tax on the consumer. Moreover, while exporting countries may regard tariffs as a hostile move designed to capture part of the rent when market prices move up again, importers can argue that this is a legitimate device against predatory pricing.

iii) A minimum import price (m.i.p.) on imported crude oil and products could be effective in protecting indigenous energy (including coal, nuclear and new alternatives as well as oil and gas) from disastrously low international prices. Indeed, this was the basis of the agreement reached in the IEA in 1976 under US leadership, when the m.i.p. was set at $7 a barrel (equivalent to about $13 in dollars of 1986). It makes little difference of mechanics whether the desired price level is achieved by a floor price or by variable tariff. The 1976 agreement left it to individual members of IEA to adopt the most appropriate means. The level at which the price is set will either act as a guarantee against disaster or, if higher, as an incentive for additional investment. Regulations would be set so as to require any importer to pay a tariff equal to the difference between his c.i.f. cost and the m.i.p. This would at the same time provide investors in each country in the OECD with some confidence that profitability of the investment would not be undermined once on stream. It would also encourage foreign exporters to limit the volume they put on the market to a level that would raise prices towards the m.i.p. Although there would no doubt be the usual cries of 'confrontation', this action would thus in reality assist the exporting countries to stabilise volume and price. OPEC itself has declared it wishes to achieve stability at around $18. A minimum import price system would also provide a windfall to OECD treasuries, although only to the extent that the external price remained below the m.i.p. If set at any level below $18, it would still leave OECD consumers with the benefit of a fall in energy prices of around half since 1982. No doubt the internal administrative complications would be immense, but they could be overcome, and the scheme could be effective, provided it was simultaneously introduced by the US, the EC and Japan and provided there were no exceptions. And it would have the advantage that it would be self-cancelling (unlike most tariffs) once the objective of stabilising the price at a reasonable level was reached. In considering such a fee, the costs and benefits would have to be carefully assessed. These would include comparing the volume of additional crude oil and petroleum products which would, in the absence of a fee, not be available, with the resulting impact on energy prices both within the 'fee region' and between the region and the rest of the world. The macroeconomic effects are also relevant. These can include the impact on inflation and the resulting change in industrial competitiveness. The opportunity and facility in introducing the fee will depend on current expectations of future prices and of course the level of the fee proposed.

d) Export restrictions. A minor but not unimportant measure to improve overall OECD energy security would be the removal of current restrictions on trade in energy within OECD, such as the export of Alaska North Slope oil to Japan, or of Australian and US steam coal to the UK and Germany (the latter at present restricted by the importing governments).

e) Oil imports from the Middle East. Even the best conceived measures to promote indigenous OECD energy production and reduce demand, however, will not entirely free OECD from the need to import large amounts of oil from the Middle East, where the Gulf states (GCC, Iran and Iraq) are the key sources. It is therefore necessary to consider what can be done to maintain good commercial relations with that region, and to promote stable trading links. Possible responses to specific political sources of instability have been discussed in the section above on the Middle East. In the specific context of oil, all that needs to be repeated here is that Europe and Japan, and eventually the US, cannot afford to alienate the Gulf countries. But equally these countries cannot afford to alienate the countries where their main market lies, nor to spoil that market either by overpricing, or by setting such low prices that they force OECD countries to respond with protectionist measures. Hence the constant cry for 'dialogue'. Dialogue, however, goes on all the time through normal diplomatic and private channels. Something more than this is implied, and here it is necessary to distinguish between exchange of information on facts, hoisting signals on intentions, and some form of negotiation with a view to an agreement of some kind.

It is an illusion to suppose that, in present circumstances, the last of these three is a possibility as between OECD as a whole and OPEC, or even the Gulf countries as a whole. Attempts at negotiation during the 1970s came to nothing. There is no organisation which could either negotiate an agreement on behalf of its partners, or deliver a bargain once made. On the first and second aspects - exchange of facts and signalling of intentions - institutions exist and are in use, both bilateral and multilateral, official and informal. They are adequate to the extent that those concerned are willing to use them singly or collectively. Such exchanges are useful if only to avoid damaging each other by mistake. But they offer no prospect of enforceable agreements on either price or volume. There are, however, smaller entities, between which such agreements might be possible. The 'special relationship' between the US and Saudi Arabia is one such, although it is always under strain because of disagreements on other Middle East issues, and in any case its exclusive features are scarcely reassuring to Europe or Japan. A Free Trade Area between the EC and the GCC, to which Iraq and Iran might eventually adhere, would strengthen the mutuality of interest between the two areas, as would the encouragement of investment by the Gulf countries in OECD-based enterprises. Co-operation among OECD energy partners in sharing the burdens as well as the benefits of trade would facilitate this process. For their part, Middle East exporters have learned the dangers of overpricing and of overproduction and some Middle East leaders may not be averse to private consultation to avoid such mistakes in the future. OPEC is not an enemy to be fought, but a group of countries with legitimate interests which need to be reconciled with those of the OECD.

f) Research and development. Energy security can be improved through promotion of research and development work into new technologies and renewable energy sources. Despite considerable achievements during the period when oil prices were rising, this work is under severe threat following the oil price collapse. Short-term commercial considerations threaten to prevent further research in important areas such as: renewables; coal liquefaction and gasification; and transport technologies, all of which could assist in reducing the demand for oil. Continued financial support for R and D and co-operation among OECD countries will therefore play an important role in ensuring future energy security. (Here again the IEA can perform a useful co-ordinating and promotional function, especially in driving forward research into subjects such as the 'greenhouse effect', with a view to getting the technical facts before panic sets in.)

g) Crisis management and stocks. Whatever efforts are made to improve relations with the Gulf, the possibility of tensions between or within single countries there, or between them and the West, leading to interruptions in oil supplies, cannot be excluded. The fact that several political crises have occurred in the last five years without any interruption in supplies is no guide for a future in which existing spare capacity elsewhere has been used up, either by increasing demand or declining production, or failure to invest. Emphasis on energy security, for example by building greater flexibility into energy networks and promoting energy efficiency, could lessen the impact of a future crisis. Handling such a situation would require the retention of the International Energy Agency, the organisation for crisis management which was set up under American leadership in 1974. The details of its functions are well known and have been described elsewhere.[13] That its organisation is adequate to its task was demonstrated in the 1980 Iran-Iraq war crisis, and in subsequent simulated tests. The system needs to be brought up to date to cope with the speed and the speculative aspects of the modern oil markets. But given the continued will of the member governments and of the oil companies to back the organisation, there is no reason why it should not cope with a major supply interruption both in the sense of damping down early price increases, and in the sense of ensuring that no member country suffers undue hardship through physical shortage of supplies. In a crisis the strength of the IEA lies in having agreed mechanisms in being, without having to wait for the improvisation and delays that normally hamper international organisations. It therefore needs to be more clearly agreed in the IEA than is now the case what proportion of total stocks is to be instantly available for release to counter price rises at the beginning of a crisis, and what proportion is to be kept to counter supply problems if the crisis persists.

Stock-holding and standing mechanisms for oil release are the key to crisis management in the short run, and the best insurance against the price being suddenly bid up towards the high levels of 1980 in the long run. The IEA agreement that requires member countries to hold stocks of 90 days of imports is probably adequate if all members fulfil their obligations and if the full 90 days' worth is in fact available on the day (and not, for example, tied up in company minimum operating and pipe-fill requirements, or kept back for some hypothetical worse crisis). But the system needs to be strengthened and understandings clarified in advance as to the circumstances and mechanisms by which all IEA members will release stock to the market. In July 1984 the Governing Board of the IEA agreed that a proportion of stocks be earmarked for early release in the event of a crisis which threatened a sudden and steep price increase, as had happened in 1979 when a relatively small shortfall was aggravated by speculation and by buying for stock both by governments and companies. But the mechanics of early release are far from clear, and even the availability of oil for this purpose is in doubt. Stocks are the key to crisis management.

Sound stock mechanisms in being are also in themselves a deterrent to arbitrary action by suppliers; but it is not realistic to suggest that they can be used as a sort of market price regulator in normal times. Stock-holding has of course to be organised in advance, but stock release comes essentially into the category of measures to be taken 'after the danger takes place'.

h) Third World energy co-operation. It is in the interest of OECD nations to assist Third World countries in the development of indigenous energy resources. This would ensure that, to the extent possible, these countries would not become dependent on OPEC oil, thus creating further competition for this source of supply.

Conclusion

The teams which have worked for over a year on these issues in Washington, Tokyo and London hope that this analysis, and the detailed studies on the three regions that accompany it, will provide a useful contribution to a continuing debate, and also a spur to action by governments, industrialists and consumers.

Governments will always be reluctant to take action to avert a future and uncertain risk, and the problems of international co-ordination which are necessary for success in energy policy are formidable. But the fact has to be faced that additional barrels of Gulf oil can for the foreseeable future be produced at an average local cost of under $2 a barrel, while few additional barrels of OECD oil can be produced for less than $15 before tax. With this discrepancy, the 'market' if left to itself will always dictate that the Gulf retains a greater proportion of total oil outlets, and that oil retains a greater share of the energy market than is compatible with OECD security. There is no quick fix. OECD governments have the choice of leaving their countries to ride the roller coaster of successive supply interruptions and price disturbances or of adopting sustained and co-ordinated measures to counter what are essentially political, not market, forces.

Notes

[1] The members of OPEC are as follows: Algeria, Indonesia, Iran, Iraq, Kuwait, Libya, Nigeria, Saudi Arabia, United Arab Emirates, Venezuela, Ecuador, Qatar, Gabon.

[2] The Organisation of Economic Co-operation and Development groups the world's main industrialised and market economy countries, including the US, Canada, Western Europe, Japan, and Australia.

[3] For purposes of this study, 'low' oil prices have been defined as $15 or less, 'high' oil prices as above $25 a barrel - in US $ of 1986. $15 is considered to be the cut-off point below which few if any investments in OECD energy sources will be made.

[4] The International Energy Agency is affiliated to the OECD and has the same membership minus France, Finland and Iceland.

[5] The members of the European Community are as follows: Belgium, Denmark, West Germany, Greece, France, Ireland, Italy, Luxemburg, Netherlands, United Kingdom. Spain and Portugal joined the Community on 1 January 1986 to make 12 members.

[6] The Gulf Co-operation Council, consisting of Saudi Arabia, Kuwait, Bahrain, Qatar, the United Arab Emirates and Oman, was set up in 1981.

[7] API (American Petroleum Institute): 'US Faces Another Energy Crisis', Oil and Gas Journal, Vol. 85, No.1, 5 January 1987, p. 24-25.

[8] Development of the Oil and Gas Resources of the United Kingdom, (The Brown Book), Department of Energy, London: HMSO, 1986.

[9] Some would argue that Soviet oil exports to OECD countries will be sustained at around 1 mbd by the end of the century (compared with around 1.3 mbd in 1986). A recent study sees Soviet exports

falling to a maximum of 0.5 mbd by 2000. Jonathan P. Stern, Soviet Oil and Gas Exports to the West: Commercial Transaction or Security Threat?, Aldershot, Gower 1987. Chinese oil exports are most unlikely to increase from the present level of 0.4 mbd and there is at least the possibility that the country will become a net importer by the end of the century. National Institute for Research Advancement, The Present State and Future of China's Energy Problem, Tokyo, NIRA 1986.

[10] See Valerie Yorke and Louis Turner, European Interests and Gulf Oil, Aldershot, Gower, 1985.

[11] CMEA member countries are USSR, Hungary, Bulgaria, Poland, Romania, Czechoslovakia and German Democratic Republic.

[12] This is understood to be the informal agreement worked out between the countries, although individual governments would not agree to any figure being published in the communiqué. Energy Policies and Programme of the IEA Countries, 1983 Review, Paris: OECD, 1984, Appendix A, Annex 1, pp. 72-3.

[13] See Wilfrid L. Kohl, International Institutions for Energy Management, Aldershot, Gower, 1983.

Table 1.1

Saudi light official crude price (US$ per barrel) 1981-85

1981		1982		1983		1984		1985	
Apr 1	Oct 1	Apr 1	Oct 1	Apr 1	Oct 1	Apr 1	Oct 1	Apr 1	Oct 1
32.00	34.00	34.00	34.00	29.00	29.00	29.00	29.00	28.00	28.00

Source: BP Statistical Review of World Energy, June 1986.

2 Japan's Energy Security to 2000 — The Dawn of an Age of Multiple Energies

Acknowledgements

The Japanese Study Group on Energy Security in the 1990s was established as part of the National Institute for Research Advancement (NIRA). This group was responsible for the Japanese group's research: their report was compiled during a total of eight meetings using extracts from the discussions and study themes of the meetings held in London in January 1986 and in Washington in January 1987. We would like to express our gratitude to the members of the study group and all other individuals who have given their full co-operation to this study.

Members of study group

Yasushi Matsuda	-	Head of study group, Institute of Energy Economics
Tsutomu Toichi	-	Institute of Energy Economics
Shunsuke Kondo	-	University of Tokyo
Hiroaki Fukami	-	Keio University
Tashashi Ikoma	-	Japanese Institute of Middle Eastern Economies
Tatsujiro Suzuki	-	International Energy Forum
Kazuaki Matsui	-	Institute of Applied Energy
Tetsuo Hamauzu	-	Institute of Developing Economies
Toshio Aoki	-	National Institute for Research Advancement
Hideaki Okino	-	National Institute for Research Advancement
Shigeo Watanabe	-	National Institute for Research

		Advancement (Former Senior Researcher)
Yoshiki Kurihara	-	National Institute for Research Advancement
Toshiaki Nakai	-	National Institute for Research Advancement
Toyoto Matsuoka	-	National Institute for Research Advancement
Hiroya Harada	-	National Institute for Research Advancement (Former Researcher)
Seiichi Kurosawa	-	National Institute for Research Advancement
Yoshinori Itoh	-	National Institute for Research Advancement

(As of March 1987)

Contributors to Japanese Report:

Sections	I, II:3, III:2,4, IV:1	H. Okino
Section	II:1,2	T. Matsuoka
Sections	II:4, III:3	T. Nakai
Section	III:1	T. Ikoma
Section	IV:2	H. Fukami
Section	IV:3	Y. Itoh
Section	IV:4	K. Matsui, Y. Kurihara
Section	IV:5	S. Watanabe, K. Kurosawa
Sections	II:5, V	T. Toichi, H. Okino

I. Why energy security in the 1990s now?

1. The uncertain future

There are two opposing schools of thought in Japan concerning the significance of the oil price collapse which began in late 1985. One views it as the start of another round of oil supply restrictions, which will be brought in in the medium- to long-term future; it predicts that the real price of crude oil may begin to go up as early as 1990.[1] The other contends that the real price will come down to the level of the historical peak of $5 a barrel, recorded in 1920 and again in 1974 (1960 dollars), and stay at this low level for a long period.[2] The differences in view stem from the perspective each side takes concerning future supply and demand.

Such very different forecasts bring confusion to energy policies and present problems for the discussion of energy security in the 1990s. As stated on p. 19 of the general tripartite introductory chapter, energy security is determined by anticipated danger (the degree of which depends on its scale, how often it occurs and how long it lasts) and countermeasures to deal with it (two types of measures, one before and the other after the danger takes place). If the anticipated danger contains too large a factor of probability, countermeasures will have to widen in scope to deal with every possible situation, and this makes the task difficult. Another factor is that energy security is a 'matter of degree'[3]; in other words what constitutes 'security' is relative in concept depending on countries, particularly when Japan, the United States and Europe discuss the matter from their respective points of view. Clarification of these problems can probably provide clues to answering the question 'Why energy security in the 1990s now?'

Political and economic changes in the Middle East and the oil glut which began in the early 1980s seem to have alleviated the need for concern over energy security. Efforts exerted by developed nations such as Japan, the US and Europe to reinforce countermeasures appear at first glance to have secured sufficient energy security.

For example, as regards the Middle East:

i) The Egyptian-Israeli peace treaty (signed in March 1979) has divided the Arab world, which renders it unlikely that oil will again be used as a political weapon for the sake of 'Arab causes'.

ii) The Iran-Iraq war has been going on for seven years now, but has not prevented either country from exporting oil. This suggests that conflict in the Gulf region could disrupt oil supply only for a while, but would not cut it off permanently.

As regards the demand and supply of oil:

iii) As diversification from oil, the introduction of new alternative forms of energy, and conservation efforts have progressed steadily, economic growth is no longer automatically linked with an increase in oil consumption: demand therefore seems unlikely to increase greatly in the future.

iv) The so-called 'oil glut' is expected to last for some time and a buyers' market should continue.

With regard to the cartel function of OPEC:

v) Commoditisation of oil demonstrates the superiority of market forces in the pricing mechanism and the cartel function of OPEC seems to have been lost.

vi) The oil price collapse since the end of 1985 is said to have occurred because of changes in supply and demand. Oil exporting countries had exploited the short-term price inflexibility of oil supply, and this encouraged exploration and development of oil reserves in non-OPEC regions, and the introduction of alternative energy and energy conservation efforts. Consequently, demand for OPEC oil decreased dramatically. OPEC countries are aware of the mistakes they have made and will probably not raise their prices without carefully considering the prices of alternative energy sources.

Finally, with regard to countermeasures:

vii) Since the developed countries now have sufficient emergency oil reserves and have instituted the International Energy Agency's emergency programme for international mutual help, temporary disruption of Middle East supplies can be dealt with.

viii) Countries with surpluses in conventional alternative fuels such as coal and natural gas are eager to export them to obtain hard currencies. Therefore, any oil price rise will encourage the introduction of conventional alternative energy.

Each of the above-mentioned factors is persuasive in its own way. If we are to come up with an answer to 'Why energy security in the 1990s now?', we have to examine these factors one by one and see if they are relevant to the energy climate of the 1990s.

Uncertainty of the Middle East situation. Since the signing of the Egyptian-Israeli peace treaty, Egypt, which had been the strongest Arab opponent of Israel, has dropped out of the war front, and the focal point has moved to the Palestinian issue. However, reconciliation of the Palestinians, who desperately want to have their rights as a people, and Israel, which demands its right to exist as a recognised state, seems remote at present. The prospect for Middle East peace is therefore bleak.[4] Some people see the oppressed Palestinians as having only two choices, either to become terrorists or to turn to Islamic fundamentalism and prepare for war against Israel.[5] In any event, they represent continued political instability.

As regards the Iran-Iraq war, the confrontation will most likely not be resolved completely even if the two countries agree to a truce, in view of the history of conflict between Persians and Arabs. It is said that because of historical, racial and religious diversity, the Middle East contains more factors of instability than any other region[6], although direct relations between these factors and disruption in oil supply have yet to be proved. On the other hand, if East-West detente prevails in the 1990s and economic reconstruction is given priority in the Middle East countries, long- and large-scale disruption in the oil supply, based on political motives, is hardly likely (see Section III, part 1). However, brief interruptions in supply cannot be ruled out completely, and a sharp price rise could still occur depending on the duration and scale of the disruption and on the response of consumer countries. And if Islamic fundamentalism sweeps the Gulf area and challenges conservative regimes in the 1990s, the danger of disruption of supply will loom large.

No-one can accurately envisage what the Middle East situation will be in the 1990s, and this inherent uncertainty signifies uncertainty about the Middle East oil supply. In this respect the present situation has not changed in the slightest since the oil crises of the past, which is significant.

Uncertainty of oil supply-demand outlook. As regards the medium- to long-term outlook (i.e. in the 1990s) there are two opposing views concerning oil demand. According to one, it will steadily increase, especially in the developing countries, as decreases in the crude oil price increase OECD members' demand.[7] According to the other, a dramatic increase cannot be expected for three reasons.

i) The demand curve has shifted downwards because of large-scale investment in energy conservation measures, the introduction of alternative energy sources and changes in the industrial structure in the main developed nations.

ii) Demand for energy-consuming durable consumer goods has peaked, and the income elasticity of energy demand has decreased.

iii) Price elasticity draws an asymmetric curve when the price fluctuates.[8]

Although the last may apply to the Japanese situation, whether or not it applies to the US is another matter. Due to the deregulation policy which the Reagan Administration is promoting, the price mechanism is expected to operate in a straightforward manner.[9] If oil consumption in the US, which consumes three times as much oil as Japan, increases more than expected, it will have a tremendous impact on the world's oil supply-demand relations.

With regard to oil supply, OPEC controls 67% of total proven recoverable reserves. Similarly, OPEC's ratio of reserves to production is 77 years compared with the non-OPEC regions' 16 years. Although considerable quantities of recoverable reserves do exist in non-OPEC regions, they are expected to be found in Arctic/Antarctic areas, the deep sea bottom, remote inland areas, etc., which renders their exploitation difficult both economically and technically. Furthermore, recently discovered oil fields are small in scale, and in spite of the sharp price rise which followed the oil crises, the number of newly discovered oil reserves, apart from the Middle East region, is diminishing. The oil supply capability of non-OPEC regions has more or less reached its peak and will level off and begin to decline gradually after 1990 at the latest.[10]

If we examine the relationship between the use of oil and gross additions to reserves in the period 1970-84, we find that apart from the years 1972, 1976, 1977, and 1979, the use of oil totalled 313.5 billion barrels as opposed to gross additions to reserves of 479.7 billion barrels. Thus, if we use more expensive forms of alternative energy instead of comparatively cheap oil, this cheaper oil could be left underground as an unexploited resource. Some academics who subscribe to this thinking assert that we should 'persuade the world at large that oil is a secure, plentiful, clean and preferable source of much of the world's energy needs for the foreseeable future instead of emphasising, as over recent years, resource availability problems and indeed even presenting quite pessimistic views on the relationships between reserves development and use'.[11]

In contrast to this view, however, one needs only to look at the Chernobyl disaster in April 1986. Negative public reaction to nuclear energy in the face of such occurrences may lead to an increase in demand for other energy sources, including oil.[12]

Thus, as we have reviewed the present situation, there is much uncertainty over the supply-demand outlook for oil. Indeed, this is the only fact that is not in doubt.

Possible restoration of OPEC cartel. The change in Saudi Arabia's oil policy in September 1985 and the subsequent decision to abandon production control at the OPEC meeting in December brought the collapse of OPEC's cartel function, i.e. the abandonment of price control of crude oil. Consequently, crude oil prices collapsed and oil producing nations other than Saudi Arabia - particularly those which were producing at their maximum or near-maximum capacity - suffered greatly. If Saudi Arabia's objectives are to re-establish a stronger foundation for OPEC price administration and to put pressure on other oil exporting countries inside and outside OPEC to co-operate in bringing this about[13], then the decision on a production ceiling taken at OPEC's general meeting (excluding Iraq) in July and August 1986, and the agreement on oil output reduction at the general meeting in December 1986, which aims at the restoration of a fixed oil price of $18b, can both be interpreted to be in line with Saudi long-term strategy. According to one calculation, if the real crude oil price of $18b is maintained until 1990, oil demand by then will increase by 5 million barrels per day (mbd). Oil supplied by non-OPEC countries will decrease by 1 mbd and demand for OPEC oil will increase to 22-24 mbd.[14] As a result, the oil supply share of OPEC and non-OPEC countries will be reversed in the mid-1990s; hence there is a good likelihood of OPEC restoring its cartel function in the late 1990s. There is one snag, however: Saudi Arabia's long-term moderate strategy may be hampered by an internal conflict within OPEC or by other unexpected events.

Insufficient adaptability. Developed countries see Japan as a country whose economy has succeeded in coping with the oil crises. The world view is generally optimistic that Japan's flexible economy can overcome another oil crisis. Is this realistic? It is true that the IEA's emergency reserves are sufficient to cover a 20% reduction in oil supply for one year, but they are not enough to deal with open-ended, untargeted disruption. For example, if OPEC supply is reduced by half, IEA emergency reserves of 90 days will run out in six months. In other words, open-ended untargeted disruption will be difficult to deal with properly.[15] Although the IEA has an emergency programme, there is some doubt that it will work in an actual emergency.[16]

What we have just reviewed indicates insufficient adaptability or the uncertainty of oil supply in the case of physical disruption. Apart from the problem of the amount of supply, the problem of price is most important. When supply becomes tight, the price goes up and people are anxious to keep sufficient stocks, which in turn increases demand in some cases.[17] The OECD's revenue reduction due to the second oil crisis between 1980 and 1981 is estimated to have been more than one trillion (million million) dollars[18], which demonstrates how serious the effect of the inflationary price rise has been on the OECD economy. Unless a proper mechanism to deal with oil price rises is established quickly, the world economy will be adversely affected.

As far as conventional alternative energy sources are concerned, they are bound by long-term production and sales agreements. The lead time between exploration and sales is long. Various kinds of infrastructure are required, whose establishment costs money and time. These requirements can be met only if the long-term oil price outlook is stable. Therefore, an oil price rise in the short term might not be restrained by the pricing of these conventional alternative energy sources.

2. Japan's special circumstances

Let us now examine the special circumstances of Japan, regarding its energy supply structure, energy trade structure and Middle East diplomacy, with a view to presenting ideas for managing its energy security in the 1990s.

Energy supply structure. Table 2.1 shows the energy supply structure of the major developed countries. It reveals the greater dependence of Japan's primary energy on imported oil from the Middle East and particularly crude oil passing through the Strait of Hormuz, as of 1984, although the figures have shown some improvement since 1973. Of course, it does not necessarily signify Japan's vulnerability in terms of energy security compared with the rest of the developed countries. Nonetheless, we can see the special situation Japan is faced with, because it is lacking in energy resources and therefore has to rely largely on imported oil from abroad, and from the Middle East in particular.

Energy trade structure. Japan's energy consumption in 1985 amounted to 365 mtoe, which constitutes 5% of world consumption, and its imported primary energy in 1984 constituted 17% of internationally traded oil, 28% of coal and 74% of LNG (natural gas) (see Table 2.2). Thus, Japan occupies an important position in the world's energy trade.

As far as coal and LNG are concerned, Japan has promoted a 'develop and import' system (development with assured importation of a certain proportion of the product), which has created a unique situation in energy trade. The number of supplying countries has been reduced to a handful, with Japan agreeing to import most of the supplier's product, such as Australian coal and Indonesian natural gas. Such an arrangement illustrates Japan's dependence on the political and economic stability of these countries, and its potential vulnerability to internal disturbances, terrorism and strikes, which could result in disruption of energy supply. However, there is also an advantage for the exporting countries, for they have secured a large and stable export market in Japan.

As regards oil, there are no similar arrangements. Table 2.3 shows the changes in quantity and percentage of Middle East oil exports. Between 1975 and 1984 the share of Japan and South East Asia combined rose to 45% (notably, South East Asia increased its net imports by 0.105 mbd, despite the price rises during that time). This means increased significance of these markets to the Middle East. Since political stability in the Middle East is yet to be established, Japan has to make an effort to develop and introduce alternative energy sources and propagate its advanced energy conservation technology in East Asia for the sake of energy security in the region.

Middle East diplomacy. Japan's Middle East diplomacy following the first oil crisis was called 'resource diplomacy', because energy security was as important an issue in terms of national interest as was a friendly relationship with the United States.[19] We are now moving away from oil as the main source to the 'age of multiple energy sources', in which there will be an equal demand for different energy sources such as oil, coal, nuclear, natural gas and other new types of energy to meet existing energy needs.[20] Accordingly, the period between the 1990s and the early part of the twenty-first century can be regarded as a transitional period. The dilemma of giving priority to friendly relationships with oil producing Arab countries or with the Western alliance, will remain a potential problem for many years to come. Since Japan has renounced all military action including the export of arms, it cannot allow itself to become directly involved in the security issues of the Middle East region. Accordingly, it has to establish a co-operative relationship with the Middle East countries based on non-military grounds, that is, on matters of economy and technology. (See Section IV for the kind of approach Japan should take towards the Middle East.) Moreover, it must assume an important role, based on its strengths in financial and technological areas, in developing energy security for the West. Through this 'division of labour', or delegation of responsibilities, concerted energy and diplomatic policies can be most effectively promoted among the OECD countries.[21]

II. Effects of low oil prices

1. Factors leading to the sharp drop in prices

Changes in the supply-demand structure. The fundamental reason for the sharp drop in oil prices is the change in the supply-demand structure. High oil prices following the second oil crisis led to a sharp fall in demand, mainly among the industrialised countries, and since there was a surge in supply among the non-OPEC producers, the proportion of oil produced by OPEC dropped. This changed the nature of the international oil market from its strongly political and cartel-like orientation when the OPEC producers were dominant to one in which oil is treated as a commodity.

Decreased demand for oil. The decrease in demand is due to the shift to other sources of energy, to changes in the industrial structure (particularly in Japan, away from heavy industries and towards those consuming much less energy), and finally, to efforts to conserve energy.

Predominance of non-OPEC oil. One of the reasons for the present popularity of non-OPEC oil is that the

OPEC suppliers are unstable and the industrialised countries, seeking political and economic guarantees, wanted to move away from them. Another is that high prices since the second oil crisis have made it profitable to develop offshore, remote, or small oil fields, or to invest in secondary or tertiary recovery efforts that had previously been unprofitable. Yet another reason is that investment by the major oil companies and others has been concentrated in the less volatile investment climate of the non-OPEC countries. For all these reasons, the share of oil produced by OPEC has gradually declined.

<u>Increased spot transactions and the appearance of an oil futures market</u>. The above conditions have led to a worldwide glut of oil. Spot prices have tended to undercut long-term contract prices, resulting in more spot market trading (Table 2.4). However, prices on the spot market can vary widely, so an oil futures market was established in 1983 to offset risk. The futures market is free, so that the price of oil, like that of other primary products, can move up or down depending on market conditions. This has attracted investors from outside the oil industry. At the same time, crude oil pricing by the British National Oil Corporation (BNOC) in the North Sea was terminated, as that body was dismantled. Accordingly, the oversupply of oil created the perfect conditions for a fall in oil prices.

<u>Changes in Saudi Arabian policies</u>. Swing producer Saudi Arabia had been the main bulwark against the downward trend in oil prices, cutting production and rigidly adhering to its GSP (government selling price) policy. However, reduced production meant a drastic fall in government revenues, and since the other OPEC producers were unwilling to co-operate, Saudi Arabia announced that it would abandon its traditional role in July 1985. Increased Saudi production from September of that year and the sale of Saudi oil on a netback basis, together with deregulated pricing due to the dismantling of BNOC and the increasingly speculative atmosphere of the spot market, produced a sharp drop in prices. As a result, prices dropped further, and the large amount of surplus funds thus generated stimulated the speculative fever on the market (Tables 2.5, 2.6). OPEC lost price leadership and the futures and spot markets assumed the function of setting the benchmark price, leading to the drop in oil prices.

2. Price scenario to the year 2000

Medium to long-term forecast. As noted in Section I, the prevailing opinion in Japan is that oil supply and demand will remain flexible for some time but that demand will begin to rise in the 1990s, resulting in a rapid price increase. The scenario envisaged by the Institute for Energy Economics (IEE), described later, agrees with this view.

A different view - but not the majority opinion - holds that oil prices will not rise in the 1990s. According to Nobuyuki Nakahara, president of Toa Nenryo Kogyo[22]:

> The real price for oil in 1960 dollars, $5 per barrel ($20 per barrel in nominal terms) is more or less historically determined. However in terms of a stock market curve, present conditions correspond to an extended low price period. Therefore, oil prices will probably hold at $15-20 for some time, and the next peak will be reached around 2030, in accordance with the Kondrachev curve.

Short-term forecast. Over the short term of the next five years or so, many observers in Japan believe that, given the nature of the free market, prices will continue to fluctuate between $10 and $20 per barrel. However, Akitaro Seki, an oil economist, points out the possibility that oil prices may not prevail uniformly[23]. In his view, the oil demand curve (Figure 2.1) is perpendicular and can shift to left or right. Past experience shows that a decrease in excess production capacity to 2-4 mbd, even if oil is in excess supply, creates a psychological danger zone; prices start to rise because of anxiety about future supplies. If this holds true, present real excess capacity of 2.5-5 mbd affords little leeway. Prices could rise sharply at the least irregularity in supply or with even a small increase in consumption. In addition, Seki points out that an upward uncontrolled price spiral might occur in these circumstances.

The forecasts of the International Energy Agency and the Institute of Energy Economics in Tokyo are representative, and are introduced here as basic information in the presentation of the various arguments.

IEA forecast. The IEA has amended its forecast to show increased demand in its member countries for oil in 2000[24]. This is because oil prices are not expected to have risen as much as previously forecast, resulting in a more optimistic outlook for economic growth. However, this forecast does not allow for the recent drop in oil prices; oil consumption would be expected to go up if this adjustment were made.

At the same time, energy production by means of coal, nuclear, and hydro electric power generation is expected to grow steadily in IEA member countries. In addition, a more optimistic view of oil production will prevail and production capacity will fall off less rapidly than expected. This is because estimates of reserves in the US have been revised upward due to the development of technology for secondary and tertiary recovery and other processes. Nevertheless, oil imports by IEA countries are expected to increase; imports of 760 mtoe in 1984 are expected to rise to 820 mtoe in 1990, and to 990 mtoe in 2000.

However, if allowances are made for recent falls in the price of oil, more imported oil will be needed because oil production in IEA countries will drop further than estimated in this forecast, as secondary and tertiary recovery becomes unprofitable, small and medium sized oil fields in the US are shut down, and new oil developments in the IEA slow down.

According to the IEA's world energy forecast, total energy demands and the demand for oil itself will continue to grow. The market will tighten up, and since non-OPEC production will decrease, dependence on OPEC sources will grow. In 2000, it is foreseen that 50% of the 26.6 mbd oil supply will come from OPEC. The IEA is also concerned that the recent drop in oil prices will result in a 2-3 mbd increase in consumption, further worsening the situation. In the short term, however, the changeover to alternative sources of energy, gains made in energy-saving technology, and higher consciousness of conservation are expected to continue. Moreover, it will take time for the savings resulting from lower oil prices to trickle down to consumers and be reflected in increased consumption. Also, because of existing environmental restrictions in many countries, increased oil consumption is expected to be concentrated in thermo-electric power plants that are now idle. Over the long term, the IEA foresees that lower oil prices will lead to lower investment in energy-saving technology and alternative sources of energy, demand for oil will increase, and dependence on OPEC sources will grow, thus setting the stage for a new energy crisis.

IEE forecast. The IEE recently developed a world energy demand simulation taking into account recent falls in oil prices.

Fixed price simulation. A simulation was run using primary energy supply and demand (Table 2.7), decrease in the supply of alternative energy (Table 2.8), and long-term potential oil supply (Table 2.9) to draw a picture of the world oil balance (Table 2.10). This simulation assumed that 1986 oil prices ($25, $20, $15, and $10 per barrel respectively) would remain constant over the ten years to 1995. According to this, at $15 per barrel, in 1995 the necessary OPEC production will be 36.4 mbd, far above OPEC's projected production capacity of 6 mbd. This indicates that OPEC will also be unable to meet demand. US oil imports at $15 per barrel (Table 2.11) show that US dependence on imported oil in 1990 will rise to 55%, surpassing 8.5 mbd. Thus dependence on imported oil will be more than it was immediately before the second oil crisis. The IEE points out that this could become a factor contributing to a sharp rise in the price of oil.

Variable price simulation. Price fluctuations are a fact of life. A drop in crude oil prices paves the way for a further price rise because of increased demand and decreased production. On the other hand, higher prices contribute to a drop in demand and increased production and lead to an eventual fall in prices. The IEE has taken this 'cyclical price fluctuation' into account in the variable price simulation shown in Table 2.12, based on the fixed price simulation. This variable price simulation assumes a V curve scenario, with 1986 prices of $20, $15, and $10 per barrel starting to rebound two or three years later. The supply-demand balance was calculated using the correlation between the average rise in oil demand based on the fixed price simulation for each of the prices at the 1986 level, and the decrease in oil supply based on the rate of decrease of non-OPEC oil production (Table 2.10) for each price. Using this, the upward movement in prices for each year was calculated, with the rebound taking place two or three years after the period of balanced supply and demand.

According to this simulation, the average price of oil will continue to fluctuate between $15 and $18 over the next two or three years. During the period from the late 1980s to the early 1990s, prices will jump to a little over $20 and hold for a time. After the mid 1990s, however, prices will start to rise, to $24 in 1995 and then to $30 in 2000 (the 1986 price in real terms). This view anticipates future prices rebounding by as much as they dropped in the past, the reason being that the drop in prices will accelerate oil field closures and reduce investment in oil field development. In addition, increased energy demands due to economic growth and lower supply of alternative energy will lead to increased dependence on OPEC oil. This trend is particularly evident in the US and could lead to an abrupt increase in US oil imports.

The IEE has formulated another variable price simulation with a flat bottomed U curve, based on the assumption that prices will remain low for the remainder of the 1980s. Calculations according to this simulation show that the price rebound would be much greater.

OECD energy needs in 2000. The IEE believes that economic growth trends will influence energy demand, and that crude oil price trends will affect the competitiveness of various forms of energy. Table 2.13 estimates the OECD's energy needs in 2000, assuming a yearly world economic growth rate of 2.8% (1985-2000) and allowing for the previously mentioned V shaped curve illustrating oil price fluctuations.

According to this, the demand for oil compared to the present would decrease by 3.4-4.4 mbd. Demand for coal would grow as it became more price competitive than oil, leading to diversification in the world's source of energy. According to the IEE's rather optimistic forecast, this would mean less reliance on any one source of energy and less concern about continuing access to energy supplies.

3. Structural changes in the market and industry

<u>From control by the majors to decisions by OPEC.</u> During the 1930-1960s period, the international oil market was controlled by a loose international structure which could be termed 'guided laissez faire'. After all, the large international integrated oil companies (majors), known as the 'Seven Sisters', controlled the exploration, development, refining and marketing of oil on a worldwide basis, and by regulating production in oil exporting countries under their control, they directed cyclical changes, changes in demand arising from changes in pricing within the international market. In other words, cyclical changes were almost entirely absorbed by the oil producing and exporting nations.

A structural turning point came in 1970 when US oil production reached its peak. This meant that the US ceased to have surplus capacity capable of supplying its allies when the flow of oil was interrupted for political reasons, as in 1956 Suez crisis and the June war of 1967.

The relative strengths of the oil companies and the governments of the oil producing countries were abruptly reversed, and during the 1970s OPEC removed the control of resources from the vertically integrated companies. By the late 1970s, both pricing and production levels were no longer determined by the majors, but by the political and commercial motivations of the oil producing nations, with the burden of changes in the market falling on consuming nations.

<u>The revival of market theory.</u> In the late 1980s, the supply-demand situation became easier for the consuming countries due to a decrease in demand brought about by the high prices of the second oil crisis. In addition, a recession in the industrialised nations, the use of alternative fuel sources and conservation, and increases in oil production by the non-OPEC countries, all combined to further ease the situation, and OPEC was forced to maintain prices by co-operative cuts in production. However, the individual quotas set under the joint production system were not adhered to by all OPEC members out of concern for their individual interests, so that Saudi Arabia, the swing producer,

suffered all the damage. When Saudi production levels fell as low as approximately 2 mbd in the third quarter of 1985, it abandoned its role of market stabiliser, and announced that it would be carrying out a price offensive to regain market share.

This meant not only the collapse of OPEC's ability to control the international oil market, but also the entrustment of price formation to market theory. This may signal a return to the period before the 1930s when the international oil cartel was established and prices stabilised. As the fluctuation in oil price increases, the need for a hedge is intensified. As a result, trading of crude oil futures on the New York Mercantile Exchange (NYMEX), which started in 1983, has grown rapidly in recent years. The concept of oil trading is reputed to have changed greatly following the development of such trading in futures. In other words, the growth of options and futures markets has increased information-oriented oil trading and has turned oil into a commodity or financial instrument. The following might be considered to be the conditions necessary to bring an end to such commoditisation:

i) Revival of sales of crude oil by oil producing countries with preferential terms for certain customers.

ii) National oil corporations of the oil producing countries enter fully into downstream activities, and provide products at lower prices than competitors.

iii) Intervention by oil importing countries in the market e.g. through the introduction of import charges/fees, import tariffs, minimum import prices and control of petroleum product prices.

<u>The market and industry in the 1990s</u>. According to the IEA forecast, presented at the time when the impact of the dramatic decline in oil prices was not fully assimilated, OPEC's share of oil supplies to the OECD countries was expected to rise from 37.7% in 1985, to 41.5% in 1990 and 49.6% in 2000 (Table 2.14). Moreover, according to the IEE's simulation results (June 1986) calculating the impact of the sudden drop in oil prices, if the actual oil price was fixed during the period 1986-95 at either $20 or $15 per barrel, the share of

OPEC oil was expected to exceed that of non-OPEC countries in either the early 1990s or the late 1980s (Table 2.10, Figure 2.2).

The sudden decline in oil prices has had an impact on oil supply and demand as shown above, and this may accelerate the time when OPEC's share of supplies overtakes non-OPEC's by over five years in some cases, from the year 2000 target previously considered. The significance of this is clear: the conditions for a revival of the OPEC cartel will be in place.

Decreases in revenues for oil producing countries as a result of low prices lead to delays in domestic economic development and worsening deficit problems for both OPEC and non-OPEC countries. The problem here is the possibility of exhausting reserves earlier than expected, in countries other than a few large oil producing nations, as a result of production at maximum capacity to make up revenues. There is speculation that Algeria, Ecuador, Gabon, and Qatar will have to drop out of OPEC by 1990. In addition, it is suggested that the larger than expected increases in North Sea oil production are likely to accelerate the pace of production decline after the peak has been attained. Taken together with the fact that reserves to production ratios are generally small for non-OPEC countries, it may well be that the low oil price will bring forward the depletion of oil resources for those countries with relatively small reserves, and bring about the concentration of world oil production capacity in the Gulf region.

This means a decline in the number of oil supplying countries, which is one aspect of the reorganisation of the international market. There is also another aspect; the full-scale entry into downstream activities such as refining and marketing by the national oil corporations of the oil producing countries, and the possibility of their entry into the international market as vertically integrated companies. At present the move into downstream activities by oil producing countries (Saudi Arabia, Kuwait, and Venezuela) has not yielded much in the way of results. This is due to the difficult conditions arising from competition in the European oil products market and the scrapping of excess refining capacity. However, there are rewards in expanding operations from crude oil to production and sales of higher value oil products. In other words, even if differences arise between the profitability of crude oil and product sales, it will be possible to limit the damage by participating in both activities. For example, during periods of low crude oil prices (particularly netback contracts), downstream activities are more profitable than the upstream division, while the reverse is true when oil prices are high. Therefore the oil producing countries will enjoy stable maximum earnings as a result of vertical integration.

It has been suggested that at a time when there is a surplus of oil in the world market, oil producing nations with high export capacities should co-operate closely with international oil companies, or promote vertical integration in oil consuming countries through their national oil corporations, or both, in order to secure minimum export volumes. This view is based on the assumption that oil producing countries need to limit their customers and markets in order to secure their sales outlets and revenues, in accordance with the scope of their export volumes. If this view is correct, those oil producers with large export capacity will rely on their own vertically integrated national oil corporations and the sales networks of existing international oil companies, while countries with a low export capability will rely more on the open (spot) market (Figure 2.3). Up to now, only Kuwait and Venezuela have attempted entry into overseas downstream activities. However, if Saudi Arabia and other countries are unable to use the distribution facilities of the existing international oil companies, the national oil corporations of these countries may appear on the international oil market in the future as global, vertically integrated corporations. Moreover, should low oil prices continue in the medium to long term, such a development may take place in order to stabilise and maximise oil revenues.

4. The influence on Japanese demand

The recent change in imported crude oil prices, which began in late 1985, demonstrates how sharp the drop has been. The average price of imported crude oil in January 1986, by which time prices had already started to drop, was $27.77 per barrel (¥35,298/kl). The price dropped to $16.46 (¥18,488) in April, and $10.34 (¥10,081) in August. Although it has also been affected by the high appreciation of the yen which took place after the meeting of the Group of Five (the US, the UK, Germany, France and Japan) Finance Ministers in September 1986, Japan is now able to buy crude oil at less than a third of its price at the beginning of 1986. This price collapse gives rise to the natural expectation that oil consumption will increase. This section will review the impact the 1986 crude oil price collapse has had on Japanese energy consumption, especially oil demand, by examining industry, transport, residential energy consumption and electricity.

Industry. Classified by industries (from the viewpoint of alternative energy). Following the oil crises of the 1970s, the steel and cement industries, which require vast amounts of energy, were the first to make the conversion from oil to coal. The paper/pulp industry and the chemical industry were quick to follow. Are these energy-intensive industries going to reconvert from coal to oil because of the recent oil price collapse? In July 1986, the IEE issued 'Choice of fuel among the main industries', which explains the issues and concerns in making the choice between oil and coal, and which gives a clue to answering this question. The borderline in terms of energy conversion is $13.20 per barrel for steel, $20.20 for cement, $23.80 for paper/pulp, and $19.00 for the chemical industry, which suggests reconversion to heavy fuel oil to be a better choice for many industries. However, up to September 1986, there has been no such move apart from the paper/pulp industry. The steel industry uses coke for smelting, because it produces useful gas as a by-product. The cement industry sees stability of supply as the more important consideration, and oil does not meet this criterion. For the time being, the chemical industry is merely suspending its conversion to coal, which it undertook later than other industries. Since the energy consumption of the paper/pulp industry amounts to a mere 4% of the total manufacturing consumption, reconversion to oil at the moment appears to be minimal.

Classified by factors of energy conservation. Energy conservation has been achieved at the level of individual companies by: conservation in a narrow sense; efficient use of energy in production processes; manufacturing products whose energy costs are lower and which have added value; and changing the industrial structure from energy-intensive to one which consumes less energy.

How will the current drop in oil prices affect these factors? Business enterprises which have learned lessons from the two oil crises are sensitive to energy cost, even though at present there is little merit or incentive for energy conservation because of low oil prices. Consequently, expected price fluctuations have become built-in to industries, enabling them to survive competition in the domestic as well as international markets. There may be further developments, since the economy is becoming more software-oriented, and the strong yen is establishing itself, if not getting stronger. Therefore, the energy demands of the industrial sector will not substantially increase unless production as a whole increases.

Transport. Passenger cars are most affected by falling oil prices; they were responsible for 79% of petroleum consumption in domestic transport in 1984. Even after the second oil crisis, passenger cars with a higher energy consumption per unit (Kcal/person-kilometre), increased their share compared with other facilities for domestic transport in terms of transported persons per kilometre. In addition, average fuel costs (km/litre) of passenger cars, which have been levelling off in recent years, may go up due to the popularity of higher-powered cars. The drop in petrol price is likely to increase petrol consumption as well as the number of transported passengers. As for diesel, there has been a shift from petrol-consuming cars for commercial use to vehicles which consume diesel. In service industries, consumption of diesel by small trucks is increasing.

Residential consumption. The oil price drop will affect the demand for kerosene, which is popular in Japan for space heating, and which can be easily substituted for other fuels. However, since the consumption ratio of kerosene to total energy consumption is only 6% (1984), the impact of the oil price drop in this respect is not important in terms of quantity. The price drop will probably release people from economic restraints as an incentive to conserve energy and encourage them to opt for a better living environment, which will then increase energy demand as a whole. Whether or not oil-based fuel will be chosen depends on overall evaluation of its economic efficiency, usefulness, safety, etc.

Electricity generation. Nuclear power plays the role of base load. Its fuel costs are cheaper, therefore it retains its present level of operation. LNG is responsible for middle or peak supply. Electricity supply is bound by contract to purchase certain quantities of LNG. Coal-fired power producers are also bound by long-term coal purchasing agreements. Hydro-electric power generation does not involve fuel costs. Therefore oil-fired power stations, which usually take care of peak supply, have little room in the short run for increasing their power output. Although some industries have switched from buying electricity from public utilities to independent power stations, no change seems to have taken place in terms of oil consumption.

What about the long-term outlook? According to computations done in 1986 by the Agency of Natural Resources and Energy of electricity costs over the life of power generation facilities, there is no particular economic advantage in oil-fired power stations, provided the crude oil price is between $30 and $40 per barrel in 2000. In view of unstable oil prices, which would undermine energy security, reversion to oil-fired power stations is unlikely.

Summary. From a management viewpoint, industries which require investment in large-scale plant and equipment, or purchase large quantities of coal and LNG under long-term contracts to ensure a stable supply, are unlikely to decide to reconvert to oil as long as uncertainty over future crude oil prices lingers. As shown above, it is unlikely that industries which use vast amounts of energy will reconvert. Households or industries with low fuel costs or ease of conversion will probably go ahead, although the scale of this conversion in terms of quantity will not be large. Industries which rely heavily on oil, such as the transport industry (excluding electric railways), will increase their demand for oil gradually, as the fall in prices removes the pressure to conserve. Therefore it cannot be ruled out that oil demand, which has hitherto fallen, may eventually turn upwards and gradually increase. However, because of the present energy situation in Japan, this trend may not surface for a while. For instance, another unusually hot summer or cold winter, as experienced in 1984 and 1985, will result in an increase in oil demand in 1987. Rapid appreciation of the yen since the Group of Five meeting has driven export-oriented industries into recession due to a loss of competitive edge in the world market. This will also work as a negative factor against energy demand. Nonetheless, low oil prices do discourage industries from switching to other fuels. In this respect, concern for energy security is still well justified.

5. Conclusion

It is extremely difficult to quantify how the present low prices will affect the supply-demand relationship of oil in the future. Many institutions have presented the results of their studies of the non-OPEC supply-demand situation, using econometric models. However, they rely on the past performance of oil supply and demand and its price elasticity, and it is doubtful whether they can predict the future correctly. For example, the price elasticity of oil demand does not necessarily follow a symmetrical curve when prices go up, as opposed to when they come down. Since development of energy requires long lead times, and is dependent on government policies, the influence of the oil price drop on energy supply will appear gradually, with some time lag. Moreover, the results of a fixed price simulation should be understood more flexibly, because supply and demand change in a dynamic way through the market, where a tight supply-demand relationship increases oil prices.

This must be taken into consideration in understanding some of the figures from the simulations cited below.

A long-term projection before the collapse of crude oil prices forecast that the supply of oil and its importance among primary energy sources in Japan, the US, and the European Community in the year 2000 would be lower than in 1984 (Table 2.15). However, when the influence of low oil prices was taken into account (Table 2.16), the forecast showed that in 1990 oil demands in the US and Europe would surpass those in 1984 and 1985, and net imports or import dependence would be increased at the same time.

The following conclusions can be drawn from the projections for oil consumption, oil imports, and oil imported from the Middle East from 1984 to 2000 in Japan, the US, and Europe (Table 2.17).

i) Oil consumption will increase only in the US (cf.b).

ii) The share of oil in final energy consumption will decrease in all three areas (cf. b/a).

iii) The volume of imported oil will increase for the US and Europe. For Western Europe, where the amount of imported oil had been decreasing from 1973 to 1984 because of increased North Sea oil production, the situation will be reversed (cf.g).

iv) The share of imported oil in oil consumption will increase for all three areas (cf.c/b).

v) The amount of oil imported from the Middle East will increase for all three areas, and especially for Europe and the US (cf.d).

vi) The share of oil imported from the Middle East in oil consumption will also be higher (cf.d/b). In Japan, the ratio may reach as high as 70%. Most of the increased amount of imported oil for the US (2.9 mbd) will be provided by the Middle East. In Western Europe, reduction of the regional supply will be offset by oil from the Middle East (cf.g/h).

vii) Competition for Middle East oil will be caused mainly by the increase in imports to the US and Europe (cf.h).

viii) The increase in oil imports to the US will be four times as large as that for Europe (cf.g). This is because the increase in US oil consumption will be 2.6 times as large as for Japan and Europe (cf.f).

As indicated above, the results of low oil prices have shown that dependence on the import of oil and on Middle East oil will increase for Japan, the US, and

Europe. This means that the threat to their energy security will become more serious. Due to the low prices, the share of OPEC oil supply may rise (see part 3 of this Section) leading to a revival of OPEC's function as a cartel. This would further endanger their energy security. However, it should pose no problem if counteracting forces are improved to meet the rising threat. An increased threat does not necessarily mean a deterioration in energy security, or to put it another way, an increase in energy fragility.

III. Increased dependence on Middle East oil

1. Political instability in the Gulf

In reaction to the oil boom of the 1970s, the Gulf oil producing countries have suffered financial setbacks in the 1980s. This section will examine future prospects for the 1990s while taking a look at the situation in the late 1980s.

The year 1985 saw a hardening of three Middle East disputes: the Iran-Iraq war, the Arab-Israeli dispute, and the Lebanese civil war. 1986 was a year when all hopes for peace were dashed by Iranian intransigence, the terrorist strategies of the Palestinian hard-liners, and the political awakening of the Shi'ites in Lebanon.

The Iran-Iraq war. In August 1985, the Iraqi air force carried out an intensive air raid on the oil facilities of Kharg Island, once believed to be immune from air attack. Since then, oil exports from Iran have been under attack by the Iraqi air force. Iraq carried out as many as 120 attacks on the oil facilities of Kharg Island, Sirri Island, and Larak Island in the Strait of Hormuz in the south, including the shuttle tankers there, up to December 1986. In spite of the raids, the damage was repaired, and oil exports from Iran are still continuing on a large scale. Even so, Iran's oil export revenue dropped sharply to less than $6 billion in 1986, down from $16 billion in 1985 as a result of the decrease in production and low prices.

Meanwhile, Iran occupied Fao on the war's southern front in February 1986, and won the battle for possession of Meheran in Iranian territory on the central front from May to July. This demonstration of the weakness of the Baghdad government, plus skilful propaganda warfare, struck a blow against the morale of the Iraqi soldiers. On the diplomatic front, Iran improved its relations with the Soviet Union, Eastern Europe, China, France and the UK, and the Irangate incident in November 1986 revealed its shrewdness in negotiating a secret arms deal with its arch enemy, the US, and its lesser foe, Israel.

Up to now, each time Iraq has attacked Iran's oil facilities, Iran has made retaliatory attacks on the ships of third nations in the Gulf, and many Western nations have suffered in consequence. In May 1986, ships related to Saudi Arabia (ships registered in Saudi Arabia, or plying between Saudi ports etc) were targeted, and since September ships related to Kuwait have become targets. The 12 mile limit off the United Arab Emirates and Qatar was frequently violated, and the offshore oil field facilities of the UAE were attacked by an unidentified aggressor in October and November. Thus, the conflicts of the Iran-Iraq war have gradually begun to involve the whole Gulf area. In this situation, the role of the Gulf oil producing countries that have been providing back-door help to Iraq and trying to avoid war damage from Iran has become increasingly difficult. However, the joint defence of the Gulf oil producing countries was not established even at the GCC summit conference in November.

The OPEC oil ministers' conference in the latter half of 1986 was noteworthy because of Iran's proposal to eliminate Iraq from OPEC's reduction plan at the August regular meeting. It has been said that Saudi Arabia's slight oil policy shift towards Iran dates from this event. Although the Gulf oil producing countries obviously have different views from that of Iran, which is to obtain the highest price and as quickly as possible, they can no longer afford to overlook Iran because of the oil and military situations.

<u>The Arab-Israeli dispute and the Lebanese civil war.</u> In February 1986, King Hussein of Jordan announced a split from PLO chairman Yasser Arafat, abandoning the solidarity which had characterised their relationship since

the Amman agreement drawn up between the two in February 1985. This had led to a rift within the PLO and to intensified terrorism. As a result, 1986 could be regarded as a year spent in continuous efforts to find countermeasures to combat international terrorism. However, faced with the present situation, many international organisations and governments have been making steady efforts to ease the strife within the PLO, to settle the Palestinian dispute through international conferences, and to develop and improve the economy and standard of living in the Gaza Strip and the West Bank of the Jordan.

Although the Israeli army withdrew from Lebanon in June 1985, this did not result in peace, but in a new and more intense struggle in Lebanon. The 'security zone' left by Israel when it withdrew with its ally, the South Lebanon army, has intensified Lebanon's efforts to liberate its national territory. Since late 1985, PLO commandos born in Lebanon and returning from Tunis etc., have caused problems with the Shi'ite Amal in the Palestinian refugee camps by trying to rebuild a nation within a nation. 1986 was a year in which prospects for peace collapsed. However, there is a small measure of hope for the future. Surprisingly, Irangate revealed the existence of a realistic faction within what was previously considered to be a closely united Iranian Government. The authorities arrested Hajatlesam Hashemi, an advocate of the International Islamic Liberation Movement, and he has been kept under house arrest. It seems that the Iranian Government was bearing in mind relations with the Soviet Union, Syria, and Israel, considering that excessive religious fervour makes enemies overseas.

As for the Arab-Israel dispute, the overwhelming feeling is that peace moved further away when the Israeli premiership changed from the dovish Peres to the hawkish Shamir. However, to keep this in perspective, it should be remembered that it was the militaristic Begin Government that signed the Camp David agreement. On the whole, the hawks are perceived as having a better chance of settling the dispute, the reason being that they will carry the doves along with them in any peace settlement.

After a period of transition in which the leadership changed frequently, the Soviet Union has been establishing the Gorbachev line, and it is reported that, besides resuming relations with Israel, it has recently started sounding out Saudi Arabia with the aim of establishing diplomatic relations. Relations had already been established with Oman and the UAE in 1985, but there were practical necessities behind the fact that these conservative countries opened relations with a communist power. This can be observed in the active non-alignment policy adopted by Kuwait which had been in a weak position since the early 1960s.

So far the Soviet Union has been strengthening its relationships with radical Arab countries through arms supplies, but it has often had meetings with nations on the rebound from the US, and has loosened its ties with Egypt, Somalia etc. The fact that the Soviet Union is an atheist country gives it little ground for acceptance in Islamic countries. However, while being fully aware of the dangers of communism, Iran, Israel and even Saudi Arabia have shown a pragmatic attitude by recognising the existence of the Soviet Union. This realism is crucial to the outlook for the Gulf area in the 1990s.

Future changes in the Iran-Iraq war. The impetus that has maintained the Gulf war has been the Ayatollah Khomeini's vision of an Islamic Jihad, in which the war has been defined as a challenge from secular Iraq to highly religious Iran, and Khomeini's refusal to end the war without victory. However, the influence of Khomeini will decrease in the 1990s, and the prediction is that after a middle-scale offensive in the spring of 1987, the war will enter an unofficial truce without an agreement. Both Iran and Iraq will face problems in rebuilding their military structures and economies. If oil prices stay at a reasonable level and if import demand by the industrialised countries increases only moderately, it will be difficult for them to secure enough oil revenues. This raises the possibility that they might aim at the properties and oil markets of the other Gulf oil producing countries. If things work out smoothly, bilateral assistance as well as assistance from the Gulf oil producing countries through international assistance organisations will be offered. In the worst scenario, a new local dispute will flare up.

Economic and political prospects for the Gulf oil producers. The economies of the Gulf, having experienced the oil boom of the 1970s, were then faced with the subsequent severe reaction of the 1980s. This had had political repercussions.

In Kuwait, Amir Jaber dissolved the national assembly in July 1986. There are many Shi'ites living along the coastal areas of the Gulf, and past experience has shown many cases where dissatisfaction with economic conditions has caused social unrest among them. Saudi Arabia has therefore gone to great lengths to ensure economic development and public welfare in the eastern province where there are many Shi'ites.

There is also the danger that insufficient oil revenue, together with a sluggish economy, may intensify the confrontation within the royal families. In many of the Gulf states, Islamic high priests, local clans, royal families, and emirates monopolise power, and that power must always be protected. The leaders of these countries also have health and old age problems, with Ayatollah Khomeini being the oldest at 87. Furthermore, Kuwait has a system whereby two branches of the ruling family take turns in wielding power, and Oman's Sultan Qaboos has no wife or heirs, so the climate is ripe for future succession disputes. There have been many of these kinds of internal disputes in the past but the real problems will probably arise in the 1990s.

What kind of confusion will occur in Iran and Iraq when the present leaders have departed? The US and European view, that the post-Khomeini period will be characterised by power struggles, has little support in Japan. Furthermore, the US and European view that the post-Saddam Hussein period will be a stable one because of the Ba'ath party in Iraq is also a minority view in Japan. According to one Japanese diplomat, Iran is like a carpet woven by the warp of Persia and the weft of Islam, so that it has a solid foundation, and this is the view held by the present author. In Iraq too, it seems that the Ba'ath party system is established both at government and private levels. Thus domestic power struggles and civil war over leadership issues are unlikely in either country.

Mutual relations between the Gulf states and domestic problems. The 1986 territorial dispute between Bahrain and Qatar left several areas in dispute, but this particular problem was settled through the mediation efforts of Saudi Arabia. Hence there is little possibility that such a dispute may lead to long-term armed conflict.

Sluggish economies and the spread of education will provide a favourable breeding ground for Shi'ites and the leftist factions. In addition, it will be essential for the authorities to police the Gulf area where the Palestinians are living. Saudi Arabia receives more than a million foreign religious visitors every year, and it is reported that political demonstrations in the streets and arms smuggling incidents have occurred under the guise of the haj. The Gulf oil producers must take care in releasing foreign workers back to their own countries, while replacing them with their own workers. In order to achieve this, the move towards industrialisation must be accelerated by making full use of the investments made so far in infrastructure. Police power must also be expanded to prepare for the unexpected.

Possible interruption in oil supplies. Previous examples of attacks on Iranian facilities in the Gulf show that complete destruction of oil facilities or stoppage of operations is difficult, while repair of any damage incurred has been mostly carried out in a short time, given available materials. As the security of oil facilities and power plants is extremely tight there would seem to be very little room for destruction.

If the 1990s are characterised by East-West detente, it will still be possible to control the various disputes in the Middle East. The area is likely to enter a period when disputes are suspended, resulting in far fewer opportunities to use oil as a political weapon. The producing countries will need to secure their oil revenues and make efforts towards stability of supplies, as the utmost emphasis will be placed on the reconstruction of their domestic economies during this period. Although domestic political instability will be intensified, it is unlikely to cause long-term massive interruptions in oil supplies.

However, there is a danger of short-term, medium-scale interruptions. One example would be if the Strait of Hormuz were to be blockaded. Another would be if some party were to occupy the oil fields and oil loading facilities of the Gulf producers. And a third case would be if civil wars were to break out in one or more of the Gulf Emirates or in the eastern province of Saudi Arabia, etc. In any of these instances, there is a danger that a sensitive reaction in the oil market would cause prices to soar and supplies to be disrupted. This could be avoided, however, if the governments of the industrialised countries were able correctly to apprehend the situation and its impact on supplies, and reassure the private sector by a prompt release of stocks. The first and second oil crises were the result of an amplification of the effects of supply stoppages, due to excessive reaction on the part of the industrialised countries. We should not forget the lessons we have learned from the past two occasions.

2. OPEC strategies

The following reasons have been given for the weakness of the OPEC cartel in restraining production and maintaining prices compared to the international oil companies[25]:

i) OPEC does not have a monopoly of crude oil supplies and increased production in non-OPEC countries tends to lead prices down;

ii) OPEC is an organisation of sovereign nations so that it cannot enforce a production ceiling which might infringe the sovereignty of its member nations, nor can it punish violators of its rules;

iii) Oil producing countries have a tendency to reduce prices in order to secure revenues as long as the situation of over-supply exists.

Oil cartel prices are being eroded by the market mechanism. The struggle over market share through price competition has been quite damaging to the oil producing countries. Saudi Arabia's policy turnabout in the autumn of 1985 actually made good its threat to the other OPEC countries of 'bringing the whole OPEC edifice crashing down on everyone's head like Samson'[26]. The movement towards co-ordinated reduction of OPEC production since August 1986 shows how effective the Saudi threat has been. There is no guarantee, however, that this will be continued successfully in the future. The latter half of the 1980s will be the testing period for OPEC as well as the time to learn the management of the international oil market by trial and error. The methods of market management include co-ordinated reduction by OPEC members; co-operation between OPEC and non-OPEC oil producing countries; a move towards international vertical integration by the national oil companies of oil producing nations by entering downstream activities; and co-operation between OPEC and the international oil companies. Whether the managing ability of OPEC, that is to say, its cartel function, will revive or not depends primarily on the level of demand for OPEC oil in the future. If demand increases steadily, as a number of forecasts have predicted, then OPEC will enter a period of co-ordinated restraint in which the production ceiling will be gradually raised in compliance with demand. On the other hand, if demand for OPEC oil does not increase as much as expected, the maintenance of a co-ordinated reduction plan will be impossible, and the trend will revert to the price wars experienced in the first part of 1986.

There are two types of co-ordinated reduction strategy in OPEC: one insisted on by the conservative Gulf states, and the other by the price-hawkish countries.

The strategy of suppressing energy conservation and alternative energy by moderate price levels. The former Saudi Arabian oil minister, Sheikh Yamani, made a new proposal in his lecture at Harvard University in September 1986. It exemplifies a strategy in which the average equilibrium price in the 7 years from 1986 to 1992 is set at \$18 per barrel (equilibrium price for each year is calculated as \$14-16 in 1986, \$15 in 1987, \$17 in 1988-9, \$19 in 1990-91, and \$20 in 1992). This is indeed a well-devised and strategic method of restraining energy conservation and alternative energy incentives in the consuming countries. It is also considered to be a part of Saudi Arabia's traditional long-term strategy[27].

It has yet to be shown whether the return to the fixed price system with the price of $18/b starting in February, 1987 will realise an equilibrium price with moderate increases. However, provided that strategic pricing is realised, it will undoubtedly have a striking impact on world oil supply and demand. First, on the supply side, costly fields in the non-OPEC countries, where the production cost for crude oil is $14/b or more, will be partially forced to close down. According to calculations (see Table 2.18) such fields exist in the US, Canada, and parts of Europe, with a capacity of 2 mbd and production at 1 mbd. Investments in exploration and development will be greatly cut at the beginning of the 1990s, and oil supply from non-OPEC countries will be reduced by 2 - 3 mbd compared with forecasts based on 1985 prices[28]. Efforts to conserve energy and to develop alternative energy and energy technologies are also expected to be promoted much more slowly from an economic standpoint. The result is estimated to be a much increased demand for OPEC oil, reaching some 22 - 24 mbd in 1990, and 26 - 28 mbd in the mid-1990s[29]. This indicates that OPEC would surpass non-OPEC countries in supplying the free world's oil needs.

As for a crude oil price, an average $18/b is a strategic price and its significance in energy security in the consumer countries should not be overlooked. However, if there is stability in crude oil prices, and uncertainty of price in the medium to long term is decreased, there will be a certain rational basis for the decision to invest in oil exploration and development, introduction of alternative energy, and development of energy technology. This will also be desirable from the perspective of energy security, as it would enable the public sector to judge how much incentive it should give to the private sector to promote alternative energy, energy conservation, and the development of energy technology which might not progress sufficiently if they were left in the hands of the private sector alone.

<u>The strategy of reducing production volume to seek higher prices</u>. The moderate price strategy is suitable for countries such as Saudi Arabia and other Gulf countries with conservative political attitudes, where oil reserves are abundant, the population is small, and domestic oil

demand does not put pressure on the amount of exports. Other OPEC countries, on the other hand, may not necessarily comply with such a strategy but may seek instead to maximise oil profits in the short term and to conserve resources. They might not insist on prices as high as $30/b or more, since they have learned that lesson previously. However, they might request a much lower production level than that proposed in the first strategy taking into account the demand for oil. Such a strategy requires co-operation not only from OPEC but also from non-OPEC countries. If prices for the first strategy are set at the equilibrium price, a cartel of all suppliers will be needed to maintain a price higher than this.

Over the medium to long term, is it possible to maintain a market price which surpasses the marginal supply price of non-OPEC countries? It may be possible in the short term, but certain non-OPEC countries (or even some OPEC countries) are likely to break the agreement. Maintenance and co-ordination of production standards will be difficult, and there is danger of the price structure breaking down. It is not welcomed by oil producing or consuming countries as it will create uncertainty as to the degree and likelihood of a price rise.

<u>The strategy of national oil companies entering downstream activities as vertically integrated entities.</u> The ultimate goal of OPEC countries entering downstream activities is to facilitate the development of their domestic economies as well as to encourage national oil companies to become vertically integrated like the majors[30]. A dominant factor hindering the national oil companies of producing countries in attaining vertical integration is their lack of expertise in finance and marketing. In order to overcome this, some OPEC countries have entered into consignment contracts with refiners in Europe for the refinement of crude oil and sales of products since 1979. Countries like Kuwait and Venezuela have acquired refining and sales operations in the European and US consumer markets. A sharp collapse of crude oil prices could potentially accelerate these trends, since the national oil companies in the producing countries would be assured of market access as the oil market becomes reintegrated[31]. The strategy's

execution might be delayed because of the difficult financial situation in the producing countries and excessive competition in the oil products market in Europe and the US. However, entering downstream will meet the economic security needs of the producing countries if the strategy is viewed as a long-term measure and executed in the 1990s or later.

What does such a strategy mean for the energy security of consuming countries? There are three differing views at present. The first insists that by entering downstream, the producing countries will directly confront market conditions, and take much more appropriate action based on market realities. As a result, so it is said, they will make efforts to secure clients and to stabilise oil prices, thus reducing the risk of interruption of supply. At the same time, the revival of the link between demand for oil products and the supply of crude oil will bring efficiency in the market, which will be seen as a side benefit as the mutual dependence of the producing and consuming countries deepens. The second view emphasises the negative factor that dependence not only on the supply of crude oil but also on refined oil products will further increase the chances that political motives in the producing countries will put supplies at risk. There is also a danger that many refiners and sales agencies in the consuming countries could not survive[32]. The third position argues that even complete downstream integration by producing countries would not bring stability of the market, but would destabilise it; production beyond agreed quotas could be hidden more easily and a cartel restriction on production volume would become extremely difficult. In addition, even in the absence of this effect, downstream integration is not enough to achieve the market stability that existed in 1972, if there is no control function over output[33].

The vertical integration strategy will certainly increase the threat to the consuming countries[34]. However, as it is also necessary for the producing countries to secure a sales market in order to secure income stability, this threat takes on less importance in the long run. Checks and balances effected through mutual dependence can be expected in the strategy of vertical integration and this will increase the counteracting force of the consuming countries. In addition, it will be necessary to take certain countermeasures such as reinforcing the stockpile of products and semi-products, or securing excess refining capacity, etc. Once these steps are put into effect, the strategy of the producing countries will not necessarily increase the fragility of the consuming countries.

3. Japan's ability to cope

The Japanese economy managed to overcome the last oil crisis and is now in quite good shape. As regards energy, Japan comes second to the US in energy consumption in the free world, and first in imported energy. The current oil situation is that supply exceeds demand, creating a buyers' market. Thanks to this favourable situation Japan is currently in a position to purchase as much energy as it needs for its economic activities. The fact remains, however, that Japanese economic security depends totally on energy resources from abroad. This is where energy security comes in. Have we learned anything from the experiences of the oil crises? In this matter, Japan can learn a great deal from Europe, which is more self-sufficient in energy and whose energy policy is more strategically oriented.

<u>Significance of controlling demand</u>. There have been three major oil crises during this century. The first (1916-17) occurred during the First World War, with the sudden increase in oil demand by the allied army. This first crisis was alleviated as big oil fields were discovered in Texas, USA. The second (1939-59) was also triggered by a world war and was not resolved until Middle East oil started to flow in abundance. Tremendous increases in oil supplies were important in resolving the first two oil crises. However, in the case of the most recent crisis, there was no big increase in supply, although production of non-OPEC oil such as North Sea oil was increased. The third crisis was remedied through reduction in oil demand in the face of the exorbitant price of oil which had nothing to do with production costs. Japan provides a good example to illustrate what has happened in recent years[35].

First, the relationship between Gross National Product (GNP) and energy consumption needs to be examined.

Figure 2.4 shows that energy consumption as compared with the real GNP basic unit had decreased by 30% in the 10 years since the first oil price rise of 1973. Next comes the relationship between production and energy consumption in the mining and manufacturing industries, whose combined share constitutes approximately half of total energy consumption. According to Figure 2.5, the graph showing changes in energy demand in the mining and manufacturing industries crossed that of the mining and manufacturing production index between 1981 and 1982, and has stayed below it ever since. The present status of energy conservation in major high energy consumption industries is shown in Table 2.19.

From the viewpoint of fuel conversion from oil to coal, the cement and steel industries have achieved dramatic improvement, as has the transportation industry, as far as effective use of energy is concerned. Average fuel consumption of passenger cars produced for domestic use, monitored in a simulation of 10 driving conditions, improved from 9.0 km/litre in 1975 to 13.0 km/litre in 1982 (See Figure 2.6).

Progress in energy consumption regarding refrigeration units, whose power consumption is outstanding among home electric appliances, is far more drastic. Electricity consumption of these appliances came down by one third during the period 1973-84 (as shown in Figure 2.7).

As the Japanese example demonstrates, the developed countries undertook fuel conservation and fuel conversion, and this reduced the demand for oil. With supply now exceeding demand, the market mechanism worked to lower crude oil prices. There are two possible cases which are capable of leading to an energy crisis: (a) production is cut for some reason, thus reducing supply, and (b) demand is gradually increased, leading to increased competition between consumers. As for (a), the crisis can be resolved if the cause of the supply stoppage is removed. However, in the case of (b), consumers have to adapt to the situation unless new sources of energy supply can be found. This requires time and great effort on the part of consumers, as we learned from the most recent crisis. Oil crises have hitherto tended to be discussed as a problem of supply, but there is an important element of demand, which needs to be pointed out.

Security of energy purchasing ability. When we look at energy security from the aspect of supply, it is important to promote self-sufficiency. Since domestic water-power resources and fossil fuels are limited, development of nuclear power, which can be regarded as a quasi-domestic resource, has to have priority. Nuclear power generation output increased seven-fold between 1974 and 1984, and its contribution in total electricity output has increased from 5% to 23%. This issue is studied in Section IV.3.

In 1985, Japan's dependence on foreign nations for the supply of its energy resources was 82%. As for oil, foreign dependence rose to 99.7% (69% being crude oil from the Middle East). On the other hand, dependence of primary energy supply on oil was 68%. Energy security therefore requires diversification of energy sources and a wide balanced selection of supplying countries. This policy would provide leverage for Japan when importing energy from abroad. These ideas are born of the bitter experiences of the recent oil crises, until which time Japan had depended on Middle East oil more or less exclusively[36].

The 'one-third principle' promoted in Europe represents one of these ideas, and can be helpful to us. However, this issue is not just a matter of arithmetic. One has to think of energy security in the context of interdependence between nations, and pay attention at the same time to the aspects of each energy purchase transaction.

As for Japan's oil supply, where foreign dependence is still high compared with other developed countries, it would be as well to mention here the issue of self-development, that is, development by Japanese investment in oil producing countries. The proportion of self-developed crude oil compared to total crude oil imports to this country in recent years is about 10%, which is quite low. It is true to say that oil developed by Japan in foreign countries provides less security than emergency crude oil which has already been brought into the country, no matter how big are the oil holdings Japan possesses abroad. Nevertheless, it is still worthwhile to buy oil fields for the future, taking advantage of the strong yen which has appreciated since the Group of Five Finance Ministers meeting in the autumn of 1985.

The significance of emergency oil stocks. The need for emergency stocks has been stressed as insurance against a possible disruption of supplies and oil stocks for the private sector have reached a 90-day level, while the target of government stocks is set at 30 million Kl. These stocks are expected to function as a reservoir in case of sudden stoppage of oil supply. Since they also perform a function of preventing sudden price fluctuations, it is advisable to increase them even further.

For the present, the economic environment surrounding Japan provides the best opportunity for increasing stocks. Thanks to three favourable conditions (low crude oil prices, the strong yen, and low interest rates), an oil stock storage base can be built with a diminished burden of interest on the construction fund, and crude oil can be purchased more cheaply. Japan, as the second highest oil importing nation in the world, has considerable influence on the oil market in the event of an emergency. In view of this, it has a responsibility to the international community to prepare for such an emergency.

There is another issue to be studied in connection with emergency oil stocks - how emergency oil stock levels are to be decided. How much oil, in terms of daily consumption, is required for Japanese economic safety? There is no definite answer to this yet. Even if a 90-day level of stocks became stockpiled in compliance with the IEA system, it should be noted that this amount of oil cannot necessarily be released altogether in an emergency. In other words, oil which remains at the bottom of the tank or in the pipeline is physically impossible to use, and oil refineries cannot afford to release all their oil stock without risking a total shutdown of operations. This kind of stock is said to constitute about half the emergency oil stocks of the IEA countries[37]. In view of this, increases in emergency oil stocks should be encouraged in a positive manner.

During the last oil crisis extra oil was bought for stock when prices had just begun to rise, and this consequently accelerated the price rise. Therefore, it should be noted that increasing emergency oil stocks could jeopardise their very purpose.

4. Conclusion - International linkage of energy security

Energy security is determined by the ratio of threat to the proper counteracting forces. The threat to energy security in Japan, the US and Europe has arisen basically from the fact that the oil supply capacity of the Western allies, and countries whose political stances are closer to the West, is less than the demand for oil, and alternative energy resources (nuclear energy including nuclear fusion, coal, natural gas, oil shale, tar sands, and renewable energies such as solar energy) are not yet practical economically and technically. OPEC countries and the Centrally Planned Economy countries have been providing the excess demand. The threat will disappear if the oil demands of Japan, the US and Europe return to the level equivalent to their supply capacity, or if supplies from the OPEC and CPE countries can be guaranteed. This may prove difficult. If so, will the counteracting forces employed by Japan, the US and Europe against the threat be sufficient?

There are two types of counteracting forces: efforts to alleviate the threat, but not eliminate the threat itself (the effort not to have the threat materialise); and efforts to minimise the damage sustained in an actual crisis. The former is the more preferable of the two. The threat incurred by increased dependence on Middle East oil may bring about a possible disruption of oil supply due to the political instability of the Middle East region. Equally threatening is the influence of politically motivated production and export policies that would impose hardship on the entire economic world through disruption of prices and supply. Intense effort to lessen dependence on Middle East oil, and to limit the possibility of political motives influencing oil production and export policies, will be required to alleviate the threat. Though it is considered impossible for Japan, the US and Europe to reduce their needs to negligible amounts for the 1990s, they should co-operate to lessen their dependence on Middle East oil. If any of them were to increase their oil consumption and import volume, this would most probably trigger an upward trend in oil prices and have a negative effect on the world economy. In this regard, the dependence of Japan, the US and Europe on Middle East oil is not only a threat to the energy security of each of them, but also a threat to the energy security of the rest of the world. The governments of Japan, the US and Europe should fully recognise the international linkage of energy security. Furthermore, although the essential solution to the Arab-Israeli dispute is not in sight, they should further stabilise the political situation by making the economic bases for the Middle East countries more substantial.

Finally, it is necessary to touch upon the self-centredness of the oil producing countries[38], as a political motive likely to pertain to oil production and export policies. It is vital that the Middle East oil producing countries stop thinking only of their own self-interest, and recognise their responsibility for supplying oil to the rest of the world. One opinion holds that the best way to secure supply is to keep the oil producing countries in poverty, thus developing a constant reliance on oil revenues[39]. However, this will only worsen confrontation with OPEC. The lesson of the oil crises of the 1970s and of the recent drop in crude oil prices is that trends in oil are not restricted to the field of energy, but inflict a greater impact on world political and economic systems, and the impact will ricochet back on the oil producing countries. Any further drop in crude oil prices would be most damaging to the producing countries. Energy security for the supplying countries means overall security of oil income. This is where the possibility exists that the energy security of the consuming countries and that of the supplying countries can meet - another form of international linkage in energy security.

IV. The direction of policy responses

1. Promoting control over dependence on the Middle East

The essential goal of policies in the US, Europe and Japan is, first of all, to gain as much control as possible over their dependence on oil from the Middle East. It is therefore necessary to promote further diversification of the sources of oil, exploration for oil in areas other than the Middle East, and reinforcement of policies discouraging dependence on oil through the use of oil substitutes and energy conservation. Future policy direction should be discussed to develop necessary countermeasures to cope with the situation after the collapse of oil prices. In this Section, the short- to medium-term political responses during the period of oil over-supply (the period of agreed reduction by OPEC), such as (i) responses to low oil prices, and (ii) responses to oil price instability will be covered. Additionally, medium- to long-term policy responses will be discussed in two other areas: (iii) promotion of energy studies and reinforced regional co-operation, and (iv) reinforcement of IEA/OECD-based multilateral co-operation on energy.

Responses to low oil prices. There has been considerable discussion on an oil-import tax, a floor price system or a tax on oil consumption. In the US, for instance, there is an opinion that an import tariff should be adopted rather than an excise tax, since the former is effective for the protection of domestic oil products and for control over consumption. Others say that, in the circumstances of oil over-supply, the unilateral imposition of such an import barrier by the US would involve disadvantages. Foreign oil could only enter the US market at the price of US domestic, minus customs duty, and this would cause damage to exporting countries like Mexico. Therefore, there is some call for an IEA-based customs alliance, which could be extended to the industrial countries as well as to Mexico. During periods of oil price competition when it is expected that low prices will continue at less than $10/b, this policy may be accepted as a self-defensive measure for consuming countries. However, if the crude oil price moves to within the $15/b to $20/b range, consuming countries must decide whether it is necessary for them to join such a customs alliance in order to protect the US domestic oil producing companies.

This question is a component of a more universal problem: who is to bear the costs of energy security in the world and in what form? Other alternatives - for example, incentives for the domestic oil industry in the

US to develop further exploration - need also to be considered in terms of comparative cost and benefit. In this instance, it is indispensable to have multilateral discussions and adjustment in such places as the IEA or the OECD, in the case of international linkage of energy security where the world's energy security cannot be achieved by relying on individual nations' policies. However, as regards those countries most affected by low oil prices, taking measures to control oil consumption seems to have a good psychological effect on other countries. Also, when oil consumption appears to be increasing worldwide owing to a fall in oil product prices, it will be necessary to investigate appropriate measures to control consumption growth.

Private oil exploration will inevitably be reduced if prices are low. Therefore, it is necessary for each nation to take appropriate measures to ensure medium- and long-term supply. For example, in the US, such measures are likely to be tax privileges for oil exploration on land, offshore and off the continental shelf, or further deregulation. In Western Europe, tax privileges for North Sea oil are also likely. In Japan, incentives can be provided such as acquiring oil licences in order to take advantage of the current high exchange rate of the yen, or maintaining a public investment fund to promote oil exploration in the US or China, etc.

Responses to oil price instability. Almost nothing can be done solely by the consuming countries to stabilise oil prices. In order to keep the crude oil price within a certain stabilised price range, two methods are available: one is to make use of regular market forces, and the other is to intervene in the market itself. As regards the former, in order to compensate for price changes in the market, accumulation and release of public oil stocks might be considered. This would mean establishing new oil stocks in order to adjust supply and demand, different from the stocks used for emergencies. The practicality of such a plan is questionable, because of the many problems which would need to be solved, such as financing, management, etc. To intervene in the oil market directly, such measures as price control or control over private stocks might be considered. However, these should be undertaken only in an emergency.

In order to stabilise oil prices, appeals to the producing countries will be necessary. In the international oil market, the following measures are believed to be indispensable on the part of the producing countries:

i. Limiting the number of participants in the market
ii. Rational product determination
iii. Oil industry integration.

In the long term, a reduction in the number of oil exporting countries can be expected due to the fact that OPEC and non-OPEC countries with small oil reserves are dropping out of the market. But in the short to medium term, if some countries were to withdraw from OPEC, the oil market would become unstable. As for (iii), from the medium- to long-term point of view, stabilisation can be expected from the fact that national oil companies in the producing nations have promoted entering downstream activities, thereby inviting the development of international vertical integration.

From the short- to medium-term point of view, the second condition, i.e. agreed reduction of production by OPEC and the adjustment of supply and demand agreed to by non-OPEC nations, seems to be the key to oil price stabilisation. Therefore, if Europe, the US and Japan all recognise the necessity of stabilising oil prices, every effort should be made to hold talks between oil producing and consuming countries, or to appeal to the non-OPEC producers - especially Mexico, Norway and the UK.

<u>Promotion of energy studies and regional co-operation.</u> Japan, which is a big energy consuming and importing country, has promoted energy substitution and conservation by investing capital and technology in the development of countermeasures for adjusting to an oil crisis. Energy efficiency has been given great prominence in industry, the residential and commercial sectors and transportation. From now on, the perspective of 'creating' energy through high technology will be important in making further gains in energy efficiency. Japan is expected to promote international co-operation actively in order to contribute to energy security worldwide, not to mention its domestic efforts. Details

on promoting energy studies are described in part 4 of this Section.

Recent trends towards regional energy co-operation among the US, Europe and Japan seem to be to promote energy security for all parties as one unit rather than for individual nations. An example of this is the decision of four West European countries (West Germany, France, the Netherlands and Belgium) to participate in the development of the Troll gas field in Norway, and to promote electricity trading between EC nations. Clearly, regional energy co-operation has definitely been developed in Western Europe. In the US, a plan for a US-Canada energy alliance is again being considered. In Japan, a plan for Pacific energy co-operation (see part 5 of this Section) is now being promoted. These types of co-operation make flexible responses within the region possible in energy conservation, substitution, or efforts to diminish dependence on oil, as well as facilitating technology transfer for energy. Eventually, these efforts will control dependence on oil from the Middle East and thus promote energy security in the world.

Reinforcement of IEA/OECD-based co-operation. In order to gain control over dependence on oil from the Middle East, while at the same time promoting IEA-based co-operation, it seems worthwhile to set up a new system in IEA/OECD to supply immediate international information regarding trends in the oil market - products, demand, and especially stock changes - and a forum for energy ministers from individual countries to discuss policies on oil consumption and control. The present IEA office 'believes in' the market mechanism (according to Secretary-General Steeg); however, it seems necessary to ensure smooth and quick circulation of information related to world energy in order to determine whether the market mechanism is working efficiently. Moreover, in the event of an emergency, it would be necessary for energy ministers to have such a forum to discuss and devise immediate responses.

2. Japan's approach to the Middle East - Towards reinforcing multiple interdependence

The common criticism from overseas - particularly from the West - that Japan is a free rider requires a look at the basic direction and actual implementation of its Middle East policy measures.

As its major policy measure, Japan should adopt a roundabout approach to the Middle East. Although it is currently restricted in its approach to mainly economic measures, it would be wise to aim at assuring and promoting smooth economic development by eliminating and alleviating economic difficulties in the Middle East, and to work towards political stability in the region by adopting a careful and diversified linkage policy at the bilateral, multilateral and international levels in all international relations. This would strengthen true interdependence, which in turn would lead to a more stable supply of Middle East oil for Japan.

Japan today has become one of the leading countries in the world with its huge current account and trade surplus which easily compares with that of OPEC after the first and second oil crises of the 1970s. Japan is therefore in a position to make a more active and positive contribution to the world as a whole. Thus, it needs to adopt a systematic and pragmatic approach to the Middle East, after it has clarified the Middle East's position and order of priority etc. in its overall global policy.

Basic premises: restrictions on Japan.

i) As a basic premise we can assume that Japan is unlikely to amend the Constitution (particularly Article 9) during the period from the late 1980s to the early 1990s. Therefore, it will continue to maintain its 'defence only' stance, and political means such as military aid or military commitment will be outside its range of possibilities.

ii) Japan will adopt a basic multi-directional foreign policy towards the world, the aim of which will be, above all,

> to promote a foreign policy that actively contributes to the peace and prosperity of the world. Japan has

> adopted a stance as a member of the free democratic nations with which it shares political and economic viewpoints, and as a nation that belongs to the Asia-Pacific region with which it is closely related geographically, historically, and culturally.[40]

Japan's present foreign policy thus centres on the US, the Western European nations, and the countries in the Asia-Pacific region with which it shares the values of free democracy and a market economy, and will continue to do so in the future.

iii) From the above, it is clear that Japan's policy approach to the Middle East will necessarily be restricted to economic measures, and the significance and role of such a policy must now be considered. From the basic standpoint of Japan's foreign policy, it must continue to place secondary significance and priority on Middle East issues, yet keep sight of their importance.

Japan's basic foreign policy. First of all, the Japanese Government has clearly stated its basic policy direction as one of

> active co-operation in the building up of nations and human resources in the countries of the Middle and Near East, as well as making efforts to promote mutual understanding through strengthening personal and cultural exchanges. With the increasing international role of Japan, there have recently been growing demands from the Middle and Near East for Japan to take a more active part not only in the economic arena, but in the political arena, as well. In line with these expectations, discussions were held with related parties on many occasions in 1985, to create an environment for peace settlements in the Middle East and bring about an early settlement of the Iran-Iraq war by peaceful means.[41]

Since Japan's major and basic policy approach lies in economic exchange and economic relations in the broadest sense of the word, including cultural and personal exchanges, its basic policy direction will be examined focusing on these aspects.

Definition of 'true interdependence'. Japan's basic policy will be to establish and strengthen multiple interdependence in the true sense of the word. Many cases of so-called interdependence are in fact one-sided dependence or subordination which are mistakenly perceived as interdependence.

In a bilateral relationship, true interdependence can be defined by looking at the cost and impact on both nations when a change - particularly a stoppage or cut-off - occurs in international economic relations or international economic exchange. If the actual cost or impact of such a break in relations is large enough to be fatal to both nations concerned, they are said to be truly interdependent. However, if the impact is great for one nation and small for the other, this is one-sided dependence. And if the impact on both nations is very small, then they are independent. Furthermore, if their ability to eliminate or alleviate the impact caused by events occurring in the other nation and by changes in economic relations is very small for both nations, then they are interdependent; if it is great for only one nation, they have a one-sided dependent or subordinate relationship, and if it is great for both nations, then they are independent.

If we analyse Japan's relationship with the Middle East - especially the oil producing nations - according to the above definition, then even if the situation has improved considerably compared to the period during the 1973-4 oil crisis, it is clear that Japan has a rather one-sided subordinate relationship of dependence. The cost and impact of a stoppage or cut-off would still be overwhelmingly great for the Japanese side.

Let us examine this in concrete terms. According to a sobering simulation carried out based on the actual situation in 1970 before the first oil crisis, Taichi Sakaiya calculated that if a cut-off in oil supplies from the Middle East had continued at 30% of the normal rate for 200 days, the outcome would have been 3 million deaths and the disappearance of 70% of the nation's assets.[42] Similar to the scenario presented in Sakaiya's novel, Japan's vulnerability around the time of the first oil crisis was such that a breakdown in relations with the Middle East oil producing nations might have had a fatal impact on Japan. Meanwhile, for the Middle East oil producers, the impact was considered to be comparatively small, as the main Japanese exports of manufactured goods were for the most part substituted by goods from the US, Europe, etc., regardless of problems over price and quality.

As a result of Japan's continuous efforts to reduce its dependence on oil, and especially on oil from the Middle East, its level of dependence on the Middle East for primary energy supply fell from 58.9% in 1973 to 31.3% in 1984, and the level of dependence on crude oil imports through the Strait of Hormuz fell from 75.1% to 63.5%, while oil inventories in June 1986 stood at 132 days. Compared to the period of the first oil crisis, the situation has improved considerably and the impact and cost to Japan have become far less. However, compared to the US (whose dependence for its primary energy on the Middle East in 1984 was 0.4%) and Europe (the UK 0%, West Germany 4.1%, France 7.1%), the impact and cost are still overwhelmingly large, and in a supply-demand emergency, there would be little possibility of switching to other oil producing nations. Japan should therefore place more importance on finding a way to establish and strengthen true interdependence by increasing the impact and cost borne by the Middle East oil producers.

<u>Implementing a two-fold strategy</u>. Basically, Japan needs to adopt the following two policy countermeasures: first, it must move towards strengthening its ability to reduce or eliminate the cost or impact of a cut-off in its relations with the Middle East, especially the oil producing nations. As for countermeasures and actual policy, measures such as increasing oil stockpiles and the diversification of oil supply sources, and changing and diversifying energy sources to alternative or new energy forms have already been outlined in this report. It will also be important to adopt a policy of reducing oil demand and consumption and decreasing the degree of dependence on oil by economising on oil and promoting its effective use.

The second policy measure needed is to change the relationship between Japan and the Middle East, especially the oil producing nations, and to nurture true interdependence instead of the former one-sided relationship of dependence and subordination. If it were felt that a drastic reduction or cut-off of relations with Japan would have a fatal impact on the Middle East, and particularly the oil producing nations, this would act as a control on any unilateral action by an individual nation. We could expect this to function as an incentive to maintain and promote as stable and smooth a relationship as possible.

Naturally, the first policy choice for Japan would be to create a situation in which, contrary to the present relationship, the Middle Eastern oil producing nations would be in a state of one-sided dependence on Japan. This would further enhance Japan's standing and negotiating ability and would thus be the best policy for Japan.

However, the reality Japan has to face is that it has a one-sided dependent and subordinate relationship with the Middle East oil producers. It will therefore have to consider adopting the second-best policy direction, in which its only choice is to aim at strengthening its negotiating power and stabilising and levelling up the relationship. Since Japan does not have an overwhelmingly superior position, and moreover has a restricted policy choice, the formation of its policy must work within these constraints.

<u>The paradox of interdependence</u>. Of course, merely aiming at establishing and strengthening a truly interdependent relationship with the Middle East does not in itself solve problems nor guarantee energy security. To believe that true interdependence can be the almighty panacea may be an illusion.

Any interdependent relationship has both negative and positive sides, or aspects of harmony and conflict: the two sides always co-exist, promoting the stability and co-operation between nations, and increasing the friction and conflict between them.

As an example, Kenneth N. Waltz writes,[43]

> Close interdependence means closeness of contact and raises the prospect of at least occasional conflict. The fiercest civil wars and the bloodiest international ones have been fought within areas populated by highly similar people whose affairs had become quite closely knit together. It is hard to get a war going unless the potential participants are somehow closely linked. Interdependent states whose relations remain unregulated must experience conflict and will occasionally fall into violence. If regulation is hard to come by, as it is in the relations of states,then it would seem to follow that a lessening of interdependence is desirable.

Just as in a relationship between two people, the well-known 'porcupine dilemma' also exists between nations. This image is taken from a fable by Schopenhauer in which, during one winter day, two freezing porcupines tried to warm each other up. However, when they realised that their quills were hurting each other, they tried staying at some distance. But then they just got cold. After several attempts, they finally found the exact distance where they would not hurt each other, and could also manage to warm each other to a certain degree. We have to rebuild our interdependent nation-to-nation relationships bearing this 'porcupine dilemma' in mind, and take a general and pragmatic look to clarify the limit of interdependence and the ideal distance between nations. We must solve the questions of how close we can get without interfering with each other, how much warmth we need from each other, and how to co-exist without hurting each other too much.

This shows the necessity and effectiveness of the two-fold strategy mentioned above. It will be essential to take into consideration the ideal distance or ideal degree of economic exchange between nations, and to make careful preparations to establish means and systems to restrict and control such interdependence as required.

Furthermore, as will be discussed below, this means not only making efforts to establish a narrow interdependence between two nations. Japan must also aim at establishing and strengthening interdependence in many diversified ways.

The significance of a drastic change in the international oil situation - increasing effectiveness of policy. As a result of soaring crude oil prices caused by the oil crises of the 1970s, the Middle East oil producing nations gained vast oil revenues. In particular, the producers in the Arabian Peninsula, where there is a concentration of low absorber nations, held large amounts of oil money. As far as an approach to these nations was concerned, it has been pointed out that the role or significance of economic means was drastically reduced and was even disappearing.

However, the situation changed in the 1980s. The demand for oil could not move upwards, and continued to decrease, so that crude oil prices remained low. In addition, the OPEC nations' share of oil production and exports was largely taken over by the non-OPEC nations. Oil revenues therefore continued to decrease and the international balance of payments dropped into deficit after 1983 even in the low absorber nations which suffered from a negative growth rate. They were forced to abandon, reduce, or postpone their development and industrialisation plans, as they lost most of their oil revenues.

As OPEC was unable to continue its policy of cutting production after December 1985, it began to compete by increasing production and cutting prices to recover its market share. The result was that, in 1986, crude oil prices continued to fall drastically, and in July fell to less than \$10/b, a level which nobody could have imagined one year previously. The oil producing nations were all faced with a difficult situation.

On 5 August 1986, OPEC agreed to co-ordinate its strategy of production cut-backs in September and October, and crude oil prices rose again to maintain a \$13 - \$15/b level. On 20 December the OPEC general meeting decided to go back to the \$18/b fixed price system from January 1987 and to strengthen co-operation in reducing production. However, it is not clear if this \$18/b rate can be achieved and maintained, and a situation where there is a rapid increase in prices as well as in demand and consumption in a short space of time cannot be expected. The economic difficulties of the Middle East oil producers are likely to continue for some time. It is in such a situation that Japan's basic policy of an economic approach can be most effective.

Scope and significance of a multiple policy. Let us now examine how actually to implement and set the course for Japan's approach to a policy of establishing and strengthening multiple interdependence with the Middle East oil producing nations.

The word 'multiple', as used here, has the following two meanings. The first is concerned with spatial and regional aspects. Japan's bilateral relations with the nations in the Middle East, especially the oil producers, are important. But more than that, the formation of diversified tripartite or multilateral relations, or relationships through international organisations or forums, is also conceivable in establishing true interdependence. Japan's relations with the Middle East should be developed along these lines through a combination of these various elements.

The second meaning of 'multiple' concerns all of the aspects in international relations, especially economic relations. Japan's approach to the Middle East must be carried out so that it includes not only the transfer of manufactured goods, i.e. not only commodity trade and services, but also the movement of the factors of production such as capital, human resources, and technology. Furthermore, it should include political co-operation and active support for direct investment by multinational corporations where all these elements are transferred as a package deal. On a higher level, it should not only include economic exchange but take into consideration cultural, academic, social exchanges, the political approach, and diplomatic efforts. All these elements must form part of Japan's concrete approach to the Middle East, so that they are combined at multiple levels.

Implementing a policy on a bilateral basis.

i) Trade aspects. The first task is to establish and strengthen interdependence in trade. Japan needs to make as great an effort as possible not only to import oil on a one-sided basis from its trading partner, but also to export consumer products, production goods, and capital goods essential to the social and economic development and industrialisation of the people in the other nation. For Japan's security, it will be important to maintain superior price and quality and to go on creating products which cannot easily be substituted by exports from other nations.

Japan used to be the leading supplier of inexpensive and high quality products, but recently other industrialised nations and the NICs (newly industrialised countries) have begun to catch up. The priority for Japan from now on should therefore be on adopting a policy to maintain and strengthen its superiority in high-tech products, and in technology and technology-intensive goods.

It is necessary to promote trust from the oil supplying nations by endeavouring to maintain a stable purchase of oil. Japan should also aim at establishing more interdependence in the commodity trade also, by increasing imports of oil products and other goods. From now on, it will be increasingly important to open the Japanese market, especially for finished products. In the service industries too, Japan should export services essential to the oil producing nations and should also in some cases promote the import of services (such as using OPEC tankers, or importing finance, insurance services and information, etc.), to strengthen interdependence in both commodities and services.

Let us examine in more detail the trade between Japan and the Middle and Near East, especially the Middle East oil producing nations. Starting with Japan's exports (f.o.b.) and imports (c.i.f.) and their share of the total in 1985 and the first half of 1986, the figures (in millions of dollars) were as follows: for the Middle and Near East as a whole, exports 12,171 (6.9%) and 5,462 (5.5%), imports 29,937 (23.0%) and 11,376 (17.6%). For the Middle East oil producing nations: exports 9,989 (5.7%) and 4,387 (4.4%), imports 26,808 (20.7%) and 10,191 (15.8%). Imports are still significant, but the ratio of exports has considerably decreased to a 4-5% level. The ratio of exports to the Middle and Near East in Japan's total exports increased from 3.3% in 1970 to

4.8% in 1973, 10.9% in 1975, 11.1% in 1980, and 12.7% in 1982. However, after 1983, exports rapidly decreased from 11.7% to 8.4%, 6.9%, and, in the first half of 1986, the figure stood at 5.5%. As for imports, there was a rapid increase from 12.4% in 1970 to 12.9% in 1973, 28.5% in 1975, 31.7% in 1980. But since 1981 they have been continuously decreasing from 29.8% to 28.6%, 26.7%, 24.2%, 23%, and, in the first half of 1986, they had decreased sharply to 17.6%.

As for the balance of trade, Japan has had its largest trade deficit with the Middle and Near East nations, and in this respect its relationship can be said to be unique. The trade deficit rapidly increased from $1.7 billion in 1970 to $3.2 billion in 1973 and to $12.2 billion in 1974, and it remained at the $10 - 11 billion mark from 1975 to 1978. In 1979 it reached $18.6 billion and in 1980 $30.1 billion, but since then it has been decreasing from $24.9 billion in 1981 to $17.8 billion in 1985 and to $5.9 billion in the first half of 1986.

Japan's exports reached a peak in 1980 ($21.2 billion) and since then there has been a definite and continuous decrease, dropping to $12.2 billion in 1985. As this actual transition clearly reflects, ever since the Middle East oil producing nations started having difficulties owing to stagnant oil prices and a decrease in exports at the start of the 1980s, Japan's interest in and recognition of the importance of the Middle East has rapidly dissipated.

Even more than with the commodity trade, we can say that with the trade in services, Japan's relationship with the Middle and Near East, especially the Middle East oil producing nations, has not been close. The truth of the matter is that the implementation of a basic policy aiming at establishing and strengthening interdependence based on trade may not be feasible.

ii) Transfer of factors of production. It would be difficult to achieve and promote true interdependence exclusively in trade in products. Therefore, the second point is that Japan should aim at multiple interdependence, including the transfer of factors of production. In order to contribute more actively and prominently in the economic development and industrialisation of other nations, it will be necessary to promote further the transfer of capital, technology, human resources, and direct investment, as well as a package of these elements. In the future, it will be necessary to stress economic, technological, and educational co-operation, etc. with the Middle East oil producing nations. At present, they are facing difficulties due to the large drop in oil revenues, and the role and significance of such economic co-operation from Japan on a broad base is greatly increasing.

Japan should not only increase transfers of factors of production and co-operation to other nations by promoting human, cultural, and academic exchanges on a one-sided basis, but should also make efforts to build up multiple interdependence in these fields. Japan is now rushing towards socio-economic internationalisation, which could be termed the second revolution of the twentieth century (the first being the defeat in World War II). It should place particular importance on building up a broader and steadier exchange basis with the Middle East, such as accepting more students, technical trainees, researchers, and scholars, and promoting joint research and academic exchanges.

Turning to Japan's actual direct investment (on an approval and notification basis), the sum total from 1951 to 1984 in the Middle and Near East was $2.927 billion. This amounts to 4.1% of total direct investment, and of that, investment in the major Middle East oil producing nations (Saudi Arabia, Kuwait, Iran, and the United Arab Emirates) was $2.823 billion (4%), which accounts for almost all of the direct investment in the Middle and Near East. Recently, however, the proportion of total investment in the Middle and Near East and the major Middle East oil producing nations has dropped considerably, and is now, respectively, 1.6% and1.3% in 1982, 2.1% and 1.9% in 1983, and 2.7% and 2.4% in 1984. Japan's direct investments are mainly in North America (the total from 1951 to 1984 was 30.1%, and from 1982 to 1984, 35.2%), Asia (25.2% and 18.7%), Central and South America (18.2% and 21.8%), and Europe (12.7% and 14.6%).

As far as intake of foreign students is concerned, out of a total of 15,009 as of 1 May 1985, only 129 (0.9%)

were from the Middle and Near East, and only 68 (2.7%) were Japanese government scholarship students out of a total of 2,502.

The fact should therefore be recognised that a large gap exists between the basic direction of this policy and its feasibility.

iii) Policy. The third point in this area is the desirability of deepening the relationship in general policy aspects and international relations, and promoting assistance and co-operation.

Japan must also consider such courses of action as supporting policies and promoting the right environment for achieving peace settlements in the Middle East and in the Iran-Iraq war. Although OPEC's oil policy - especially in the Middle East oil producing nations - looks rather shaky as witnessed by the dismissal of the Saudi oil minister Sheik Yamani, Japan must clarify its basic stance with regard to oil policy and co-operate wherever possible in helping other nations achieve complementary policy aims.

On the bilateral basis too, Japan's approach to the Middle East, especially the oil producing nations, should be carefully planned to help establish and strengthen multiple interdependence.

Implementing a diversified and multilateral policy. A bilateral policy is hardly sufficient, and there is the danger of the paradox of interdependence (see p. 83 above) if it is based only on that. However, in addition to bilateral interdependence, by continuing to work at establishing and strengthening a more diversified, tripartite or multilateral interdependence, a more stable and definite relationship can be developed.

For example, we could first consider establishing diversified interdependence between three nations that would include not just Japan and a Middle East oil producing nation, but also a Middle East non-oil producer. This strategy would aim at economic development and industrialisation by building factories and manufacturing industries combining the oil money and oil resources of the Middle East oil producing nations with Japan's technology, human resources (mainly managerial), and plant, etc. and would also look to the abundant manpower and markets in the Middle East non-oil producers.

Second, it is important to secure third-nation markets for the goods and oil products produced from the industrialisation of the Middle East nations, by fully utilising the marketing ability and information of the Japanese general trading companies.

Of the total sales of 9 major Japanese general trading companies, transactions among third nations reached 19.6% in 1985, which is nearly 20% (Y19 trillion out of Y97 trillion). Together with transactions within Japan, and exports and imports from and to Japan, transactions among third nations are already significant. The percentage of transactions among third nations for each of the general trading companies are as follows: Mitsubishi Corporation 16.1%, Mitsui & Co. Ltd 20.9%, C. Itoh & Co. Ltd. 19.0%, Sumitomo Corporation 11.1%, Marubeni Corporation 20.5%, Nissho-Iwai Co. Ltd. 24.8%, Toyo Menka Kaisha Ltd. 19.0%, Nichimen Co. Ltd. 46.3%, and Kanematsu-Gosho Ltd. 17.8%.

In addition, in any approach to the Middle East centring on the Middle East oil producing nations, we should also consider co-operation and role-sharing between Japan and the NICs. In this course of action, Japan would be in charge of capital, technology, basic design, and management, and the NICs would undertake actual construction work and provide the human resources.

Finally, there is a multiple approach to the Middle East by Japan, the US and the European nations through mutual sharing and co-operation. For this, it would be desirable to have concrete discussions when conferences are held between the three areas.

Implementing a policy through international/world organisations.

One approach could utilise existing international organisations, and another could be based on establishing new international organisations and forums.

i) Using existing international organisations. First of all, Japan's foreign policy up to now has been centred on the United Nations, and so long as the organisation of the United Nations is revised and becomes more effective, Japan will basically continue to maintain such a policy. Working out a rough framework for peace in the Middle East should be done through the United Nations, and as Japan has also been selected as a non-permanent member of the Security Council of the United Nations, it should play an even more active role.

Further promotion of Japan's economic co-operation should be carried out not only on a bilateral basis but also globally and multilaterally through the International Monetary Fund, the World Bank, the UNDP, etc. Another desirable policy direction would be to take a greater initiative in solving today's major problems by establishing special funds provided by Japan to the IMF and the World Bank.

From the standpoint of contributing towards solving the world's oil and energy problems, directions such as the following should also be emphasised: establishing special funds for the exploration and development of world energy and oil resources, especially in the developing nations, and establishing special funds to alleviate the accumulated debt problem caused by the sharp fall in oil, energy, and primary product prices. Japan should call for world participation and co-operation, particularly from the West, in establishing these funds.

In September 1986 Japan announced that it would make an additional contribution to the eighth capital replenishment of the International Development Association (IDA - commonly known as the 'Second World Bank'), and would grant a loan of 3 billion SDR (approximately $3.6 billion) to the IMF for the purpose of helping nations with cumulative debts (financing this from its foreign exchange special account). Furthermore, the World Bank and the Japanese Government agreed to establish a special 'Japan fund' to promote the movement of capital in the World Bank to help recycle Japan's trade surplus back to the developing nations.[44]

Thus, it is worth noting that, albeit a little late in the day, Japan's stance is to shoulder more responsibility in the international sphere as befits an economic power with a huge current account and trade surplus.

On 20 September 1986, the Conference of GATT Ministers adopted their opening resolution in the new round of multilateral trade negotiations ('The Ministers' Resolution Concerning the Uruguay Round'), and negotiations are due to start aimed at preventing protectionism in trade in commodities and services and at constructing a more open and permanent multilateral trading system. Here, too, Japan should take an active lead and demonstrate initiative.

ii) Exploring new organisations and forums. The approach of establishing new international organisations and international forums should also be considered.

Although the necessity of holding talks with the oil producing nations has been pointed out for some time, it has not actually occurred so far. Indeed, there seems little possibility of actually doing so judging from the major differences and conflicts of interests, opinions, and speculation between the oil producing and consuming nations and within these nations.

However, the costly experience of the sharp fall in oil prices since the beginning of 1986 served to some extent as a lesson to the major oil producing and exporting nations (excluding the UK), so there is a growing basis for co-operation. One could also say there has been a common realisation on the part of the major oil importing and consuming nations (excluding the US) of the necessity for talks and policy co-operation between the producing and consuming nations.

Is it really impossible to think of talks or a conference between IEA and OPEC? OPEC has even begun to reconsider the price rises in the oil crises of the 1970s, saying that the first rise in 1973 was fair as it compensated for the unfairly low oil price up to then, whereas the rise in 1979 was wrong and unnecessary as it caused oil prices to be overestimated and finally led to the most recent drastic fall. Former oil minister Sheik Yamani of Saudi Arabia concluded in a speech given on the occasion of the 350th anniversary of the establishment of Harvard University that[45]

> if the market is to be stabilised in the long term, OPEC and non-OPEC producers should co-operate in aiming at the establishment of a price structure which takes into account the economics of equilibrium between supply and demand. Producers as well as consumers should adopt policies that shun drastic interference in the market forces which may disturb the much sought for long-term stability. It is only through the achievement of long-term free market equilibrium that stability can be attained.

However, this direction was eventually rejected by King Fahd. Sheikh Yamani was removed from office, and King Fahd and the Saudi Government have opted for the adoption of a fixed price system of $18/b from January 1987. Toward this end, they will implement a policy of strengthening the strategy of co-ordinated reduction of oil production.

However, it is hard to believe that the $18/b price can be smoothly realised and that the price will continue its upward trend, or that co-ordinated reduction by OPEC can be achieved and maintained, or that the non-OPEC oil producers will go along with it. On the contrary, it is predicted that there may be some hitches in the pace of the co-ordinated reduction and that some disruption may occur among the non-OPEC producers. So, taking advantage of the situation, we may well have reached a stage where concrete proposals on holding an international forum for co-operation between the producing and consuming nations can be put forward.

Although the idea of establishing a new international organisation is almost a dream, it is worth considering how Japan could work on the West and take the initiative in starting talks between the two sides and make bold plans to set out the possibilities.

<u>Feasibility and executors.</u> In Japan, the actual major executor of such a policy would be the private sector. Since the policy would not simply be implemented in principle or as a general proposition, but practically and in detail, the crucial point is whether it can be done on a commercial basis and whether it would be profitable or not.

As regards the approach to establish and strengthen true multiple interdependence with the Middle East, if this were an attractive commercial proposition for the private sector, many of these actions would have been carried out and such a relationship would already exist. However, as we have seen, the reality of such a policy direction is far from this, and the truth of the matter is that without co-operation, aid, and initiative on the part of the government and public policy, such an approach is not feasible.

It requires various active aid policies by the government, and official development assistance (oda) should play the central role.

With regard to oda, Japan has been making efforts through the first mid-term objective (the plan for doubling oda in the three years from 1978 to 1980) and the second mid-term objective (doubling oda in the five years from 1981 to 1985), and by setting up the third mid-term objective (a total of more than $40 billion in oda in real terms for 7 years from 1986), Japan is continuing its efforts to strengthen its official aid. Although total oda for 1984 reached $4.32 billion, as a percentage of GNP it only amounted to 0.35%, and the proportion of oda for the Middle East was only 1.8% (a 2.7% decrease compared to the previous year when it was 3.1%), which is very low indeed when compared to that for Asia (65.7%), Africa (15.7%), and Central and South America (9.4%).

Therefore, regrettable as it may be, one has to admit there is very little possibility of actually organising and boldly implementing an effort to establish and strengthen multiple interdependence as outlined here.

The need for new concepts and new countermeasures.
In Japan the priority is on promoting small government, administrative reforms, and solving financial deficits, so it is unrealistic to move toward large increases in the amount of foreign contributions overseas centring on oda.

However, the Japanese Government is making some efforts as can be seen in the 1987 budget (Government Bill drawn up on 30 December 1986). Official development assistance is increasing to approximately ¥658 billion, which is a 5.8% increase over the previous year; the number of foreign students in Japan on government scholarships will increase to 2,045 (up by 230); the number of foreign trainees to 4,920 (up by 260) and the defence budget will be up by 5.2% over the previous year, while general expenditure is reduced.

In addition, Japan is profiting from the large decrease in import values due to the recent drop in the price of crude oil and primary products.

The current high appreciation of the yen has added to this situation, and the arguments are mainly focused on how to return to Japan these marginal profits as a result of the drop in oil prices and the high yen. However, the huge trade and current account surplus has become a major international issue. Now that Japan has become one of the leading world nations, priority should be placed on discussing the issue of how to return these marginal profits or 'presents from the poor' to overseas countries.

Although, as has been stated earlier, the Japanese Government is making efforts in its own way, such as increasing the amount of official development assistance, and announcing new loans and the establishment of funds for international organisations, it is essential at the present time to consider measures dealing with some totally new concepts and systems, rather than with the conventional framework and ideas.

For example, Japan could conceivably set up a standard c.i.f. price for crude oil and enforce something like a new second oil tax with a system of graduated tax increase below the standard price and graduated tax decrease above it. This tax revenue could be returned to the rest of the world by putting it into what we might call a World Peace Co-operation Fund. To avoid possible criticism of why only crude oil should be the object of this taxation, it might also be necessary to consider the application of the same kind of taxation on imports of other mineral fuel and primary products. Then those nations that export and produce these items would not raise objections to the present oil tax, as it would not be collected for Japan's benefit, but to be recycled back to the rest of the world.

As for the funds donated and used for something like a World Peace Co-operation Fund, management measures, such as entrusting them to international organisations or using them jointly with Japan, could be considered. One direction could be to eradicate absolute poverty and achieve Basic Human Needs (BHN) by utilising the funds for agricultural development leading to food self-sufficiency; the funds might also be used to solve the problem of accumulated debts and economic hardships caused by the sharp drop in oil prices. If the latter were chosen, it would greatly contribute to achieving the basic direction of establishing and reinforcing multiple interdependence with the Middle East area.

We should also note that, if a minimum import price and new inverse progressive oil taxation were implemented, it would also have the effect of controlling large price fluctuations and help to stabilise prices.

The government, economic, and industrial worlds together should take a long-term view of the future and adopt a basic stance to deal with wider perspectives, rather than sticking to narrower and short-term interests. Japan in particular has not yet completed its move away from oil, OPEC, and Middle East oil, and compared to the US and Europe is overwhelmingly dependent on oil and the Middle East oil producing nations. The situation is still delicate, so the maintenance and reinforcement of stability in the Middle East are an essential prerequisite to the development and normal operation of the Japanese economy.

Moreover, it has been predicted that as we enter the 1990s, the significance of OPEC oil supplies, particularly from the Middle East oil producing nations, will recover and continue to grow. A time like the present, just when the Middle East oil producing nations are facing difficulties, is a good opportunity for Japan actively to plan and work at the establishment of true interdependence and a relationship of trust.

The main theme of Japan's policy is how to bridge the gap between the present, when there is a growing disregard for the Middle East oil producing nations, and the future in the 1990s, when the need for the Middle East, centring on the oil producing nations, will begin to grow once more.

In this respect, the present joint research is significant. In order to achieve the direction of the policies put forward here, we need to begin with an earnest study of Middle East issues and the problem of energy security and continue and develop the study in order to change people's understanding.

3. Research and development in nuclear energy

After experiencing two oil crises in the 1970s, Japan has been aggressively promoting an alternative energy policy to free itself from an overdependence on oil. The electric power industry has also been striving to become less dependent on oil, especially from the Middle East. Nuclear power has replaced oil as the main alternative energy source. Figures for fuel consumption in generating electric power between 1973 and 1984 show a decrease in oil usage of about 220,000 bd, and an increase in the use of nuclear power to about the equivalent of 630,000 bd. In 1973, 2.4% of the power generated in Japan was supplied by nuclear power. In 1985 it was 26%, the first time electricity generated by nuclear power surpassed the 25% share of oil.

However, the recent sharp drop in crude oil prices that began towards the end of 1985 has raised the question of whether Japan should choose nuclear power as the main energy source for the future. In the 1990s, will nuclear energy continue to provide energy security?

It is estimated that there are enough uranium resources available worldwide to meet demand until the year 2005, which can be exploited at the cost of less than $30 per pound of refined uranium (U_3O_8). Japan's electric power industry has secured about 170,000 short tons of natural uranium through long-term contracts and approximately 20,000 short tons by the overseas develop and import scheme; therefore, for the time being, there is no fear of a shortage. However, by the late 1990s more resources will be required. Since the lead time for the development of uranium must be taken into consideration, it is necessary to continue to seek out as yet unexploited deposits for the future. As long as the exploration and development of overseas uranium resources continue, Japan's energy supply is secure up to the year 2000.

With this in mind, it will be necessary to diversify energy sources for the future, since Japan's natural resources are so limited. At present, 82.8% of the primary energy supplied depends upon imported fuel. This high figure emphasises Japan's need to diversify and establish a flexible energy supply foundation.

Realistic alternative energy sources must be technologically safe as well as economically feasible. Nuclear power meets these requirements. The highest operating percentage of nuclear power facilities in Japan was in 1985, at 76%. Compared to other countries, the number of reactors in Japan forced to shut down due to accidents and malfunctions is extremely low. The cost of generating power utilising nuclear energy is less than other methods, and it is generally agreed that an alternative will not materialise in the near future. For these reasons, nuclear power should continue being used and developed as Japan's most economical and viable energy source.

The Chernobyl accident. A special investigation committee set up by the Nuclear Safety Commission in Japan came to the following conclusion regarding the causes of the Chernobyl accident, based on a report presented by the Soviet Union to the IAEA Special Evaluation Meeting on the Chernobyl Accident held in Vienna in August 1986.

The causes of the accident can be attributed to the lack of an appropriate back-up system or emergency plan during experiments on the reactor. In addition, the reactor's design and safety features were considered to be insufficient. The committee also concluded that such an accident could not happen in Japan, after analysing issues such as differences in structure and characteristics of the nuclear reactors, safety designs, and operation administration systems.

The impact of the Chernobyl accident on nuclear energy development in major countries. Although no countries so far have expressed a policy abandoning nuclear energy as a means of generating power after the accident, public fear and pressure are turning it into a political issue, especially in Europe. Austria and Sweden were already gradually reducing the use of nuclear energy prior to the accident. However, in other countries, apart from France, which has not been affected, the opposition parties are advocating a freeze on the construction of new nuclear power facilities and the closure of those already in existence.

In the US, where about 30% of the world's nuclear power facilities are concentrated, no new commercial nuclear power plants have been built since 1979. Thus though the US has not been seriously affected, opposition to nuclear reactors at present under construction has increased. On the other hand, in countries such as France, Canada, Korea and the Soviet Union, the scene of the accident, there have been no moves towards reduction in the development and utilisation of nuclear power.

The impact on Japan's nuclear energy development. Compared to European countries, it seems that there has been no direct impact of the Chernobyl accident on Japan. There have been no significant changes in the policies of nuclear energy development, nor has an increase in the activities of anti-nuclear energy movements been observed. Since food contamination by the radioactive fallout was not considered great enough to be harmful, the government did not take any precautionary measures limiting the intake of certain foods. After the accident various organisations dealing with nuclear energy issued detailed reports regarding the safety of nuclear power plants in Japan, pointing out differences in reactor types and safety designs. Also, nuclear power was not a disputed point during the elections to the Upper and Lower Houses of the Diet in July 1986.

Lessons from the Chernobyl accident. As noted above, it is not likely that a similar accident will happen in Japan. Regarding nuclear power in Japan, there is no direct lesson to be learned from the accident. However, running a nuclear plant with high safety and operational standards in one country is not enough to ensure responsible nuclear energy development worldwide. Since radioactive fallout knows no national borders, it is obvious that nobody can remain indifferent to nuclear power accidents in other countries.

Direction of Japan's nuclear energy development policies. It is necessary for Japan to promote energy security for the 1990s, while keeping the safety issue concerning nuclear power in mind.

Nuclear Energy Vision[46] categorised the process of development and the application of nuclear energy into the following phases:

Phase 1: The phase for light water reactors to take root. (Nuclear power generation using Light Water Reactors is stabilised. The nuclear fuel cycle is in the stage of technological development.)

Phase 2: The phase in which the nuclear fuel cycle is to be established and take root. (LWR are advanced and the Fast Breeder Reactor is developed for practical use. The nuclear fuel cycle takes root in Japan.)

Phase 3: The phase in which FBR is put to practical use. (FBR is applied practically, and the nuclear fuel cycle shows further developments.)

Thus it is very important, for the sake of energy security, to continue research and development in nuclear energy. The goal is practical use of the FBR and forming a nuclear fuel cycle. If practical use of the FBR is promoted, the utility efficiency of uranium resources will be increased and nuclear energy's role will be transformed from one of semi-domestic energy to domestically produced energy.

The most important issue for the 1990s will be the comprehensive improvement of the performance of nuclear energy technology, including accumulated operating experience, and knowledge gained from safe and efficient operation of previously existing plants. It is also important to increase efficiency and accountability, development and stabilisation of nuclear fuel cycle technology, and safety assurances in the development of the FBR. In the international situation following the Chernobyl accident, priority is placed in every country on the maintenance and improvement of nuclear energy technology and promotion of the research and development of nuclear energy. 'Safety 21', issued by the Agency of Natural Resources and Energy, shows one approach in viewing the direction of nuclear energy development policies in the 1990s. 'Safety 21' is a programme to attain advanced safety in nuclear plants, in which new emphasis is placed on studies to prevent human errors and to promote technology development, along with the conventional studies of fuels, reactor structures, loss of coolant accidents, etc. It seems that it will be especially important in the future to apply Japanese state-of-the-art technology, such as artificial intelligence, to the operation and management of nuclear plants in order to further improve safety.

Japanese nuclear energy technology has reached the same level as that of other advanced nations. Since research and development require an enormous amount of funds and resources, and, as the Chernobyl accident revealed, mutual dependence has been increasing in the development and promotion of nuclear energy, Japan will have increasingly to share the costs and risks. Moreover, along with the increasing energy consumption in developing countries, many countries will actively engage in nuclear energy development.

The decreasing dependence of developing countries on oil contributes towards the energy security of Japan. At the same time, it helps contribute to the lasting advancement of the developing countries. It is necessary to support and co-operate technologically with these countries in the development of nuclear energy. This co-operation should be undertaken not only in nuclear energy but also in the management of other energy resources in accordance with the varied circumstances of each country in terms of naturally-occurring energy resource distribution, technical standards, etc.

Japan is well known for its high standards of operation and management of nuclear plants. It should make a positive contribution by sharing this technology with the rest of the world.

4. Research and development in alternative sources of energy and energy conservation

Research and development programmme. Energy research and development by the Japanese Government is being promoted according to the Prime Minister's 'Basic Program for Energy Research and Development' (designated on 11 August 1978 and revised every year since). It is based on the following concepts:

i) environmental preservation and safety;

ii) public understanding and co-operation;

iii) intensive and efficient implementation of research and development programs (in implementing the research and development programs, the feasibility of a wide variety of programs shall be studied for the purpose of defining the possibility of utilising all forms of energy, including the effective utilisation of indigenous energy resources. When such studies advance to the stage at which the economic and technical feasibility of each program can be assessed more clearly, however, the program shall be evaluated in a comprehensive manner to assure intensive and efficient implementation of such programs);

iv) international co-operation;

v) the nature of energy research and development (Those R&D tasks which have relatively short lead times should be promoted with due consideration for the nation's energy demand-supply outlook. Those R & D tasks which have extremely long lead times should be steadily promoted in stages, flexibly taking into account their relation to the nation's energy supply-demand outlook and assessing the probable outcome of the R & D at each stage along the way);

vi) social science research (technological forecasts, technology assessment, etc.);

vii) organic co-operation among governmental, educational and private institutions.

Priority is given to the following:

i) With regard to the development of nuclear energy, the establishment of a nuclear fuel cycle (on which the future of nuclear power generation depends) will be pursued, as well as development of advanced thermal reactors and fast breeder reactors, which will enable the nuclear fuel cycle to complete itself. Research and development of nuclear fusion will also be vigorously pursued.

ii) With regard to the development of technology for utilising fossil fuels and natural energy efficiently, the liquefaction and gasification of coal, solar power generation systems, geothermal energy, and fuel cell power generation will take priority. Development of technology utilising natural energy as well as biomass conversion technology in the fields of agriculture, forestry and fisheries, will also be matters for further promotion.

iii) Other research and development projects will also be continued according to existing programmes for the time being. When technological and economic possibilities have become clearer, they will be evaluated and given preferential treatment according to their merits.

Economic efficiency of the main technology. The average power generation cost of each system over the total operational period of its legal life has been estimated assuming an increase in fuel costs of 3% per year: it comes out at ¥11/kWh for nuclear power, ¥13/kWh for coal-fired or hydroelectric power, ¥18/kWh for LNG (natural gas) fired power, and ¥19/kWh for oil-fired power generation. The calculation of nuclear power generation costs does not include the costs of decommissioning old reactors and the disposal of radioactive wastes, though these costs are estimated to be less than 10% of the total. Another calculation estimates the cost of nuclear power generation, including that for decommissioning old reactors and disposal of radioactive wastes, at ¥11.5/kWh, with coal-fired power generation at ¥12/kWh and oil-fired power generation at ¥12.6-14.8/kWh. If the fuel costs of thermal power [47] generation are computed at a rate equal to nuclear power generation .costs, assuming all other conditions remain constant, the crude oil price must be $20/b and that of coal $44 per ton in the year 2000. Such estimates are unrealistically low, and therefore unlikely to occur. Furthermore, as far as nuclear power generation is concerned, unit capacity will enlarge, continuous operational hours will lengthen, combustibility will improve, etc. Thus cost efficiency is anticipated as technological development progresses. Taking all factors into consideration, new nuclear power generators as baseload power sources will remain economically superior to other systems in spite of any future sudden drop in the price of oil or the consequent fall in the price of coal.

Liquefaction of coal will remain economical as long as oil prices remain between $30 and $43/b. Especially since fixed charges such as facility costs are quite high, it is unlikely that low prices of coal would contribute to a reduction of production costs. Therefore, liquefaction of coal cannot be competitive when oil prices are less than $30/b.

As for solar cells, the poly-crystalline type has achieved 12-13% energy conversion efficiency and the amorphous type 7-8%, and power generation cost has come down to ¥1,200 per watt at present. Research and development work is under way to achieve a target cost of ¥500 per watt before long, and possibly one as low as ¥100-200 per watt by the year 1995 or 2000, which would be competitive with other existing power sources at that time. If a wide application of solar cells is to be promoted, costs must come down to the level of ordinary electricity charges. Although costs for solar cells, which are semiconductors, can be reduced comparatively easily, a reduction in peripheral costs such as for batteries and inverters will be difficult. In other words, costs concerning core technology can come down substantially, while costs for peripherals cannot. Consequently, cost reduction for the system as a whole cannot necessarily be achieved, which is an important point to note.

Prospects for the introduction of alternative sources of energy and energy conservation. Assessment regarding the introduction of new energy has been carried out by the government in terms of quantity (security of energy supply), quality (efficiency and usefulness of the energy concerned), and price (cost competitiveness with existing energy). From the viewpoint of economic security, ways to rectify a weak primary energy supply through the introduction of new energy sources were also studied. The result is shown in Table 2.20. The first five years constitute a starting stage, when various problems have to be overcome. Based on achievements made during the starting stage, the year 1990 onwards will be the taking-off stage, during which new energy will be put to practical use, with further expansion following.

In August 1985, the Advisory Panel on Thermal Power Generation to Meet the Requirements of a New Age presented the following points as concrete measures for the promotion of coal and LNG (natural gas) fired power generation.

i) Coal-fired power generation. Improvement of its image as a 'clean power source' through implementation of environmental measures; improvement of load follow-up as a middle or peak electricity source. Improvement of economic efficiency through reduction of construction and operational costs.

ii) LNG (natural gas)-fired power generation. Improvement of operational characteristics such as improvement of load follow-up of vaporiser and establishment of suppression technology of boil-off gas. Improvement of economic efficiency through research and development of highly efficient combined cycle power generation.

Solar batteries can be utilised on a small scale for residential use as well as for generating commercial power on a large scale. For residential use apart from pocket calculators, cameras, and watches, solar batteries are already being used to operate some radio transmitters and traffic lights. While solar power constitutes improved energy quality, it is also more appealing than other energy sources. Although overall energy consumption is minuscule for these types of devices, the social and cultural aspects of solar power's appeal will contribute to its growing popularity, which will reach a significant level in the twenty-first century.

As for large-scale production of electricity via solar energy, a 1,000 kW pilot power station is already in operation. Experiments are being conducted to study problems associated with supplying electricity to private homes, entire communities, factories, and schools.

For the time being, the potential for utilising solar energy for residential use is considered to be much greater than for generating commercial power.

Direction of R & D in alternative energy and energy conservation. As our information-oriented society develops and the quality of people's lives improves as we approach the twenty-first century, a demand for high quality, clean energy is expected to increase, not to mention a demand for security of the energy supply. Therefore, an energy policy which balances security, cost, and quality has to be promoted on the basis of sound research and development programmes along with international co-operation.

In the long run, it is imperative to pursue alternative energy development and energy conservation, for a decrease in oil prices, such as we are experiencing now, is a temporary phenomenon. These prices will eventually rise, and since some dependence on Middle East oil is unavoidable, some uncertainty remains about the reliability of our oil supply. It is thought that oil crises occur not as sweeping global phenomenona, nor do they occur all of a sudden, but rather they begin as local phenomenona, later growing to continental and global proportions. If this is the case, then Japan, which has a weak energy supply structure, is more vulnerable to such crises than other countries.

Although energy resources are naturally occurring, and are thereby beyond human control, energy technology, which is developed by science, does fall within our control. We must therefore overcome lack of natural resources by using technology.

Below are some of the technologies and measures to be studied, developed and promoted for future benefit.

i) Technology through which new energy is to be exploited, and more self-sufficiency gained, in order to avoid relying too much on foreign energy:

Nuclear-related technology for fast breeder reactors, nuclear fuel cycle, etc.;

Technology which will exploit readily available but hitherto under-utilised energy sources such as solar power and wind power;

Oil sand and oil shale production technology;

Exploitation of entirely new energy sources, such as nuclear fusion, which has a huge potential and will create a revolutionary impact on the future of mankind.

ii) Technology which will enable conventional energy resources to be used more effectively, enhancing the flexibility of the energy supply-demand relation, such as liquefaction and gasification technology for coal, fuel methanol production technology, hydrogen production technology and more efficient utilisation of oil;

iii) Energy conservation measures undertaken at the level of machinery, as well as improvement of overall energy efficiency in the context of total energy flow:

Improvement of power generation efficiency, such as fuel cells and combined power generation with the use of highly efficient gas turbines;

Energy loss reduction technology for co-generation, heat pumps, etc.;

iv) Provision of a highly reliable, safe and useful energy, indispensable for a high quality of life: development of electrical machinery adaptable to diverse energy sources, voltage-increasing technology to accommodate high electricity consumption apparatus, etc.

A radical change is taking place concerning our perception of the potential use of energy. For instance, ten watts of electricity used to be required to operate just one electric calculator, but today this is sufficient to operate a million pocket calculators. In other words, technological innovation has created a situation in which a given amount of electricity has applications which were once thought to be possible only with a resource of much greater proportions. This kind of change in our energy paradigm has a tremendous impact, especially in the wake of the recent oil crises. Although it is important to increase our knowledge of the confirmed amount of fossil fuel deposits, from a strategic point of view, it is also important to preserve these fossil fuels by reducing production, since they will eventually be depleted.

In this regard, it is essential that we develop a new R & D programme to bring about a major shift towards energy conservation, while also promoting the restructuring of existing technology.

A calculation of energy flow as of 1984 reveals that just over 50% of all energy produced was successfully used as power or heat at its final stage, while the rest was wasted. Energy resources are limited, so their conservation and the reduction of energy costs are paramount. Reducing energy loss to a minimum is the primary objective of contemporary research and development on energy efficiency.

In Japan, budgets for the development of alternative energy sources and energy conservation are stretched to the limit. Projects such as the Sunshine Project, which was set up to deal with the 1970s oil shocks, are faced with difficulties due to the change in the economic climate since then. Research and development of energy was spurred by the oil crises, the circumstances of which have changed completely. Hence, a strategic approach is now required to keep such projects functional. In West Germany, research and development of solar energy is carried out not for Germany, but to provide technology for those countries which have abundant solar energy. Japan should follow suit in this respect.

Japan is lagging behind the US and West Germany in some fields of energy research and development. In the area of liquefaction of coal, both countries have been operating pilot plants and have thus accumulated considerable know-how. As far as utilisation of coal is concerned, different types of coal require different plant designs and operating conditions, as well as different catalysts. Therefore, even if development in this field becomes slowed down or suspended in Europe and the US, Japan ought to continue the effort until sufficient technology is accumulated, as a hedge against future need.

We also need to promote research and development of coal gasification for the more widespread use of non-polluting coal.

Generally speaking, energy research and development requires extremely long lead times. For instance, it is 14 years since the Sunshine Project was started, but at present only solar technology for personal use or limited industrial use has been commercialised. Liquefaction and gasification of coal are still at the pilot plant stage. In the wake of the second oil shock, research and development of new alternative energy sources was accelerated. Nonetheless, commercialisation of technology which can contribute to industry in terms of quantity was targeted to be achieved between 1995 and 2000. Energy research and development requires long-term commitment. As stated in the Basic Program for Energy Research and Development, we should take note of the special nature of energy research and development and promote it based on the long-range perspective it demands.

Once projects are suspended, dispersion of researchers and engineers, not to mention technical know-how and dismantling of plants, will cause tremendous problems when the projects are reactivated, as recent events have demonstrated.

Oil prices in the past have fluctuated widely. It is extremely difficult to predict the movement of oil prices, which can rise or fall depending on different factors. However, the economic efficiency of established technology does not change as much as oil prices. Therefore, technological developments, once established, will enable new types of energy to compete financially with oil in the event of an oil supply problem. Once the technology is established, new types of energy will at least have the potential and flexibility to adapt themselves to changes in the energy situation. Economic efficiency of the technology concerned will be assessed in comparison with the oil prices of the time, and this will be followed by the development of demonstration plants and commercial plants.

As already stated, it is important not to be preoccupied with the present energy situation and present needs only, but to develop long-term alternative energy and energy conservation measures that can be commercialised as soon as possible in the future.

The following points should be recognised in the promotion of research and development of alternative energy and energy conservation:

i) Although it is often stressed that research and development of new energy requires long-term vision, the successful introduction of alternative energy and energy conservation measures largely depends on the market mechanism. Therefore, the focal point of research and development of alternative energy boils down to whether or not a given alternative can compete economically with conventional energy sources. While oil prices stayed high, efforts for the development of alternative energy and energy conservation measures were producing results. Regrettably, this phase did not last long, due to lack of incentives as oil prices tumbled and the yen started to appreciate.

The pursuit of economic efficiency is not, however, the sole objective of research and development. Development of regionally adapted energy technology (utilising natural energy available in a particular region) can ease the pressure of economic efficiency and also contribute to regional development. Although the concept of 'small is beautiful' (or 'soft pass') seems unlikely to prevail nationally or internationally, it should be allowed to co-exist with large-scale mass production energy systems to a certain degree. The advantages of such compact and independent energy systems are particularly apparent in remote areas of developing countries.

Another approach to the research and development of alternative energy and to energy conservation measures is to let them lead the technological field as a whole. They have hitherto come into being as contingency measures against energy crises; however, they should not be thus limited. They should now play a pioneering role and lead other fields of industry by demonstrating how to improve related technology and production processes. This expanded role should include the leading technologies in fields such as microelectronics, new materials, biotechnology, etc., and promote research and development by interaction among these related fields. If this were the case, as it should be, people working in research and development would have to be recruited from within as well as from outside the existing framework of organisations.

The promotion of energy research and development in the future requires not only consideration of energy policy, but also consideration of the impact on scientific, technological and regional development policy, etc.

ii) Because of the nature of public funds, assets tend to be evenly distributed among various companies. Since resources are limited, no one company has enough incentive to achieve results. A new system should be instigated, such as a contract in which one particular company is appointed as a prime contractor, thus increasing the incentive to make progress in earnest. It would also be effective partially to shift project-oriented research and development efforts to a seed discovery system, in order to encourage more fruitful results.

Japan's R & D contribution to world energy security. Japan is trying to establish itself as a secure world power on the basis of science and technology. Since access to and production of energy require interdependence between nations, and since the problems Japan is tackling are also the problems of other countries, Japan can greatly contribute to international co-ordination and co-operation if it provides the technology which can resolve these problems. The developed countries are all faced with massive economic responsibilities due to the mammoth scale on which energy research and development work is undertaken. This necessitates co-operation between them. However, since increasing future energy demand is expected to result mainly from the needs of developing countries, helping these countries is also important. If a strategic target is set up on a small scale, to meet a demand scattered throughout a region, and research and development are concentrated on that target, it will eventually bring additional benefits besides the obvious economic ones. For example, solar energy can be exploited in countries where daylight hours are long. As far as solar power generation is concerned, the conversion rate has gone up considerably. If the technology of electricity storage is developed further, utilisation of solar energy will improve enormously. Therefore, it is of great significance that Japan is conducting research and development in this field. Highly efficient wind power generation technology and geothermal energy utilisation technology can also be extremely useful to developing countries in establishing small-scale power generation systems in remote areas. These alternative sources of energy will not only provide light and power but will also enable these developing countries to contact different cultures through telecommunications and broadcasts. Of course, they will also significantly improve living standards in these countries as well.

Air pollution used to be a huge problem in Japan. Because of the urgency of the problem, the technological response to it produced results quickly compared to other countries. These technological advances have restored coal to its former glory as an important energy source in Japan. European countries may also benefit from these advances to solve their air pollution problems, such as acid rain. Furthermore, if this technology is provided to developing countries such as China, where there is a large demand for coal-fired power, it will not only protect the environment but also reduce the world's dependence on oil. These are significant considerations.

Research and development, as practised in Japan, are basically oriented toward process innovation. Now, attention should be directed to product innovation systems, or from co-operation for devising new means of production to co-operation for devising new applications to daily life. There is plenty of room for utilising new energy in different ways from those in which it has been used, by taking advantage of government aid and making the most of technological and economic co-operation. This kind of new energy seems attractive enough to have caught the interest of industries. For example, Japan may be the sole supplier of the technology for producing solar-cell battery-operated radios.

The Japanese innovation cycle is not a linear type (Research -- Development -- Production -- Marketing), but a spiral type, and this is attracting the attention of other countries. If international joint research and development projects promote the Japanese-style innovation cycle as well as other types, the parties involved will stimulate each other to produce better results, and Japan's contribution will be appreciated all the more.

The budgets for energy research and development allocated by the governments of IEA member countries increased rapidly until 1980, then started to decline, and have been levelling off since 1983. This trend is particularly noticeable in the United States. This is due to a recent change in US government policy, based on the idea that when energy research and development have reached proven stages, further development ought to be left to the judgement of the commercial sector. Consequently, despite a gradual increase in basic expenditure on science, space and defence, the budget for energy reseach has been reduced since 1981. Countries other than the US have also been compelled to reduce their budgets for energy research and development because of the current economic recession, although it has been easing since 1983. Since it is one of the world's leaders in the fields of science and technology, Japan's role in the research and development of energy is now more important than ever.

5. Energy in the developing countries

Forecast of energy supply-demand. For the world as whole, the 1970s were marked by two oil crises and high prices for energy. By contrast, the 1980s saw a softening of prices and a trend towards reduced consumption of energy. However, the net decline in oil and energy consumption has been confined to the industrialised countries of the West. For developing countries and for the Eastern bloc, energy consumption, while lower than forecast at the beginning of 1980, is continuing to increase every year (Table 2.21).

In the developing countries, industrialisation, urbanisation, the use of motor vehicles, mechanisation of farming and electricification of rural villages all increased rapidly after World War II. Consequently, energy consumption in the developing countries grew at a faster rate than in the industrialised countries, and accounts for a fast-growing share of worldwide consumption. According to the 1983 World Development Report, one-third of the forecast increase in energy consumption by the West between 1985 and 1995 will come from developing countries, and will account for almost one-fourth of the total energy consumed in the West. Even forecasts based on the average rate of increase between 1973 and 1985 show that energy consumption in the developing countries will be close to one-fifth of consumption worldwide, while consumption of oil alone will be more than one-quarter of the worldwide total. Clearly, demand in the developing countries will have an important impact on future energy prices and supply-demand conditions (Table 2.22).

However, two important factors must be kept in mind. One of these is the developing countries' growing debt problem. The two oil crises, in 1973 and 1979, dealt these countries severe economic blows. The non-oil producers among them were able to get through the first crisis by borrowing funds abroad to buy oil and other commodities necessary for economic growth, but this became much more difficult after the second crisis. In addition, high interest rates in the US made repayment of past borrowings very expensive. The oil producers, on the other hand, embarked on expansive development projects, borrowing from overseas in expectation of increased revenues through higher oil prices. They had to pay the price for this lax fiscal policy, however, when oil exports plunged during the 1981-82 worldwide recession. The debt-service ratio of the developing countries began to rise during the early 1980s, and the number of countries delaying repayment of their loans has increased. Notwithstanding the steep drop in oil prices and lower interest rates in the last few years, the debt position has not improved, since prices for primary commodities have plunged and demand for them has been stagnant.

The second factor to remember is the widespread consumption of non-commercial forms of energy in numerous developing countries, which contributes to environmental breakdown worldwide. Many people in those countries rely on charcoal or plant and animal residues to provide fuel for cooking and heating. Excluding the newly-industrialising countries (NICs), developing countries were battered by the two oil crises, which boosted the price of commercial energy, particularly oil. This made the changeover from non-commercial to commercial energy difficult. The use of non-commercial forms of energy has wide-ranging effects. For example, using cow dung as fuel means there is less of it to use as fertiliser, leading to less productive soil, poorer crops, and food shortages. The use of charcoal means wholesale deforestation, which causes floods and surface erosion of topsoil. The widespread burning of fossil fuels contributes to acid rain, gradual warming of the earth, changes in rainfall patterns, higher concentrations of carbon dioxide in the air, and other detrimental effects all over the world.

Seen from the viewpoint of energy needs, these two problems are important factors as far as worldwide energy requirements go: the former because foreign debt restricts economic growth in developing countries, and the latter because continued use of non-commercial energy means no increase in demand for commercial energy. However, the developing countries cannot expect their economies to grow unless their growing debt problems are resolved. Further, the use of non-commercial forms of energy only underscores poverty and the lack of economic development; so long as such conditions exist, they contribute to political unrest, which may in turn cause serious disruptions to the supply and transport of energy to the West.

Developing countries thus face many difficulties, present and future, with regard to energy. The most promising measures for dealing with them are development of domestic energy sources, energy conservation, and policies regarding alternative sources of energy, carried out by the developing countries themselves. At the same time, development aid from international institutions and the industrialised countries, to help these countries obtain financing and develop their technology, will contribute to global energy security.

<u>Countermeasures to energy problems</u>. In the past 10 years, developing countries have succeeded in developing various forms of domestic energy, and their dependence on imported energy has dropped. However, development of these domestic sources of energy is restricted mainly to oil, gas, hydro, coal, and geothermal energy, all areas where the technology for commercial production is available. There are only a few examples of new or recyclable energy in use, such as the production of alcohol fuel from sugar cane in Brazil, and the construction of solar ponds in Israel. Efforts are under way to develop practical applications for new forms of energy (e.g. solar heat, power generation through solar rays, wind power, biomass, power generation through temperature differentials in sea water, wave power). Adapting these to the natural conditions in individual countries will contribute greatly to alleviating the anticipated crunch in world energy needs.

Another way of tackling the energy problem is by restricting energy demand through an energy conservation policy. The most important factor contributing to the recently improved world oil supply-demand picture and lower oil prices has been the more efficient use of energy in the industrialised countries. Economic growth and energy consumption are no longer synonymous. Energy-saving measures are fairly widespread in NICs like Korea and Taiwan, but energy conservation is often not accorded sufficient priority in overall energy policy in other developing countries, due to the lack of investment funds and of technical and managerial expertise. These countries are still quite far behind in energy conservation; after 1980, the rate of energy consumption per unit of Gross Domestic Product was higher in the developing countries than in the industrialised nations. However, this also means that there is much room for improvement in energy conservation, and energy consumption can be greatly reduced, depending on future energy conservation policies.

Funding is a necessary ingredient in putting these policies into effect. Foreign loans borrowed for energy in the developing countries come from various sources. More than half are private funds, in the form of export-related credits and loans from commercial banks. Another 25% is comprised of funds borrowed from the World Bank, the regional development banks, and other international financial institutions, and the remainder is development aid from foreign governments. However, many developing countries have been forced to reschedule repayment of loans from private sources, so it will be difficult for them to borrow more there. International financial institutions and official overseas aid will therefore play an important role in the future. The suggestion of an 'energy loan organisation' endorsed by former World Bank chairman Robert McNamara is worth reconsidering. However, smooth operation of this plan on a worldwide scale would probably be hampered by political considerations. One good recent example of regional co-operation is the San Jose Agreement, signed in August 1980 by Mexico, Venezuela, and a number of central American and Caribbean countries.

The concept of a Pacific Basin region. The grouping of industrialised and developing countries takes on a new aspect when reordered on a regional basis. The Asian region (Asia and Oceania) enjoys the highest rate of economic growth in the world. This trend is expected to continue in the future, so increased demand for energy will be concentrated in this region. The pattern of energy consumption in Asian countries also shows that many of them depend heavily on oil, and that this oil comes mainly from the Middle East. Some authorities expect that the oil supply-demand situation will tighten up again in the mid-1990s, so the question of reliable sources of supply arises. Establishing a stable energy supply base is a prerequisite to sustaining high growth in the Asian region.

Expanding the Asian region to take in the Pacific Basin, including North America (the US and Canada) and China, would involve an area with abundant energy resources. The Pacific Basin region contains approximately 50% of the world's coal reserves and three of the world's four largest producers of uranium or sites of uranium deposits. The risks of political upheaval or localised warfare that could jeopardise the stability of energy supplies or the possibility of a cartel forming similar to that once formed by OPEC are low in these countries. Appropriate resource development in this region would be extremely effective in ensuring a stable supply of energy.

Content. The main energy resource in the Pacific Basin region is coal. A 'coal flow concept' to expand the development and use of coal resources is currently under consideration in Japan (Tables 2.23 and 2.24, Figure 2.8). This concept calls for development of coal resources in Indonesia, Thailand, the Philippines, China and other countries. At the same time, Japan would provide assistance in building coal-fired power plants in ASEAN and other countries, and transfer coal-utilisation technology to ensure balanced supply and demand and use of coal in the region. Some authorities also advocate the establishment of regional centres involved in the general management of coal, overseeing stockpiling, supply, ash disposal, and other areas of coal management. Natural gas is another promising resource, and plans are currently under way for projects in Alaska (North Slope), the USSR (Sakhalin), and Thailand that will export LNG to Japan. Preparing for construction of LNG terminals and building a pipeline network to meet anticipated increases in demand in East Asia and the ASEAN countries will stimulate more active trade in natural gas. It gives rise to great expectations that natural gas will become, along with coal, another Pacific Region-based energy resource, whose major suppliers are located in the Pacific Basin.

Developments in new energy technology in the Pacific Basin region include a Japan-US exchange of information on solar energy and wind power technologies, and joint research projects on the technology of power generation using hot, dry rock. Japan and Australia are working on solar energy and planning a system of power supply to remote areas, but closer co-operation in all these areas is needed (Table 2.24). Also, since oil will remain the main source of energy in the Pacific region for some time, the establishment of an 'emergency oil supply system', as is currently being considered by ASEAN, will be of even greater importance if it is expanded to include other countries in the region.

V. Conclusions - Direction of OECD policy responses

1. A lesson of the times

The Japanese Government's 8th Coal Policy (fiscal years 1987-91), which contains drastic measures for halving the present annual production level of 20 million tons to 10 million tons by FY 1991, is one example of the way the administration is attempting to readjust the industrial structure by prompting uncompetitive industries to redirect their efforts. This policy is also worth considering from the point of view of energy security. In addition to the social problems which will be brought about by the closure of a majority of the nation's eleven coal mines and the resultant 10,000-plus unemployed workers, there is also the question of how such a substantial reduction in domestic coal production (in 1984 it constituted 2.7 percentage points of Japan's self-sufficiency ratio of 17.2%, 10.3 mtoe) will affect an energy policy which has hitherto sought to achieve an optimal mix of security and cost. In Japan's case, supplies of foreign coal can generally be said to be reliable, and this is important to bear in mind. There is also the price differential - due to the strong yen, domestic coal is three times the price of foreign coal. In order to retain their own international competitiveness, domestic industries such as steel are unable to ignore this differential. As a result, we are faced with a situation where factors of economy outweigh those of security. While it is probably inappropriate to draw any simple generalisations from this example, it does suggest that, in the field of energy at least, there is a limit to the long-term continuation of protective measures in the face of market principles.

2. Implications of Japan's shift in energy policy

From the 1930s until the early 1970s the petroleum market was controlled by the international oil companies. When, however, control passed into the hands of OPEC, the cost-orientation of Japan's energy policy between 1960 and 1972 was largely subordinated to a new emphasis on security. In 1983, when OPEC lowered the basic price of oil by $5/b, Japan carried out a general examination of its energy policy, followed by a redirection aimed at achieving the optimal mix of security and cost. Further steep drops in the basic price of oil mean that policy-makers now have to consider not only security and cost, but must also formulate a vision of energy policy for the twenty-first century based on the adaptability of industrial and residential needs. As the subtitle of this paper - 'The Dawn of an Age of Multiple Energies' - suggests, the early twenty-first century is seen as a time when the main energy sources of oil, coal, nuclear power, natural gas and the new technologies will play appropriate roles in a considerably diversified market, as they compete against each other to supply the same demands.

While this change in emphasis in Japanese energy policy from security (emphasis on supply) to an optimal mix taking into account cost (emphasis on demand) is in some measure undeniably the characteristic response of a country with poor energy resources, we believe that in broad terms it does suggest one typical example of the road that any country's energy policy may travel as a result of shifts in the international energy situation. The implication is that the basis for medium- to long-term energy policy must be laid on market principles. There is, of course, the possibility of this approach inviting market failure and large-scale readjustments, which will have to be met by later policy responses. It is necessary to take some policy measures if these market failures and large-scale readjustments are likely actually to occur.

3. Direction of OECD policy

The OECD includes countries both with and without their own domestic energy resources. Also, the positions of these countries vary depending on the degree of power their capital and technology give them in influencing energy supply and demand. Consequently there are differences between these countries in their view of what constitutes a 'threat' to energy security and the forcefulness of the responses that they can make. Furthermore, as the international oil situation in recent years has clearly shown, basic energy prospects are always shrouded in great uncertainty, and this is a big problem in any consideration of energy security. As our analysis has concluded, there is a possibility that the sharp decline in oil prices will have the effect of increasing the dependence of Japan, the US and Europe on OPEC (particularly Middle East) oil. This poses a threat not only to the energy security of these countries, but also to the energy security of the rest of the world. The governments of Japan, the US and Europe should fully recognise the international linkage of energy security.

Given these trends, what sort of policy should the OECD adopt? Let us consider two categories - one aiming at alleviating an existing threat and the other at controlling the impact of a crisis which has actually occurred.

Alleviating the threat. The threat raised by increasing dependence on Middle East oil is this: in the event of oil supplies being disrupted by political instability in the area, or of politically motivated changes in production and export policies, there is the probability that the resultant fluctuations in supply and price (the latter is perhaps the more significant) will impose the need for great and costly economic readjustments on the entire world. The basic measures that can be taken to alleviate this threat are:

i) optimal effort to lessen dependence on Middle East oil;

ii) improvement of stability in the Middle East region; and

iii) limiting the scope of political motives in influencing oil supply and export policies.

In Section IV we suggested some of the practical ways in which dependence on Middle East oil can be reduced: by (a) formulation of a policy towards low oil prices; (b) formulation of a policy to combat oil price instability; (c) promotion of nuclear energy development and utilisation; (d) promotion of energy research and development; (e) increased regional co-operation in energy matters; (f) improvement of energy supply and demand in developing countries, and (g) increased multinational co-operation on energy through the IEA and OECD.

Let us now look at some of these points in more detail:

Direction of OECD oil policy. Oil prices should be determined primarily through the market mechanism and government intervention in the market should be avoided. However, if the determination of oil prices is left entirely to the market mechanism, there is the danger that short-term imbalance in supply and demand combined with speculative movements will cause wild fluctuations. This situation is desirable neither to oil importing nor producing nations. However, in order to combat this problem, there are few effective measures that oil importing countries can adopt at present. The task of stabilising oil prices is for the moment best left to the oil exporting countries, the OPEC nations in particular. They should face reality and make efforts to avoid excessive competition in the oil producing market. At the industrial level, the hedging facilities of the futures market could be used, while at the consumer level there could be a flexible system allowing free choice of fuels in response to energy prices. As for alternative energy, priorities have to be more clearly identified at the government level and positive funding made for its development.

OECD development and promotion of nuclear energy. It will take some time for the effects of the Chernobyl accident to die down. Nevertheless, the OECD should reaffirm the future importance of nuclear power as an alternative source of energy to oil after coal and natural gas. At the same time, it is both natural and necessary to ensure the safety of nuclear energy facilities in each country and to promote international co-operation for the purpose of increased safety and for improving the potential emergency response.

In regard to improving political stability in the Middle East and limiting the possibility of political motives interfering with oil production and export policy, what is necessary is not so much an energy policy but rather a diplomatic policy which includes economic and technical co-operation, or the promotion of deeper bilateral and multilateral relationships of mutual dependence on the basis of an OECD market liberalisation policy. In part 2 of the previous Section, we proposed that Japan's approach to the Middle East should be directed towards strengthening multi-layered mutual dependence. Practical thought should first be given to policy development on a bilateral basis, involving such topics as:

(a) reinforcing interdependence in trade in products and services;

(b) reinforcing interdependence in the transfer of factors of production like capital, technology and human resources; and

(c) creating conditions for the achievement of peace in the Middle East and negotiations in the Iran-Iraq war.

Topics for policy development on a multilateral basis could be:

(d) strengthening and diversifying interdependence among Japan, the oil producing nations and non-oil producing nations of the Middle East; and

(e) establishment and support of third-country markets for industrial and petroleum products from Middle East countries.

Topics to be dealt with through international organisations are:

(f) possible roles and activities to be carried out by existing institutions like the IMF, World Bank and IDA; and

(g) opening of new international forums for the purpose of establishing discussion and co-operation between producers and consumers.

Some of these proposed policies are still in the conceptual stage and realisation will be difficult, the main problem being delegation of responsibility. However, they deserve to be discussed not only in Japan, but in individual OECD countries and by the OECD as a whole.

This concludes the main discussion on how the threat to world energy security can be alleviated. It should be emphasised that for OECD policy co-ordination to succeed, it is essential that each country fully exercises the resources of its 'comparative superiority' (capital, technology, military, diplomacy, culture, etc.), thus doing all it can to increase energy security through optimal responsibility and contribution.

Improving crisis management. If, despite the above efforts, a threat to energy security develops into an actual imminent or incipient crisis, the following efforts might be made to control the impact:

(a) prevention of psychological instability and panic by the prompt circulation of reliable information;

(b) governments should increase strategic reserves of oil which can be used in the case of a possible short- or medium-term stoppage in the supply of Middle East oil;

(c) establishment of an agreed-upon mechanism by which the IEA can make an early release of oil stocks to counter price rises during the early stages of the crisis; and

(d) reinforcement of IEA emergency measures in the case of a prolonged crisis.

Such attempts to control the crisis are beyond the capabilities of one country. Effective action requires the concerted action of all OECD nations.

The above comments represent our views on the directions that OECD policy response should take in order to contribute to energy security. It is our hope that in the near future the countries of the OECD will hold thorough discussions leading to practical and effective policy co-operation on energy security. We shall be glad if this joint Japanase, US and European study contributes to that end in any way.

Supplement - on minimum import price (m.i.p.)

Minimum Import Price (m.i.p.) may well be one of the means by which the OECD as a whole can cope with low or unstable oil prices. Here it is useful to examine m.i.p. by addressing the following questions:

i) Is the introduction of m.i.p. desirable for the OECD?

ii) Even if m.i.p. is desirable, what is a reasonable m.i.p. level?

iii) Even if agreement is reached on a reasonable m.i.p. level, is it actually feasible?

i) Is the introduction of m.i.p. desirable?

Advocates of a m.i.p. for oil claim that it will prevent a reduction in exploration, development, and production investment by the OECD or non-OPEC countries, and will thereby prevent any future increase in dependence on Middle East oil. Furthermore, they believe that m.i.p. would bring certain incentives to the development and introduction of alternative forms of energy. On the other hand, those opposed to a m.i.p. point out that using oil, which can be purchased at a lower price, at the artificial m.i.p. or a higher level, not only results in economic loss but would artificially distort both the energy and the economic system. This would be more harmful and would ultimately result in a system that lacks efficiency. Let us start by considering the impact of m.i.p. on the energy system.

Possibility of double pricing. Devising m.i.p. as a countermeasure to low oil prices means setting the m.i.p. at a level higher than the equilibrium price of oil supply and demand in a theoretically perfect competitive market. That is to say, such a level as $18/b should be higher than the equilibrium price in the short to medium term. This level is based on the assumption that marginal oil wells in the US and the UK would provide the oil supply. Judging from the present supply and demand situation, this m.i.p. level cannot be achieved unless there is a reduction in production by OPEC, particularly the oil producing countries of the Middle East. However, there is no guarantee that OPEC would be satisfied with production and exports at this price level. Conversely, it is more likely that they would be dissatisfied, because countries with a large supply potential, and a need for hard currency to ensure their own political and economic stability or that of their neighbours, require maximum income. What would be the OPEC reaction if OECD introduced m.i.p. in such a situation? Would they not sell at a higher price than m.i.p. to the OECD, and at a lower price to non-OECD nations in order to achieve the desired volume? If the OECD's oil demand decreases due to the introduction of m.i.p., and OPEC's revenue also decreases, would it not further spur price competition in the non-OECD market? The development of spot markets in oil dealings may encourage such a situation (see Appendix).

The impact of double-priced oil on energy systems. If oil prices are set lower in the non-OECD countries than in the OECD, it will probably lead to an increase in oil demand, and is likely to act as a disincentive to the development and introduction of alternative energy in the developing countries, particularly the Asian NICs, because of the reduced cost in acquiring oil and oil products. Also, the oil majors which have refinery plants in non-OECD countries may try to gain profits by exporting and selling the oil products which have been refined there to the OECD.

Implications of no double pricing. Having considered the impact of double-priced oil, it is appropriate to examine the implications of the theory which claims that there will be no double pricing of world oil prices if m.i.p. is introduced in the OECD. The OECD accounts for approximately three quarters of the entire oil demand in the free world (OECD oil demand in 1985 was 34 mbd while the total demand for the free world was 45.6 mbd). As has been clearly shown, it is when OPEC and/or non-OPEC oil producing countries reduce production that there is no double pricing of world oil prices; in other words, when the introduction of m.i.p. by the OECD and reduction of OPEC production are carried out simultaneously. This carries the implication of energy security for the OECD and OPEC through the establishment of tacit co-ordination between the producing and consuming countries without dialogue, without an international commodity agreement, and without the sacrifice of non-oil producing developing countries which could have purchased cheaper oil.

As outlined above, the introduction of m.i.p. in the OECD carries a risk of double pricing of oil, and it may aggravate the condition of dependence on Middle East oil by the non-OPEC countries. If double pricing does not occur, it forces a sacrifice on non-oil producing developing countries. This is not as simple as saying that it is preferable for the assurance of energy security at a global level. Recognising the issue's complexity, we should also look at its effect on the economic system.

Accelerated industrial adjustment in OECD due to double pricing of oil. If the cost of oil acquisition by non-OECD nations is lower than in the OECD, there will be a gap in energy costs so that the industries where product cost is largely determined by energy cost would shift operations from OECD to non-OECD countries, particularly to the Asian NICs, bringing about a hollowing of the economy and an accelerated adjustment of the structure of these industries in the OECD.

Effects on world economy. If oil prices go up because of the introduction of m.i.p. by the OECD, there is a danger of bringing about inflation and rising interest rates, and this would have a bad effect not only on developing countries, which have large cumulative debts, but also on the US, which has become the world's largest debtor nation today.

As we have seen, further discussion by the OECD is essential before the introduction of m.i.p. to decide whether it is really desirable, and due attention should be paid not only to its effects on the energy system but on the economy of each country, as well as on the world economy.

ii) Even if m.i.p. is desirable, what is a reasonable m.i.p. level?

This issue is basically one of which country should bear the cost, and to what degree, for the assurance of the free world's energy security. In other words, it concerns finding the price level that allows the compromise of interests between consumer countries with no oil resources like Japan, and countries which do have oil resources of their own like the US and the UK. The oil producing countries of the OECD such as the US and the UK may, for instance, advocate setting the m.i.p. at the average production cost of a North Sea oil field set by the UK's Department of Energy, which is currently $18/b before payment of royalties and taxes (The Brown Book, 1986). However, non-oil producing countries in the OECD like Japan choose to set the m.i.p. at the break-even point between oil and alternative energy. For instance, in Japan's case, according to the calculations by the IEE, the short-term break-even point (bep) between oil and coal in coal-fired power generation using existing facilities with wholly imported coal is $12/b at c.i.f. crude oil price. In the steel industry, which has the lowest bep of the general industries, it is $13/b at c.i.f. crude oil price. After the $1/b for freight and insurance between the Middle East and Japan has been taken into account, Japan may well advocate setting the m.i.p. at $11-$12/b at f.o.b. crude oil price. As this shows, where there are differences in the m.i.p. level advocated by countries within the OECD, the discussion on a reasonable price level must go deeper.

iii) Even if agreement is reached on a reasonable m.i.p. level, is it actually feasible?

The agreement in 1976 on the IEA's Minimum Safeguard Price (MSP) might provide an answer to the above question. The agreement stipulated $7/b (f.o.b.?) as a reasonable level of MSP, and the measures to be taken by each country were also described. However, will it function well when actually implemented? Can we really decide on reasonable coefficients (oil products prices/minimum import crude oil price), including how to handle oil products to be used as feed-stocks for the petrochemical industry? Can the m.i.p. level really be appropriately adjusted to account for the price fluctuation that accompanies the short- to medium-term shifts in supply and demand of oil and oil products?

And is it all right to change the m.i.p. in the short term when it forms the basis for exploration and development of energy resources in the medium to long term? Clearly, the feasibility of m.i.p. needs further detailed discussion.

Finally, it will be necessary to examine whether the m.i.p., while being a useful countermeasure to low oil prices, is really effective or not as a countermeasure to unstable oil prices. If a situation of oil double pricing occurs, would it not cause greater fluctuation in the oil prices of non-OECD countries? And even if double pricing of oil does not occur, why would oil prices stabilise at a price higher than the m.i.p.?

In conclusion, the above discussion indicates clearly that there are still too many uncertainties involved to discuss the introduction of m.i.p. by the OECD. It would be irresponsible and would go against our own good sense to propose introducing m.i.p. without tackling these issues. Therefore, serious discussions should be held now in every sphere including the governments of the OECD countries, the IEA, industry, and academic circles on measures to promote the free world's energy security.

Appendix: Medium- to long-term oil supply and demand curve

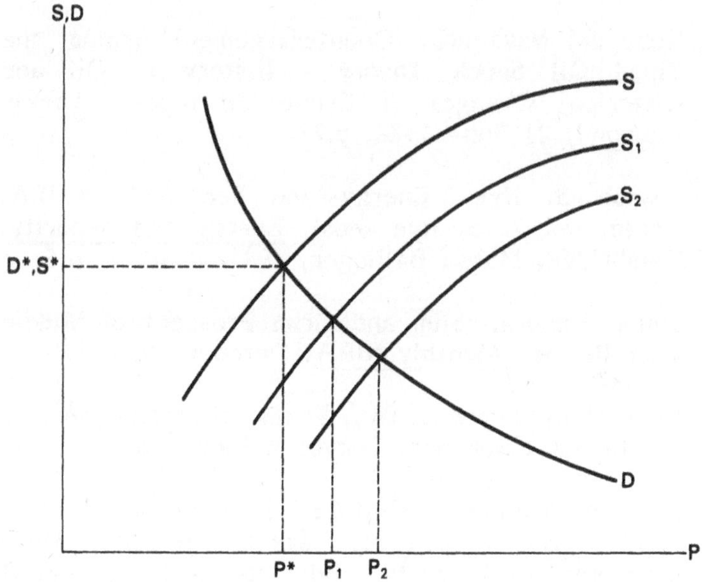

S = fs (p): supply function
Here f's (p) > 0
(f"s (p) < 0 is unknown)

D = fd (p): demand function
Here f'd (p) < 0
(f"d (p) > 0 is unknown)

i) If the equilibrium price is p* in a perfect competitive market, then the demand D* = fd (p*) and the supply S* = fs (p*) are equal, D* = S*.

ii) If OPEC reduces production, the supply curve shifts downwards from S to S_1, and price rises from p* to p_1.

iii) If p_2 as the m.i.p. is set at a level $p_2 > p_1$, in order for supply and demand to be in equilibrium, the supply curve must shift further downwards from S_1 to S_2. This is only possible if OPEC reduces production or the OPEC and non-OPEC countries co-ordinate in reducing production.

Notes

[1] MITI, Energy Vision for the 21st Century, Trade and Industry Research Foundation, December 1986, pp.98-100.

[2] Nobuyuki Nakahara, 'Counterargument Against the Third Oil Shock Theory - History of Oil and Historical Changes of Crude Oil Price', Weekly Diamond, 21 June 1986, p.77.

[3] Joseph S. Nye, 'Energy and Security' in D.A. Deese and J. S. Nye (eds), Energy and Security, Cambridge, Mass.: Ballinger, 1981, chap. 1, p.6.

[4] Shuzo Kimura, 'Slim and Grim Prospect of Middle East Peace', Monthly NIRA, October 1986.

[5] Lecture by James A. Bill, Texas University, at 13th Middle East Seminar, Tokyo, 9 June 1986.

[6] Foreign Ministry, Cultural Information Bureau, Middle East Conflict, World on the Move Company, 1981; J. F. Dunnigan and A. Bay, A Quick and Dirty Guide to War, 1985 and its translation by Satoshi Ogawa, How to Understand International Conflicts in Perspective, New Kawade Publishing, 1986.

[7] MITI, op. cit., pp.93-4.

[8] Nakahara, op. cit., p.78.

[9] Akitaro Seki, 'What went wrong with crude oil price predictions?' Energy Forum, October 1986, p.59.

[10] MITI, op. cit., pp.94-5. See also Seki, op. cit., pp.57-8.

[11] Peter R. Odell, 'Back to Cheap Oil?', Lloyds Bank Review, April 1985, No. 156, pp.11-13.

[12] The London consultancy Petroleum Economics Ltd estimates the quantity of alternative fuels which would be consumed in the world instead of nuclear

energy due to the after-effect of the Chernobyl accident to be 280,000 barrels per day of oil equivalent in 1990, 400,000 bd in 1995, and 680,000 bd in 2000, Petroleum Intelligence Weekly, 3 November 1986.

[13] Edward R. Fried, 'World Oil Markets: New Benefits, Old Concerns', The Brookings Review, Summer 1986, p.34.

[14] Ibid., p.35.

[15] Edward N. Krapels, Oil Crisis Management, Baltimore: Johns Hopkins University Press, 1980, p.117.

[16] Raymond Vernon, Two Hungry Giants, Cambridge, Mass.: Harvard University Press, 1983. Translation by Ryuzo Sato and others, Hungry Giants - US-Japan War Over Oil Resources, Nihon Keizai Shimbun, 1984, p.176.

[17] Seki, op. cit., p.54.

[18] OECD/IEA, World Energy Outlook 1982. Translation by International Energy Issues Study Group, World Energy Outlook, Trade and Industries Research Foundation, 1983, p.87.

[19] Valerie Yorke, 'Oil, the Middle East, and Japan's search for security', in Nobutoshi Akao (ed.), Japan's Economic Security, Aldershot: Gower, 1983, chap. 3.

[20] MITI, op. cit., p.111 and pp.215-17.

[21] Robert J. Lieber, 'Cohesion and Disruption in the Western Alliance', in Daniel Yergin and Martin Hillenbrandt (eds), Global Insecurity, Boston: Houghton Mifflin, 1982, chap. 11, which reviews the case of France, where bilateral relationships with Arab countries failed to improve the situation or the predominance of American energy and Middle East diplomatic policy.

[22] Nakahara, op. cit., p.77.

[23] Seki, op. cit.

[24] International Energy Agency, Energy Policies and Programmes of IEA Countries, 1985 Review, Paris: OECD/IEA, 1986, p.61.

[25] Tetsuo Hamauzu, 'Into an Era of Fluctuating Oil Prices', The Economist, 8 July 1986, p.80. Also refer to Vernon, op.cit. p.65 '...Too many suppliers are participating in the market and their interests are too far away ... national companies are, despite differences to varying degrees, enterprises established by the governments of their respective countries ... and most governments do not wish to be placed under the restraint of elaborate long-term treaties required to stabilise the market. ...'

[26] Louis Turner, 'OPEC', in Joan Pearce (ed.), The Third Oil Shock - The Effects of Lower Oil Prices, London: Routledge and Kegan Paul, 1983, Chap. 6, p.86.

[27] Refer, for example, to the speech by oil minister Sheikh Yamani in January 1981 under the title 'Petroleum: A Look into the Future' - 'As far as Saudi Arabia is concerned, our interests are clear. First, we do not intend to exhaust this wealth quickly and deprive our future generations of it. On the other hand, we do not want to shorten the life span of oil as a source of energy before we complete the elements of our industrial and economic development, and before we build our country to be able to depend on sources of income other than oil.' Quoted in William B. Quandt, Saudi Arabia's Oil Policy - A Staff Paper', The Brookings Institution, 1982, p.8.

[28] Fried, op. cit., p.36.

[29] Ibid., p.36. The figure of demand in 1990, 22-24 mbd, indicates that OPEC surplus capacity (mostly the Gulf nations) would then be approximately 6-8 mbd. However, the figure of 26-28 mbd in the mid-1990s signifies a reduction of surplus capacity to 2-4 mbd. The calculation of surplus capacity

might be slightly overestimated, considering the downward revision of OPEC production capacity presented by the recent PIW journal. Its meaning is clear: the end of world surplus oil production capacity.

[30] Tsutomu Toichi, 'OPEC Export Oil Refining and its Implications for Oil Policy in Japan', IEE, Energy-Keizai (Energy Economics), August 1985, p.5.

[31] Edward L. Morse, 'After the Fall: The Politics of Oil', Foreign Affairs, Spring 1986, p.810.

[32] Toichi, op. cit., pp.5-6; Charles K. Ebinger, The Critical Link: Energy and National Security in the 1980s, Cambridge, Mass.: Ballinger, 1982, chap. 6, pp.132-5.

[33] Philip K. Verleger, 'The long term implication of oil as a commodity', in William F. Thompson and David J. DeAngello (eds), World Energy Markets: Stability or Cyclical Change?, Proceedings 7th Annual North American Meeting, IAEE, Philadelphia, Pennsylvania, December 1985, chap. 10, pp.143-4.

[34] According to Toichi, op. cit., p. 6, (i) when the oil market becomes tight in the future, the vertically integrated national oil companies of the producing nations will be able to exercise their political influence quite effectively. It is possible that they will force refinery facilities in the importing countries to close down by requiring the importing nations to buy a 'package' of crude oil and oil products; (ii) the increase in exports of oil products from OPEC nations, especially from the Middle East, will detract from flexibility in the emergency measures of the importing countries, as the influence of oil products in the consumers' market is much more direct and serious than that of crude oil.

[35] Study made by Tetsuo Hamauzu of the Institute of Developing Economies.

[36] LNG supply, whose main suppliers are Indonesia and Borneo, had increased nine-fold between 1974 and 1984, and its share of primary energy jumped from 1.3% to 8.9%.

[37] 'Present status of oil emergency measures of IEA', International Resources, June, 1986, compiled by the International Resources Study Group.

[38] For example, a typical view - Sheikh Ali Khalifa al-Sabah of Kuwait said in September 1979, 'the oil producing states must shift production policies away from being essentially oriented to world markets ... to policies based on a long-range vision of the economic and social transformation of their societies.' Quoted in Yorke, op. cit., chap. 3, p.49.

[39] A view of Professor M. A. Adelman of Massachusetts Institute of Technology, quoted in Hamauzu, op. cit., p.81.

[40] 'Basic Tasks for Japan's Foreign Policy', Diplomatic Blue Book, 1968 edn, Ministry of Foreign Affairs, p.3.

[41] Ibid., p.52. (The Japanese Government's concept of the Middle and Near East is the Middle East and North Africa including Egypt, Algeria, Libya, Morocco, etc.)

[42] Taichi Sakaiya, Yudan, Nihon Keizai Shimbun, 1975

[43] Kenneth N. Waltz, 'The Myth of National Interdependence' in C.P. Kindleberger (ed.), International Co-operation: a Symposium, 1970, p.205.

[44] Nihon Keizai Shimbun, 22 December 1986 evening edition.

[45] Sheikh Ahmed Zaiki Yamani, 'Oil Markets: Past, Present and Future', speech at Harvard University, 4 September 1986.

[46] Nuclear Energy Vision - Thinking about Nuclear Energy for the 21st Century, Nuclear

Sub-Committee of Advisory Committee for Energy, 18 July, 1986.

[47] Thermal power conventionally refers to non-nuclear forms of electricity generation.

Additional references

'The Effect of Oil Price Reduction on Alternative Energies', (material for the regular study group of the Institute of Energy Economics), 2 July 1986.

Electric Industry Vision for the 21st Century - aiming at a new era of electric civilization, The 21st Century Vision of Electric Industry - Research and Study Committee, 15 October 1986.

Feldstein, Martin and Kathleen, 'The Risks of a Falling Dollar', The Washington Post, 19 January 1987.

Hamauzu, Tetsuo, 'Into an era of fluctuating oil prices', The Economist, 8 July 1986.

Inoue, Tomoo, 'Oil: moving away from politics and turning into a general commodity', Japan Economic Journal, 14 May 1986.

Investigation Report of Soviet Atomic Power Plant Accident - primary report, Nuclear Safety Commission, The Special Investigation Committee on the Soviet Nuclear Plant Accident, 9 September 1986.

Investigative Report of the Impacts of the Chernobyl Accident, The Science and Technology Agency, Atomic Energy Bureau, Office of Atomic Energy Policy Research, Japan Electric Power Information Center, Inc., July 1986.

Luciani, Giacomo, The Oil Companies and the Arab World, Beckenham: Croom Helm, 1984.

Matsuda, Yasushi, 'Nuclear Energy Policy after the Chernobyl Accident', International Energy Analysis, December 1986, No. 107, The Institute of Energy Economics.

Morse, Edward L., 'An Overview: gains, costs, and dilemmas' in Joan Pearce, (ed.), The Third Oil Shock - The Effect of Lower Oil Prices, Routledge and Keegan Paul, 1983.

Naito, Masahisa, 'Japan's Oil Policy', Lecture at the 10th Oxford Energy Seminar, 10 September 1986.

Nara, Yoshihiro, 'Competitive Energies in the Major Industries', IEE's Energy Economics, October 1986.

Neff, Thomas L., 'The changing oil market' in David A. Deese and Joseph S. Nye (eds), Energy and Security, Cambridge, Mass.: Ballinger, 1981.

NIRA OUTPUT, Formation of Nuclear Power Policy of the United States and France, Application System Laboratory Co. Ltd., September 1985.

Nuclear Energy Pocket Book, Japan Atomic Industrial Forum, Inc., 1987 edition.

Nuclear Energy Yearbook, Japan Atomic Industrial Forum, Inc., 1986 edition.

Samuelson, Robert J., 'Keep Watching OPEC and Try a Sales Tax', Herald Tribune, 2 January 1987.

Steeg, Helga, 'Lower Oil Prices: The Impact on Energy Policy', The OECD Observer, No. 140, May 1986, and 'Energy and the Role of Governments', Cannes, 6 October 1986.

'Summary of the Chernobyl Nuclear Power Plant Accident', Energy Forum, October 1986.

Suzuki, Shinji, 'Impacts of the Soviet Chernobyl Power Plant', Analysis of International Energy Trends, July 1986, No. 102, The Institute of Energy Economics.

Table 2.1 Energy supply structure of the main developed countries (mtoe, %)

	Japan		USA		West Germany		France		UK	
	1973	1984	1973	1984	1973	1984	1973	1984	1973	1984
Primary energy supply quantity	343	377	1,772	1,800	268	263	180	191	221	192
Dependence of primary energy on imports	88.0	82.8	15.5	9.6	54.7	51.1	77.3	58.9	50.9	- 6.5
Dependence of primary energy on oil	75.7	59.0	45.3	39.7	55.6	42.3	68.3	44.7	50.5	45.9
Dependence on oil imports	99.7	99.8	35.4	30.4	95.4	95.1	98.8	96.7	99.6	-46.7
Dependence on imported crude oil passing through the Strait of Hormuz	75.1	63.5	24.5	12.3	47.3	13.2	54.6	25.8	66.7	19.5
Dependence of primary energy on the Middle East	58.9	31.3	4.0	0.4	26.2	4.1	48.2	7.1	37.5	-

Sources: OECD, Energy Balances (1973, 1984), Quarterly Oil and Gas Statistics; (1973, 1984)

Table 2.2 <u>Changes in energy trade</u>

	1975		1980		1984	
	World inc. Japan	Japan	World inc. Japan	Japan	World inc. Japan	Japan
Oil (1,000 b/d)	30,335	4.945	31,935	4,985	24,750	4,305
%		(16.3)		(15.6)		(17.4)
Coal (million tons)	(1978) 199.3	52.9	(1981) 271.6	78.0	307.2	87.2
%		(26.5)		(28.7)		(28.4)
LNG (Natural Gas) (1,000 tons)	9,368	4,560	22,841	16,842	35,199	25,892
%		(48.7)		(73.7)		(73.6)

Note: Coal includes that used as coking coal

Sources: Oil: <u>BP Statistics</u>
Coal: <u>Coal Information, 1986</u>
LNG (Natural gas): <u>Petrol. Customs Statistics</u>

Table 2.3 Changes in oil exports from the Middle East (1,000 b/d, %)

	1970	1975	1984
USA	175 (1)	1,140 (6)	615 (6)
Latin America	240 (2)	1,525 (8)	700 (7)
Western Europe	6,220 (49)	8,815 (48)	3,045 (31)
Southeast Asia	800 (6)	1,450 (8)	1,555 (16)
Japan	3,485 (27)	3,675 (20)	2,830 (29)
Others	1,795 (15)	1,900 (10)	1,100 (11)
Total Exports	12,715 (100)	18,505 (100)	9,845 (100)

Note: Share percentage in total oil exports from Middle East is shown in the parentheses

Source: BP Statistics

Table 2.4 Spot dealings reported by 'Petroleum Argus' (1,000 b/d)

	1981	1982	1983	1984	1985
Brent	35	360	1,190	4,355	8,430
Other North Sea	120	290	470	730	920
Gulf	210	305	655	1,875	2,630
Africa	140	220	540	710	980
USA	5	70	590	950	610
Others	5	25	25	275	450
TOTAL	515	1,270	3,470	8,895	14,020

Notes 1. Gulf includes Syria, Africa, and Egypt
2. USA includes only WTI and North Slope (Alaska) crude

Table 2.5 Trends in production of North Sea Brent blend and paper transactions (1,000 b/d)

	Crude Oil Production		No. of Transactions Reported to *Petroleum Argus*(a)		
	UK North Sea Total	Brent Blend	Total	Forward Delivery	Same Month Delivery
1981	1,801	530	35	-	-
1982	2,056	665	360	130	230
1983	2,267	785	1,190	660	530
1984	2,480	940(b)	4,355	3,415	940
1985	2,532	960(b)	8,430	6,750	1,680

Notes: a) Estimates from 11 January 1985 and 13 January 1986 issues. *Petroleum Argus* does not report all transactions, so these figures are probably underestimated. However, the figures for changes reflect the true situation more or less accurately.
b) IEE estimates.

Source: Japan Institute of Energy Economics

Table 2.6 Trends in actual deliveries and exchange of futures for physicals (EFP) accounted for by crude oil futures contracts (Unit: 1,000b)

	Month	EFP[a]	Deliveries	Total	1,000 b/d
1983	June	-	64	64	2.1
	July	124	107	231	7.5
	August	220	219	439	14.2
	Sept	256	145	401	13.4
	Oct	1,289	467	1,756	56.6
	Nov	1,116	460	1,576	52.5
	Dec	1,911	157	2,068	66.7
1984	Jan	2,291	320	2,611	84.2
	Feb	2,956	773	3,729	128.6
	March	3,499	1,174	4,673	150.7
	April	4,463	1,075	5,538	184.6
	May	2,729	1,494	4,223	136.2
	June	4,701	1,308	6,009	200.3
	July	3,634	1,768	5,402	174.3
	August	4,293	1,783	6,076	196.0
	Sept	4,750	1,311	6,061	202.0
	Oct	4,351	1,888	6,239	201.3
	Nov	5,567	2,110	7,667	255.9
	Dec	6,680	2,261	8,941	288.4
1985	Jan	7,104	2,668	9,772	315.2
	Feb	6,408	3,966	10,374	370.5
	March	8,747	1,780	10,527	339.6
	April	9,761	2,395	12,156	405.2
	May	8,305	3,230	11,535	372.1
	June	9,813	2,919	12,732	424.4
	July	12,217	1,564	13,781	444.5
	August	12,332	1,232	13,564	437.5
	Sept	13,044	852	13,896	463.2
	Oct	13,262	1,469	14,731	475.2
	Nov	15,437	1,870	17,307	576.9
	Dec	16,092	1,884	17,976	579.9

Note: a) Exchange of Futures for Physicals
Source: Energy in News (NYMEX)

Table 2.7 Forecast of world (excluding Communist bloc) primary energy supply/demand (Unit: mbd, %)

(real price fixed for 10 years)

Average 1985 market price for crude oil of $26.50/b falls to $25/b, $20/b, $15/b, and $10/b and remains constant for 10 years.

At $25/b

	1985	1990	1995	90/85	95/90	95/85
Oil	45.6 (46.9)	48.2 (44.7)	51.0 (43.1)	1.1	1.1	1.1
Coal	20.8 (21.4)	23.4 (21.7)	27.5 (23.3)	2.4	3.3	2.8
Nat. Gas	17.4 (17.9)	18.9 (17.5)	20.5 (17.3)	1.7	1.6	1.7
Nuclear	5.6 (5.8)	9.0 (8.4)	10.6 (9.0)	9.9	3.3	6.6
Hydro etc.	7.9 (8.1)	8.2 (7.6)	8.7 (7.4)	0.7	1.2	1.0
Total	97.3(100.0)	107.7(100.0)	118.3(100.0)	2.0	1.9	2.0

At $20/b

	1985	1990	1995	90/85	95/90	95/85
Oil	45.6 (46.9)	49.2 (45.0)	53.2 (43.7)	1.5	1.6	1.6
Coal	20.8 (21.4)	23.7 (21.7)	28.2 (23.2)	2.7	3.5	3.1
Nat. Gas	17.4 (17.9)	18.9 (17.3)	20.5 (16.8)	1.7	1.7	1.7
Nuclear	5.6 (5.8)	9.1 (8.4)	10.9 (9.0)	10.3	3.6	6.9
Hydro etc.	7.9 (8.1)	8.3 (7.6)	9.0 (7.4)	1.0	1.5	1.3
Total	97.3(100.0)	109.3(100.0)	121.8(100.0)	2.4	2.2	2.3

Table 2.7 cont'd <u>Forecast of world (excluding Communist bloc) primary energy supply/demand</u> (Unit: mbd, %)

(real price fixed for 10 years)

Average 1985 market price for crude oil of $26.50/b falls to $25/b, $20/b, $15/b, and $10/b and remains constant for 10 years.

At $15/b

	1985	1990	1995	90/85	95/90	95/85
Oil	45.6 (46.9)	51.6 (46.4)	57.7 (45.7)	2.5	2.3	2.4
Coal	20.8 (21.4)	23.9 (21.5)	28.7 (22.7)	2.8	3.7	3.3
Nat. Gas	17.4 (17.9)	18.1 (16.3)	19.7 (15.6)	0.8	1.7	1.2
Nuclear	5.6 (5.8)	9.3 (8.4)	11.1 (8.8)	10.7	3.6	7.1
Hydro etc.	7.9 (8.1)	8.4 (7.5)	9.1 (7.2)	1.2	1.6	1.4
Total	97.3(100.0)	111.3(100.0)	126.3(100.0)	2.7	2.6	2.6

At $10/b

	1985	1990	1995	90/85	95/90	95/85
Oil	45.6 (46.9)	55.3 (48.6)	64.4 (48.9)	3.9	3.1	3.5
Coal	20.8 (21.4)	22.5 (19.8)	26.6 (20.1)	1.6	3.4	2.5
Nat. Gas	17.4 (17.9)	18.1 (15.9)	20.1 (15.2)	0.8	2.1	1.4
Nuclear	5.6 (5.8)	9.3 (8.2)	11.4 (8.7)	10.7	4.2	7.4
Hydro etc.	7.9 (8.1)	8.6 (7.5)	9.4 (7.1)	1.6	1.9	1.7
Total	97.3(100.0)	113.8(100.0)	131.9(100.0)	3.2	3.0	3.1

Source: <u>Energy Economics</u>, Vol. 12, No. 8.

Table 2.8 Decrease in supply of alternative energy (mbdoe)

	$20/b		$15/b		$10b	
	1990	1995	1990	1995	1990	1995
Coal						
Decline in production						
USA	-	-	-	-	1.4	2.8
Western Europe	-	0.1	0.1	0.2	0.2	0.4
Others	-	-	-	0.1	0.1	0.2
Decline in exports	-	-	0.2	0.4	0.5	0.7
Sub-total	-	0.1	0.3	0.7	2.2	4.1
Natural gas						
Decline in production						
USA	0.2	0.4	1.2	1.8	1.6	2.2
Others	-	-	0.1	0.2	0.2	0.4
Reductions in LNG supply	0.1	0.2	0.1	0.2	0.1	0.2
Sub-total	0.3	0.6	1.4	2.2	1.9	2.8
Nuclear power	-	-	-	0.2	0.2	0.4
Hydro, etc.	-	-	0.1	0.2	0.1	0.3
Total	0.3	0.7	1.8	3.3	4.4	7.6

Source: Energy Economics, Vol. 12, No.8.

Table 2.9 Long-term potential crude oil supply by price (Unit: 1000bd)

1990	1985 real	$25/b	$20/b	$15/b	$10/b
OPEC total	16,063	29,000	29,000	29,000	29,000
Saudi Arabia	3,209	8,500	8,500	8,500	8,500
Kuwait	846	2,000	2,000	2,000	2,000
UAE	1,203	2,130	2,130	2,130	2,130
Iraq	1,433	3,500	3,500	3,500	3,500
Iran	2,193	3,000	3,000	3,000	3,000
Other	7,180	9,870	9,870	9,870	9,870
Non-OPEC total	24,182	23,785	21,894	20,467	18,476
USA	8,932	8,191	7,387	6,589	5,639
North Sea	3,394	3,121	2,770	2,539	2,402
Mexico	2,725	3,302	3,132	2,999	2,859
Other	7,531	7,906	7,404	7,209	6,517
Communist bloc exports	1,600	1,265	1,200	1,131	1,058
NGL etc. Total	5,355	5,564	5,330	5,159	4,939
Non-OPEC	4,218	4,365	4,030	3,864	3,616
OPEC	1,137	1,199	1,300	1,295	1,323
World Total	45,600	58,349	56,224	54,626	52,415

Table 2.9 cont'd Long-term potential crude oil supply by price (Unit: 1000bd)

1995	1985 real	$25/b	$20/b	$15/b	$10/b
OPEC total	16,063	29,000	29,000	29,000	29,000
Saudi Arabia	3,209	8,500	8,500	8,500	8,500
Kuwait	846	2,000	2,000	2,000	2,000
UAE	1,203	2,130	2,130	2,130	2,130
Iraq	1,433	3,500	3,500	3,500	3,500
Iran	2,193	3,000	3,000	3,000	3,000
Other	7,180	9,870	9,870	9,870	9,870
Non-OPEC total	24,182	23,682	20,150	17,760	14,600
USA	8,932	7,512	6,110	4,860	3,560
North Sea	3,394	2,870	2,260	1,900	1,700
Mexico	2,725	4,000	3,600	3,300	3,000
Other	7,531	8,300	7,280	6,900	5,640
Communist bloc exports	1,600	1,000	900	800	700
NGL etc. Total	5,355	5,782	5,377	5,015	4,640
Non-OPEC	4,218	4,518	3,850	3,540	3,100
OPEC	1,137	1,264	1,487	1,475	1,540
World Total	45,600	56,728	55,556	51,775	48,240

Notes 1. Calculated according to supply curve: by costs (capital + conversion costs + reasonable profit (taxes + dividends+ interest).

2. Estimated supply in 1990 and 1995 when price scenario continues constant to 1995.

Source: Energy Economics, Vol. 12, No. 8.

Table 2.10 <u>World oil balance</u> (mbd)

(assuming Real Price is constant)

1986 Real Price	Year	Oil Needs OECD	LDC	Total	Oil Supply OPEC	Non-OPEC	Total
(26.5)	(1985)	(34.0)	(11.6)	(45.6)	(17.2)	(28.4)	(45.6)
at	1990	35.0	13.2	48.2	20.0	28.2	(48.2)
					(.0)	(.0)	(.0)
$25/b	1995	36.1	14.9	51.0	22.8	28.2	51.0
					(.0)	(.0)	(.0)
at	1990	35.8	13.4	49.2	23.3	25.9	49.2
					(.0)	(.0)	(.0)
$20/b	1995	37.8	15.4	53.2	29.2	24.0	53.2
					(.0)	(.0)	(.0)
at	1990	37.8	13.8	51.6	27.3	24.3	51.6
					(.0)	(.0)	(.0)
$15/b	1995	41.3	16.5	57.7	36.4	21.3	57.7
					(5.9)	(.0)	(5.9)
at	1990	40.9	14.5	55.3	33.2	22.1	55.3
					(2.7)	(.0)	(2.7)
$10/b	1995	46.9	17.7	64.4	46.7	17.7	64.4
					(16.2)	(.0)	(16.2)

Notes:
1. OPEC production includes NGL. NGL represents difference with supply curve in times of low growth.
2. ( ) represents a shortfall.
3. Excludes Communist bloc.

Source: <u>Energy Economics</u>, Vol. 12, No.8.

Table 2.11 US oil imports (1,000 bd)

	Oil Needs	Domestic Supply	Net Imports	Dependence on imports (%)
1965	11,513	9,014	2,281	19.8
1973	17,308	10,975	6,025	34.8
1978	18,847	10,328	8,002	42.5
1985	15,697	10,597	4,264	27.2
at $25/b				
1990	16,020	9,502	6,518	40.7
1995	16,510	8,714	7,796	47.2
at $20/b				
1990	16,340	8,569	7,771	47.6
1995	16,700	7,088	9,612	57.6
at $15/b				
1990	17,000	7,643	9,357	55.0
1995	17,690	5,638	12,052	68.1
at $10/b				
1990	17,330	6,541	10,789	62.3
1995	18,300	4,130	14,170	77.4

Note: Constant for 10 years at 1986 real price. Domestic production includes NGL.

Source: Energy Economics, Vol. 12, No.8.

Table 2.12 Development of price scenario and oil needs/needed OPEC production (Unit: 1,000bd)

(V-curve variable simulation)

	1986	1987	1988	1989	1990	1991	1992	1993
1) at $25/b								
needed OPEC production	16,213	16,223	15,560	15,121	15,178	14,730	14,487	14,736
non-OPEC production	29,537	29,537	29,685	29,982	30,131	30,282	30,585	30,738
total	45,750	45,760	45,245	45,102	45,310	45,012	45,072	45,474
2) at $20/b								
needed OPEC production	16,467	17,576	18,644	19,694	20,747	21,803	22,851	23,890
non-OPEC production	29,352	28,921	28,502	28,088	27,681	27,280	26,884	26,494
total	45,819	46,497	47,146	47,783	48,428	49,083	49,735	50,384
3) at $15/b								
needed OPEC production	16,713	18,456	19,892	21,008	22,119	23,225	24,314	25,386
non-OPEC production	29,215	28,464	27,732	27,330	26,934	26,544	26,159	25,779
total	45,928	46,920	47,624	48,339	49,053	49,769	50,473	51,165
4) at $10/b								
needed OPEC production	18,260	23,476	25,044	25,920	26,766	27,143	27,479	27,771
non-OPEC production	27,819	23,810	22,810	22,479	22,153	22,264	22,375	22,487
total	46,079	47,286	47,853	48,399	48,919	49,407	49,855	50,258
price fluctuation at $25/b	25.00 (25.00)	27.56 (26.50)	30.38 (28.09)	30.33 (26.97)	30.28 (25.89)	33.71 (27.44)	33.98 (26.34)	34.25 (25.29)
price fluctuation at $20/b	20.00 (20.00)	22.05 (21.20)	23.85 (22.05)	25.30 (22.49)	26.31 (22.49)	27.62 (22.49)	29.30 (22.71)	31.07 (22.94)
price fluctuation at $15/b	15.00 (15.00)	17.16 (16.50)	22.71 (21.00)	23.62 (21.00)	24.81 (21.21)	26.31 (21.42)	28.18 (21.85)	30.18 (22.29)
price fluctuation at $10/b	10.00 (10.00)	14.56 (14.00)	25.96 (24.00)	27.67 (24.60)	29.50 (25.22)	31.75 (25.85)	34.33 (26.62)	37.13 (27.42)

Table 2.12 cont'd Development of price scenario and oil needs/needed OPEC production

(Unit: 1,000bd)

(V-curve variable simulation)

	1994	1995	1996	1997	1998	1999	2000
1) at $25/b							
needed OPEC production	15,059	14,852	14,999	14,617	14,608	14,944	14,791
non-OPEC production	30,323	29,914	29,525	29,141	28,762	28,388	28,005
total	45,382	44,765	44,523	43,758	43,370	43,332	42,796
2) at $20/b							
needed OPEC production	24,909	25,906	26,869	27,690	28,005	27,811	27,082
non-OPEC production	26,110	25,732	25,358	24,991	24,653	24,321	24,004
total	51,019	51,638	52,228	52,681	52,659	52,132	51,087
3) at $15/b							
needed OPEC production	26,427	27,435	28,385	28,918	28,923	28,392	27,352
non-OPEC production	25,406	25,037	24,674	24,316	23,988	23,676	23,368
total	51,832	52,473	53,059	53,234	52,911	52,068	50,720
4) at $10/b							
needed OPEC production	28,241	28,661	29,030	29,176	28,754	28,088	27,174
non-OPEC production	22,375	22,263	22,152	22,041	22,261	22,484	22,709
total	50,616	50,924	51,181	51,217	51,015	50,571	49,583
price fluctuation at $25/b	38.12 (26.81)	42.43 (28.42)	42.77 (27.28)	47.60 (28.92)	47.298 (27.76)	48.36 (26.65)	53.83 (28.25)
price fluctuation at $20/b	33.27 (23.40)	35.64 (23.87)	38.54 (24.58)	41.68 (25.32)	45.95 (26.59)	50.66 (27.92)	55.86 (29.31)
price fluctuation at $15/b	32.64 (22.96)	35.30 (23.64)	38.92 (24.83)	42.91 (26.07)	47.31 (27.37)	52.16 (28.74)	57.51 (30.18)
price fluctuation at $10/b	40.16 (28.24)	43.43 (29.09)	46.97 (29.96)	50.80 (30.86)	54.94 (31.79)	59.42 (32.74)	64.26 (33.72)

Notes
1. ( ) is the 1986 real price. Inflation average 4% for 1986-90 and 5% for 1990-95.
2. Non-OPEC production includes OPEC and non-OPEC NGL.

Source: Energy Economics, Vol. 12, No. 8.

Table 2.13 Energy needs in 2000 (Unit: mbd, %)

Economic growth rate: 2.8%(a) Crude oil price: scenario(b)

		Coal	Oil	Gas	Hydro, etc	Nuclear	Total	Rate of growth	Elasticity Value
OECD		23.51	35.50	15.99	7.48	10.52	93.00	1.54	0.62
(share)		25.3	38.2	17.2	8.0	11.3	100.0		
Developing countries		6.62	15.04	5.42	3.33	1.50	31.89	2.77	0.73
(share)		20.8	47.2	17.0	10.3	4.8	100.0		
West bloc		30.13	50.54	21.41	10.78	12.04	124.89	1.83	0.65
(share)		24.1	40.5	17.1	8.6	9.6	100.0		
OECD	r.g.	2.38	0.65	0.69	1.50	5.78	1.54		
	e.v.	0.95	0.26	0.28	0.60	2.31	0.62		
Devlp. countries	r.g.	2.77	1.83	4.09	3.16	13.60	2.77		
	e.v.	0.73	4.82	1.08	0.83	3.58	0.73		
West bloc	r.g.	2.47	0.96	1.37	1.96	6.36	1.83		
	e.v.	0.83	0.34	0.49	0.70	2.27	0.65		

Notes a. Economic growth rate: from 1983 to 2000 in the industrialised nations, 2.5%, and 3.8% in the developing countries in the same period. World total 2.8%. (Assuming no major disruption in economic activity and continuation of present trends.

b. Crude oil price scenario is as follows: ($/b)

	1985	1990	1995	2000
nominal	26.5	25.5	37.3	59.5
real	26.5	21.0	24.0	30.0

(Inflation 1985–90: 4%; 1990–2000: 5%)

Source: IEE – 'Prospects for World Energy Supply and Demand, and Study of International Cooperation in Various Energy Sectors'.

Table 2.14 IEA projection

Projected World Oil Supply and Demand(a)

	1984	1985	1990	2000
IEA Energy requirements (mtoe)				
TPER(b)	3,480.6	3,536	3,896	4,488
Non-oil requirements	1,984.2	2,063	2,331	2,881
Oil requirements(b)	1,496.3	1,473	1,564	1,608
Net oil imports	760.3	700	819	988
Bunkers	49.2	51	51	52
World oil requirements (mbd)				
IEA	32.6	32.1	33.8	34.8
Other OECD	1.9	1.9	1.6	1.5
OPEC	3.0	3.0	3.7	5.5
Non-OPEC LDCs	8.5	8.6	9.8	11.8
World total (excl. CPEs)	46.0	45.6	48.9	53.6
World oil supply (mbd)				
IEA	16.7	17.2	16.2	13.7
Other OECD	(c)	(c)	0.1	0.1
OPEC	18.5 (40.2%)	17.2 (37.7%)	20.3 (41.5%)	26.6 (49.6%)

Table 2.14 cont'd <u>IEA projection</u> (continued)

Projected World Oil Supply and Demand(a)

	1984	1985	1990	2000
World oil suply (mbd)				
Non-OPEC LDCs	8.0	8.5	10.0	11.2
CPE net exports/imports	1.8	1.6	1.3	1.0
Processing gains	1.0	1.0	1.0	1.0
Other (incl. stock changes)	0	0.1	0	0
World total (excl. CPEs)	46.0	45.6	48.9	53.6

Notes: a. Data for 1985 and for non-IEA countries are IEA Secretariat estimates.

b. Including bunkers and refinery fuel.

c. Less than 100,000 barrels per day.

Source: IEA: <u>Energy Policies and Programmes of IEA countries</u>, <u>1985 Review</u>, p.81.

Table 2.15 Long-term outlook for Japan, USA and Europe for energy before the price collapse of crude oil (Units: actual numbers in mtoe, ratios in %)

1. USA and Japan

Country	Energy Resources	1980 Actual Number	1980 Ratio	1984 Actual Number	1984 Ratio	1990 Actual Number	1990 Ratio	1995 Actual Number	1995 Ratio	2000 Actual Number	2000 Ratio
USA	Oil	794.1	43.1	723.9	40.2	676	38.7	674	36.2	682	34.6
	Natural Gas	507.1	27.5	458.0	25.4	388	22.2	408	21.9	402	20.4
	Coal	393.2	21.3	433.9	24.1	420	24.1	472	25.3	538	27.3
	Nuclear Power, Hydraulic Power, etc.	147.6	8.1	184.7	10.3	262	15.0	308	16.6	350	17.7
	Total	1.842.0	100.0	1,800.5	100.0	1,746	100	1,862	100.0	1,972	100.0
Japan	Oil	245.4	66.4	223.8	59.6	245.4	61.9	219.2	48.0	217.1	42.0
	Natural Gas	22.2	6.0	34.5	9.2	27.7	7.0	54.8	12.0	56.9	11.0
	Coal	61.7	16.7	69.5	18.5	69.4	17.5	82.2	18.0	103.4	20.0
	Nuclear Power, Hydraulic Power,etc.	40.3	10.9	47.7	12.7	53.9	13.6	100.5	22.0	139.6	27.0
	Total	369.6	100.0	375.5	100.0	396.4	100.0	456.7	100.0	517.0	100.0

Notes:
1. Japan: Fiscal Year: Other countries: Calendar year.
2. Figures for 1980 and 1984 are actual numbers; other figures are estimated.
3. Sources of actual numbers: Japan: 'Energy Statistics', the Agency of Natural Resources and Energy Other countries: statistics by BP.
4. Sources of estimated numbers: Japan: 'Long-term Outlook for Energy Supply and Demand'.

Table 2.15 cont'd <u>Long-term outlook for Japan, USA and Europe for energy before the price collapse of crude oil</u> (Unit: mtoe)

2. Outlook for 10 EC countries for energy supply.

	1980	(%)	1984	(%)	1990	(%)	2000	(%)
Primary Energies								
Solid fuel	222.7	(23)	201	(22)	242	(23)	264	(23)
Oil	520.0	(54)	446	(48)	441	(43)	439	(39)
Natural gas	169.3	(17)	175	(18)	190	(18)	196	(17)
Nuclear power	42.7	(4)			145	(14)	215	(19)
Hydraulic power, geothermal power, etc.	15.4	(2)	112	(12)	16	(2)	21	(2)
Total	970.1	(100)	934	(100)	1,034	(100)	1,136	(100)
Oil share	54%		47.7%		43%		39%	
Degree of import dependence	55%		43.5%		46%		46%	

Source: 'Energy 2000', EC Commission, February 1985; actual numbers in 1984.

Table 2.16 Outlook for USA and Europe for oil supply and demand after the price collapse of crude oil

1. USA (IEE fixed price estimate) (Units 1,000bd)

	Oil Demand	Domestic Supply	Net Import	Import Dependence %
1965	11,513	9,014	2,281	19.8
1973	17,308	10,975	6,025	34.8
1978	18,847	10,328	8,002	42.5
1985	15,697	10,597	4,264	27.2
Assuming $20/b				
1990	16,340	8,569	7,771	47.6
1995	16.700	7,088	9,612	57.6
Assuming $15/b				
1990	17,000	7,643	9,357	55.0
1995	17,690	5,638	12,052	68.1

Notes: The real prices in 1986 are fixed for 10 years.
Domestic supply includes NGL.

Table 2.16 cont'd Outlook for USA and Europe for oil supply and demand after the price collapse of crude oil

2. Outlook for 10 EC countries for energy demand (assuming $15/b). (Unit: mtoe)

	1984		1990 (forecast)			
	Actual figure	%	'Energy 2000'	%	Assuming $15/b	%
Primary energies						
Solid fuel	201	(22)	242	(23)	212- 223	(21-22)
Oil	446	(48)	441	(43)	464- 493	(45-48)
Natural gas	175	(18)	190	(18)	190- 203	(18-19)
Nuclear power			145	(14)	140	(13-14)
Hydraulic power, geothermal power, etc.	112	(12)	16	(2)	15	(1- 2)
Total	934	(100)	1,034	(100)	1,031-1,067	(100)
Oil share	47.7%		43%		45-48%	
Degree of import dependence	43.5		46%		47-51%	

Note: The influence of coal strikes in UK is evident in the actual 1984 figures.

Table 2.17 Comparison of oil dependence in Japan, USA and Europe brought about by lower oil prices (IEE)

	1973		1978		1984		2000	
	mbd	%	mbd	%	mbd	%	mbd	%
Final Energy Consumption(a)								
USA	36.3	-	38.1	-	36.0	-	44.0	-
W. Europe	24.9	-	25.6	-	25.0	-	32.0	-
Japan	7.0	-	7.1	-	7.2	-	9.1	-
Total	68.5	-	70.8	-	68.2	-	85.1	-
Oil Consumption(b)		b/a		b/a		b/a		b/a
USA	16.9	46.1	18.3	47.9	15.	42.2	17.3	39.3
W. Europe	15.2	60.8	14.6	57.0	12.3	49.2	11.8	36.9
Japan	5.5	78.2	5.4	76.1	4.6	63.9	4.3	47.3
Total	37.6	54.9	38.3	54.1	32.1	47.1	33.4	39.2
Oil Imports(c)		c/b		c/b		c/b		c/b
USA	6.3	37.1	8.2	45.1	5.4	35.5	8.3	48.0
W. Europe	15.4	101.6	13.1	89.5	8.6	69.9	9.4	79.7
Japan	5.5	100.4	5.3	98.4	4.3	93.5	4.2	99.3
Total	27.2	72.3	26.6	69.5	18.3	57.0	21.9	65.6
Dependence on Middle East oil supply(d)		d/b		d/b		d/b		d/b
USA	0.8	4.9	2.3	12.6	0.6	3.9	3.5	20.2
W. Europe	10.4	68.1	8.7	66.3	3.0	24.4	6.3	53.4
Japan	4.4	79.7	4.0	74.0	2.8	60.9	2.9	69.4
Total	15.6	41.5	15.0	39.2	6.4	19.9	12.7	38.0

Table 2.17 cont'd **Comparison of oil dependence in Japan, USA and Europe brought about by lower oil prices (IEE)**

Amount of increase and percentage contribution	1973 - 1978		1978 - 1984		1984 - 2000	
	mbd	%	mbd	%	mbd	%
Final Energy Consumption(e)						
USA	1.5	65.2	2.1	80.8	8.0	47.3
W. Europe	0.7	30.4	0.6	23.1	7.0	41.4
Japan	0.1	4.4	0.1	3.9	1.9	11.3
Oil Consumption(f)						
USA	1.4	200.0	3.1	50.0	2.1	161.5
W. Europe	0.6	85.7	2.3	37.1	0.5	38.5
Japan	0.1	14.3	0.8	12.9	0.3	23.0
Oil Imports(g)		c/b		c/b		c/b
USA	1.9	316.7	2.8	33.7	2.9	80.6
W. Europe	2.3	383.3	4.5	54.2	0.8	22.2
Japan	0.2	33.4	1.0	12.1	0.1	2.8
Oil imported from Middle East(h)						
USA	1.5	250.0	1.7	19.8	2.9	46.0
W. Europe	1.7	283.3	5.7	66.3	3.3	52.4
Japan	0.4	66.7	1.2	13.9	0.1	1.6

Sources: 1973-1984 actual figures from BP statistics.
Figures for 2000 are projected ones estimated by the IEE (cf. Table 2.3. They correspond to standard cases of energy supply and demand in the world.

Table 2.18 Provisional estimate of production cost of crude oil

Crude oil production cost ($/b)	Production capacity (mbd)	Production volume (mbd)	Areas of production
2 or lower	15	8	Middle East
2- 4	15	12	Middle East, Africa, Indonesia, Mexico, North Sea, South America
4- 6	10	10	North Sea, USA, Africa, South America
6- 8	6	6	North Sea, USA, Canada, Asia, South America
8-10	4	4	USA, Canada, Asia, Europe
10-12	2	2	USA, Canada Europe
12-14	2	2	USA, Canada, Europe
14-24	2	1	USA, Canada, Europe
Total	56	45	

Source: Texas Eastern, Nov. 1985.

Table 2.19 Present status of energy conservation and energy conversion in high energy consumption industries (%)

Industries	steel	petrochemical (ethylene)	cement	paper/pulp
Energy basic unit	80.5	69.1	73.6	77.7
Reduction in energy requirements in 1984 from 1973	(25.2)	(76.1)	(0)	(52.4)

Note: Reduction in oil basic unit is shown in parentheses.

Source: Energy 1986.

Table 2.20 Forecast for introduction of energy application

Energy	Applied uses by 1990	Fields of application in or about 1990
Solar power generation	Small independent electrical source	Complement to generator in remote area
Fuel cells	Experimental on-site fuel cell	On-site type fuel cell
Wind power generation	Small scale system	Complement to diesel power generators on remote islands
Solar heating system	System for general public	System expanded for public use and adapted for industrial use

Table 2.21 Rate of increase in world consumption of primary energy (%/yr)

Oil consumption indicated in ( )

	1966 - 73	1973 - 79	1979 - 85
Industrialised countries	5.0 (7.4)	1.1 (0.3)	-0.7 (-3.5)
Developing countries	6.9 (8.1)	5.5 (4.7)	4.4 (1.9)
of which Southeast Asia	12.3 (16.4)	7.7 (7.4)	3.9 (-0.2)
South Asia	4.5 (7.1)	3.4 (3.1)	7.5 (6.0)
Africa	5.1 (7.0)	7.4 (4.9)	4.4 (4.6)
Latin America	6.2 (6.5)	5.3 (4.1)	2.9 (0.5)
East bloc	4.9 (9.5)	4.8 (5.3)	2.7 (0.2)
World total	5.1 (7.8)	2.7 (1.9)	1.1 (-1.8)

Source: BP Statistical Review of World Energy, June 1986.

Table 2.22 Forecast of world primary energy consumption by region

Oil consumption indicated in ( )

	Actual Figures (mtoe)			Average yearly rate of increase	Future forecast based on simple extrapolation			Average yearly rate of increase	Future forecast based on simple extrapolation		
			%	%	%			%	%		
	1973	1985	of whole	1966-85	1990	1995	2000	1973-85	1990	1995	2000
Industrialised countries	3,621.3 (1,939.9)	3,718.8 (1,590.7)	50.2 (56.6)	1.95 (1.60)	46.9 (52.4)	43.7 (48.2)	40.6 (43.9)	0.22 (-1.64)	45.4 (50.9)	40.7 (45.2)	36.2 (39.7)
Developing countries	620.0 (378.9)	1,104.4 (559.1)	14.9 (19.9)	5.64 (5.06)	16.7 (21.8)	18.6 (23.6)	20.5 (25.6)	4.93 (3.30)	17.0 (22.9)	19.3 (25.9)	21.4 (29.0)
of which											
Southeast Asia	94.5 (74.2)	186.3 (112.8)	2.5 (4.0)	8.16 (8.10)	3.1 (5.1)	4.0 (6.4)	4.9 (7.9)	5.82 (3.55)	3.0 (4.7)	3.2 (5.4)	3.6 (6.1)
South Asia	103.3 (31.3)	196.1 (53.4)	2.6 (1.9)	5.14 (5.47)	2.9 (2.1)	3.1 (2.4)	3.4 (2.6)	5.49 (4.55)	3.1 (2.3)	4.8 (2.8)	6.3 (3.3)
Africa	98.1 (49.5)	195.1 (82.8)	2.6 (2.9)	5.33 (5.32)	3.0 (3.3)	3.2 (3.6)	3.5 (3.9)	5.9 (4.38)	3.1 (3.6)	3.5 (4.3)	4.0 (5.0)
Latin America	235.6 (160.3)	380.9 (209.5)	5.1 (7.4)	4.87 (3.81)	5.5 (7.7)	5.9 (7.8)	6.3 (8.0)	4.08 (2.26)	5.6 (8.1)	5.9 (7.9)	6.3 (5.6)
East bloc	1,667.9 (479.2)	2,591.1 (659.6)	34.9 (23.5)	4.15 (5.16)	36.4 (25.8)	37.7 (28.2)	38.9 (30.5)	3.74 (2.70)	37.6 (26.2)	40.0 (28.9)	42.4 (31.3)
World total	5,909.2 (2,798.0)	7,414.3 (2,809.4)	100.0 (100.0)	3.08 (2.84)	100.0 (100.0)	100.0 (100.0)	100.0 (100.0)	1.91 (0.03)	100.0 (100.0)	100.0 (100.0)	100.0 (100.0)

Source: Actual figures: BP Satistical Review of World Energy, June 1986.

Table 2.23 Total investments in Pacific coal flow (1985-95) (Unit: US$ billion, 1984 prices)

	Total	Rep. of Korea	Taiwan	Hong Kong	ASEAN Total	Phili-pines	Thai-land	Malay-sia	Singa-pore	Indo-nesia
Total	27.9	7.3	3.2	4.1	13.3	1.5	1.7	1.6	0.5	8.0
Coal-fired power (related infrastructure	17.1 (2.5)	4.7 (0.8)	2.5 (0.5)	4.1 (0.7)	5.8 (0.5)	0.5 (0.02)	1.0 0.12	0.5 (0.08)	0.5 (0.11)	3.3 (0.16)
Cement (related infrastructure)	7.3 (0.2)	2.6 (-)	0.7 (-)	- (-)	4.0 (0.2)	0.8 (0.04)	0.6 (-)	1.1 (0.01)	- (-)	1.5 (0.11)
Coal-mine development (related infrastructure)	3.5 (0.8)	- (-)	- (-)	- (-)	3.5 (0.8)	0.3 (0.02)	- (-)	- (-)	- (-)	3.2 (0.77)
For reference:										
1984 GDP	383.4	83.3	57.5	31.8	210.8	32.9	42.0	34.0	18.2	83.7

Source: Pacific Coal Flow Concept, April 1986.

Table 2.24 Co-operation between Pacific Basin countries and NEDO (New Energy Development Organisation)

Country	Project name	Description
USA	Exchange of technological information with the US Electric Power Research Institute	- Agreement signed with the US Electric Power Research Institute (EPRI) for exchange of information, and information exchange begun. - Fields of information exchange: solar energy technology, wind power technology, coal liquefaction technology, gasification technology, geothermal technology, fuel/storage technology, planning and evaluation of R & D for new energy. Agreement signed August 1984.
	IEA research and development in hot dry rock (HDR) technology	- Implementation of joint R & D effort by the US, Japan, and West Germany of Fenton Hill (US) HDR, under the terms of an IEA implementation agreement. October 1980 Signing of IEA implementation agreement (from 1980 to September 1983) September 1983 Agreement to 2-year extension (to September 1985) September 1985 Agreement to one-year extension (to September 1986)
Canada	Japan-Canada co-operation in coal liquefaction	- Under an agreement between the Japanese and Canadian governments as part of co-operation between Japan and Canada in coal liquefaction, tests of the suitability of Canadian coal for liquefaction, resource surveys, and information exchanges were carried out. October 1980 Agreement at the 4th Japan-Canada Science and Technology Co-operation Council Phase I (experiments in suitability for liquefaction) 1980-83 Phase II (experiments in suitability for liquefaction and resource surveys) 1983-86
China	Japan-China joint development of coal liquefaction	- As part of technological co-operation between Japan and China, a coal liquefaction plant (0.1 t/day) was built in Peking, and testing of liquefaction of Chinese coal was begun. November 1981 Signing of Japan-China Technological Co-operation Agreement (1981-84) November 1982 Installation of liquefaction plant completed and test operation begun March 1983 Full-scale operation for research begun July 1984 Agreement for 3-year extension (to 1987) signed

Table 2.24 Cont'd Cooperation between Pacific Basin countries and NEDO (New Energy Development Organisation)

Country	Project name	Description	
Australia continued	Plan for a power supply system to remote areas (RAPSS)	- Implementation of feasibility study and construction of plant for an electric power supply system to remote areas of Australia, using renewable energy.	
		1984	Agreement under the 7th Japan-Australia Scheduled R & D Council
		1984	Confirmation of guidelines between DRE and NEDO
		1984-1985	RAPSS Phase I - implementation of F/S for electric power supply system to remote areas
		March 1986	Two-year extension of Phase I between NEDO/DRE
ASEAN countries	Co-operation in research on solar ray generating systems for medium-size settlements	- Implementation with the Indonesian government of on-site testing of electrical solar pump systems in farming villages Period of co-operation: 1984-88 (5 years)	
		May 1985	Meteorological monitoring equipment installed and collection of data begun
		fiscal 1985	Installation of solar pump system
		fiscal 1986	Solar ray electric generating system under construction
	Feasibility study for overseas technological development in developing countries	- Implementation of boring surveys for new energy joint development projects in developing countries such as Thailand, Malaysia, etc. (1983 -)	
		1983	Installation of weather monitoring systems and experimental solar cells, and collection of data begun (Thailand, Malaysia)
		1984	Addition of study on comparative economical efficiency of solar ray power generating system costs, etc. in Indonesia
		1985	Installation of solar pump system in Malaysia
		1985	Collection and analysis of data from above facility
		1986	Feasibility study and development of use technologies for new energy in the ASEAN countries
	Japan-Indonesia joint coal exploration	1986-1990	Implementation of joint coal exploration with the Indonesian government of Mid-Sumatra is expected. Period of exploration:

Table 2.24 cont'd Cooperation between Pacific Basin countries and NEDO (New Energy Development Organisation)

Country	Project name	Description
China cont'd	Japan-China joint coal exploration	- Under an agreement with China National Coal Development Corporation, joint coal exploration began at the Liuzhuang Section of the Huainan Coal Mining in the Anhui Province. February 1982 — Signing of agreement (1982-1986) January-March 1983 — 1st joint site survey October-December 1983 — 2nd joint site survey October-December 1984 — 3rd joint site survey October-December 1985 — 4th joint site survey January-March 1986 — analysis of joint site survey results
Australia	Japan-Australia development of brown coal liquefaction technology	- Under an R & D agreement between the Japanese and Australian governments, a brown coal liquefaction plant (50 t/day p.p.) was built at Morwell, Victoria and operated for research purposes. November 1981 — Basic construction begun March 1982 — Ground-breaking ceremony June 1985 — First stage (primary hydrogenation) construction completed fiscal 1986 — Second stage (secondary hydrogenation) construction expected to be completed
	Japan-Australia technical co-operation in solar energy	- Under an agreement between the Japanese and Australian governments, co-operation was implemented in the fields of solar energy power generating FS, development of a solar ray power generating system, and the development of high density flat plate collectors. 1980 — Agreement on framework for technological co-operation on solar energy between the Ministry of International Trade and Industry (MITI) and the Department of Resources and Energy (DRE) 1980 — Testing of solar cells and high density flat plate collectors under extreme local conditions in Australia August 1984 — Agreement to a two-year extension (to 1986) for testing of solar cells March 1985 — Joint report drawn up on development co-operation for high density flat plate collectors

Figure 2.1 Oil demand curve

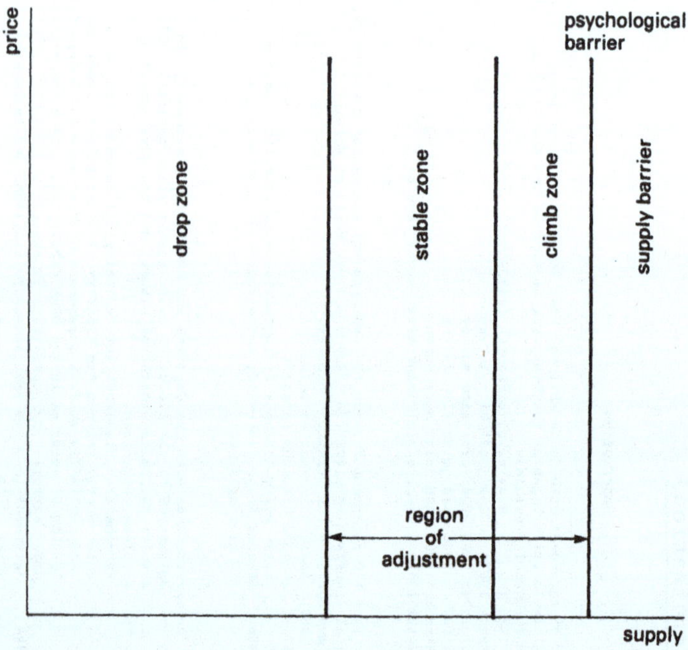

Source: Energy Forum, October 1986.

Figure 2.2 IEE's fixed price simulation results

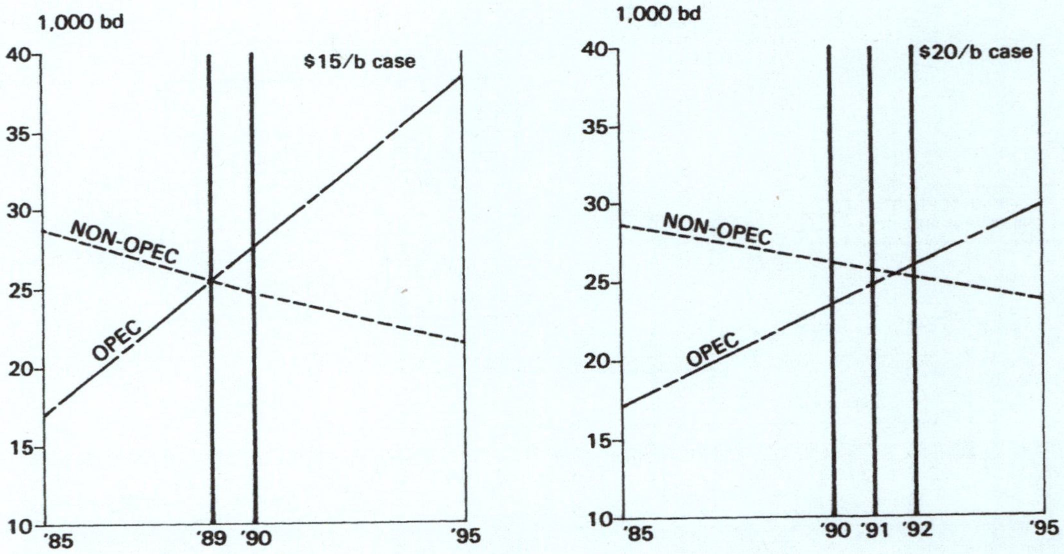

Figure 2.3 The structure of the international oil market

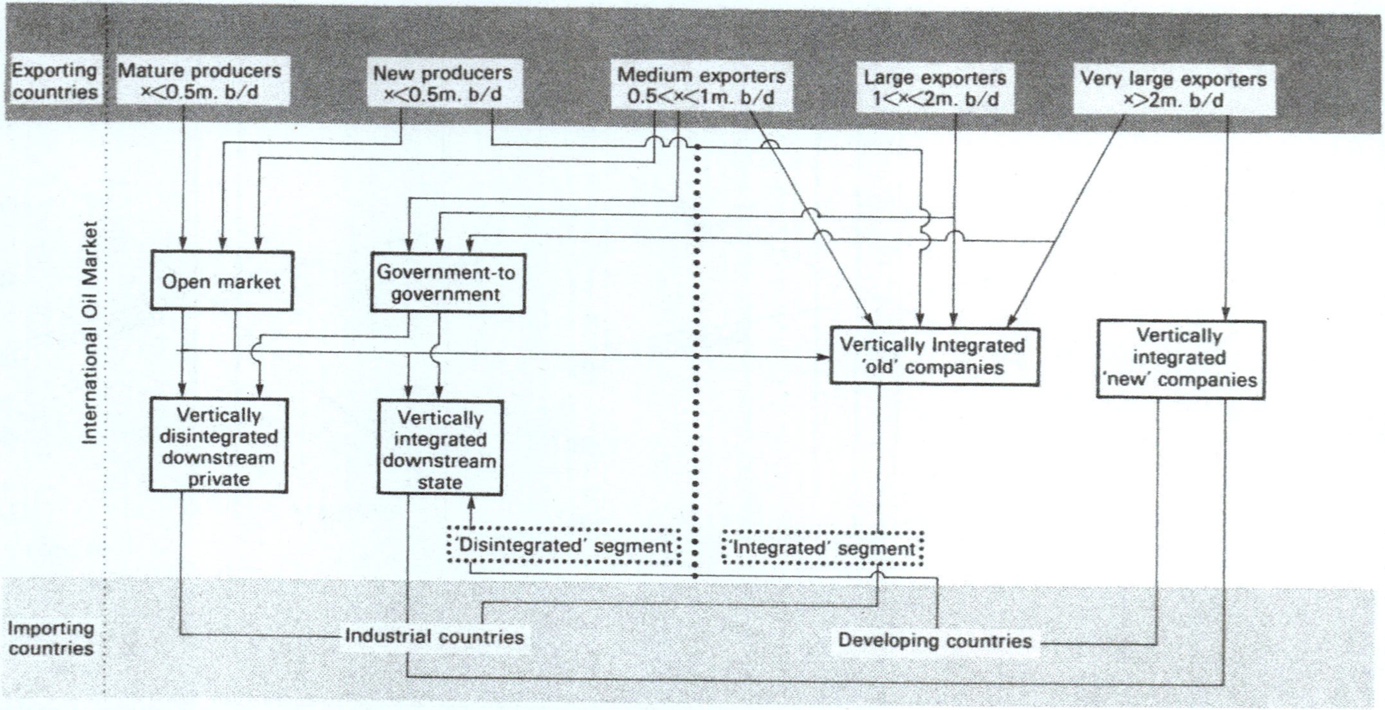

(G. Luciani: The Oil Companies and the Arab World, p. 176)

Figure 2.4 Changes in primary energy consumption against GNP basic unit

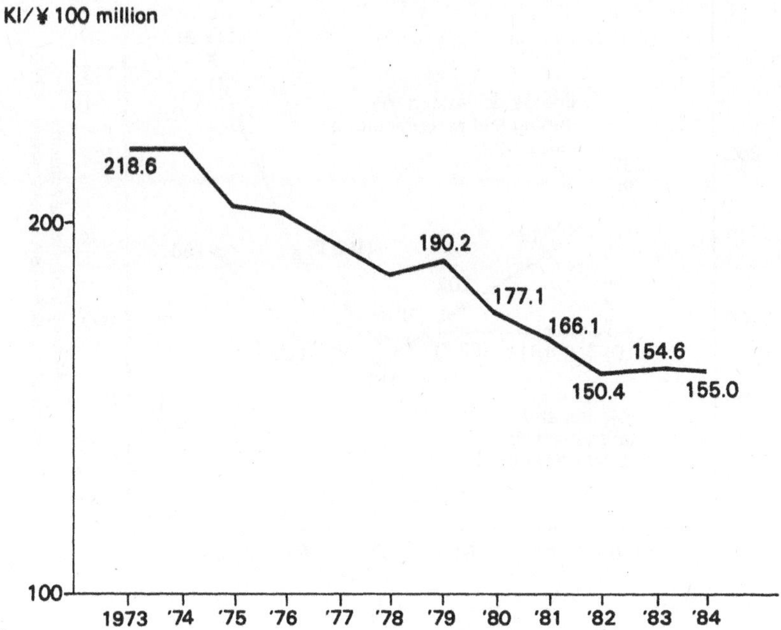

Note: Energy consumption against GNP basic unit is the energy required to produce one unit of GNP.

Source: Energy 1986.

Figure 2.5 Changes in energy demand in the mining and manufacturing industries and in the mining and manufacturing production index (production weight)

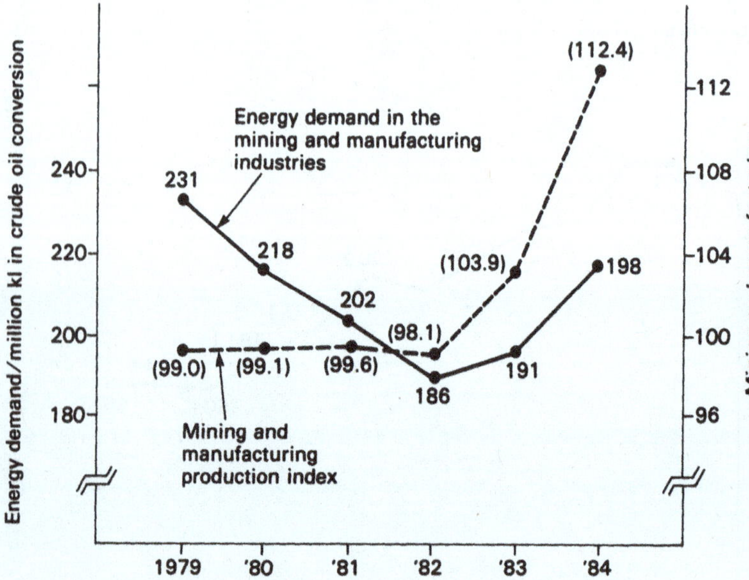

Source: Energy 1986.

Figure 2.6 Change in fuel consumption of Japanese cars

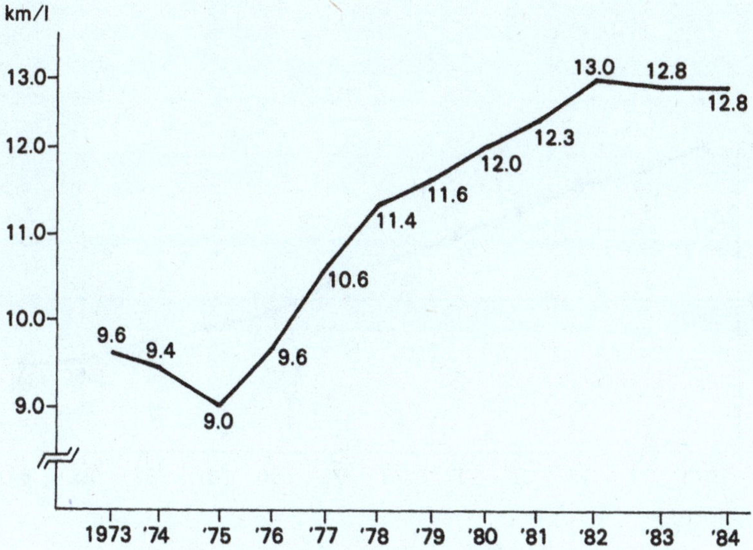

Note: Fuel consumption of passenger cars for domestic use - average of 10 simulated driving conditions.

Source: Energy 1986.

Figure 2.7 Change in average monthly electricity consumption of a 2-door freezer refrigerator with 170-liter capacity

1973 = 100)

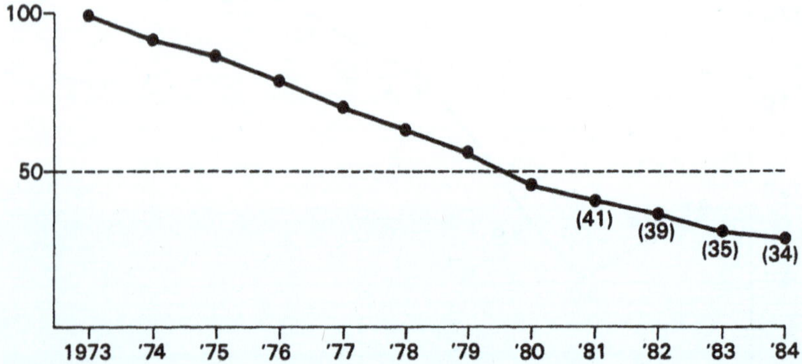

Source: Energy Handbook of 1985.

Figure 2.8 Trade forecast for ordinary coal in the Asian region 1983 (actual)

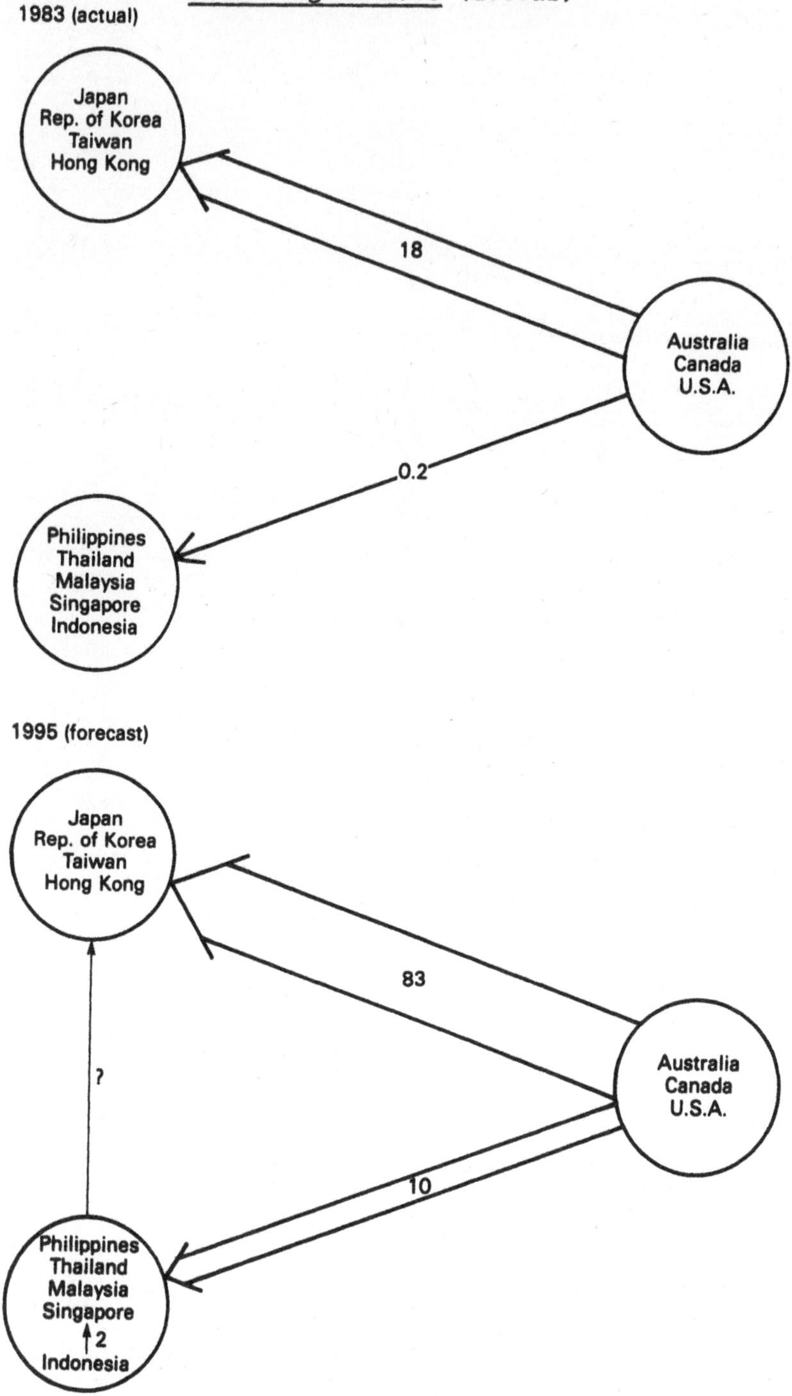

Source: Pacific Coal Flow Concept, April 1986.

3 Western Europe's Energy Security to 2000

ROBERT BELGRAVE
A. NEIL JAMIESON
JUDITH NICHOL

3 Western Europe's Energy Security to 2000

The purpose of the European chapter of this report is to examine the European energy security situation in greater detail than in the introductory chapter, but still in the light of the three major energy issues - the uncertain oil price, the political instability of the Middle East, and the effect of the Chernobyl accident on European electricity generation.

While most Europeans might accept the definition of security in the introductory chapter, the diversity of European countries, the differences in resource endowment, the absence of any underlying consensus on economic philosophy as between belief in the free market economy and in state intervention, the existence of competing commercial interests and the differences of historical relations with the oil exporting countries, all make it impossible to generalise about Europe's energy security. Moreover, the various countries (even leaving Eastern Europe aside) belong to a variety of international organisations in varying combinations. For example, all Western European countries belong to the Organisation for Economic Co-operation and Development (OECD) along with the US, Japan and most other industrialised countries. But France alone of the OECD members does not belong to the OECD's affiliated organisation, the International Energy Agency, although its headquarters are in Paris. France, however, by virtue of its membership of the European Community and its administrative organs in the European Commission, enjoys many of the advantages without necessarily accepting the responsibilities of membership of the IEA whilst having to some extent a freer hand in its dealings with international energy issues. Norway, on the other hand, another key country from an energy supply point of view, whilst belonging to the IEA, is not a member of the European Community; nor is Sweden, an important consumer. Even for members of either of those two organisations, the very limited extent to which their decisions and recommendations are mandatory means that, in practice, decisions on the priority to be accorded to energy security are largely left to individual governments, whose actions may or may not faithfully reflect the consensus hammered out at ministerial meetings of this or that international organisation or the aspirations of international officials. This diversity is particularly apparent in differing attitudes to government intervention in the energy markets, some regarding this as a last resort only to be adopted when reliance on the free market has demonstrably failed, others recognising that in practice governments will always intervene in the pursuit of particular political interests, to determine the distribution of the 'rent' to be had from energy supply, or to counter foreign governmental pressures from groupings such as OPEC. Ultimately, however, the responsibility of government to ensure the continued functioning of society, and for defence, provides an incentive for collective as opposed to individual action within Europe on energy matters. It is for this last reason that this report examines European energy security policy in the light of the activities of the two representative groupings referred to above: the European Community and the International Energy Agency.

These organisations can rightly claim that since the first 'oil shock' of 1974 they have important progress to their credit and that their objectives have to a large extent been achieved. It is the theme of this report that the need for continued vigilance, and for a sustained policy by member governments to support common actions, remains as strong as ever.

The European Community

The Community places great value on explicit energy objectives. In its own words: 'strong energy policies bring clear rewards'. 'Clear rewards' evidently refers back to previous accomplishments. There have indeed been improvements in oil imports and energy consumption, increased energy efficiency and indigenous production, and improvements in the fuel mix. These took place at a time when energy prices were high and economic growth stagnated. Nevertheless, despite changes in the energy market, both the European Community and the IEA believe it is necessary to follow a series of energy objectives in order to avoid an energy security crisis in the future.

In September 1986 the Council of the European Communities passed a resolution concerning energy policy objectives for 1995.[1] These objectives were based on a study by the Directorates of Energy and Research and Development known as 'Energy 2000'[2] and on a series of Commission reports submitted to the Council of Ministers during 1985 and 1986. The objectives cover all aspects of energy both 'horizontally' through general aims of energy strategy, and 'sectorally' through specific targets for different fuels. The objectives are not new, but refined versions of previously stated ones used in the past to try and deal with energy problems faced following the 1974 and 1979 oil crises. Of course the Community had energy interests before that, via the European Coal and Steel Community (set up in 1952) and Euratom (1958), but it was not until the first oil shock that specific energy targets were thought necessary. It must be borne in mind that policies and objectives issued by the Council and the Commission are directed at the Community as a whole, and the ways in which each member country applies them may not be uniform. Still less does the Community purport to control energy markets.

<u>1974 and 1980 objectives.</u> A summary of these objectives and how far the Community managed to achieve them is given in Table 3.1. Both sets of objectives were responses to energy crises caused by the market interference of an outside party. They were not safeguard measures to avoid such an incident. The objectives for 1974 were highly fuel-specific, with emphasis on avoiding excessive dependence on an increasingly expensive and insecure source of energy, namely oil. The 1980 objectives, however, had a different perspective. Since economic growth remained a

primary objective, the emphasis was on avoiding a corresponding increase in energy consumption. Energy security was defined as an 'adequate and secure availability of energy on a satisfactory basis'. Oil imports were the primary concern of energy security. Energy saving, use of renewables, further research and development were all encouraged. The Commission was to monitor progress made by asking the member states to submit annual statements of their energy policies and programmes (like those submitted to the IEA) with projections up to 1990. In 1981 the first annual review of members' programmes was sent by the Commission to the Council.

It will be seen that by 1985 the Community had gone some way to attaining the objectives set out in 1974 and 1980. Total oil as a percentage of total primary energy requirements (TPER) had gone down from 62% in 1973 to 44%, and imported oil from 61.6% to 30% (the latter of course due to the North Sea). The relationship between GDP growth and energy demand growth had improved. Coal and nuclear power were providing 65% of total electricity generated compared with the planned 70-75%, although coal production had declined and advances in nuclear power had been very uneven within Europe. Certain members of the Community, however, did not always manage to meet the objectives. For example, Belgium, France, and Italy were unable to reduce their oil imports significantly, while the UK and the Netherlands were able to do so through the exploitation of indigenous resources of oil and gas. Italy was also unable to reach the targets set for reduced oil consumption or for the use of coal and nuclear power in electricity generation.

Tables 3.2 and 3.3 describe the energy situation in the Community. The biggest energy users were Germany, France, Italy and the UK. They also tend to be the largest energy importers. The exceptions are the UK because of its oil and gas and, to a lesser extent, the Netherlands because of its gas reserves.

Objectives for 1995. Council Resolution of 16 September 1986. Although the Community had been successful in reducing oil imports, the Council emphasised that member countries should make sure that imports would not increase again. However, they had to face a very different situation from that which prevailed when the objectives of 1974 and 1980 were set.

'Sectoral'. Specific numerical objectives for 1995 followed the pattern set by previous objectives, save that they were expressed as percentages rather than as numbers. The oil target was for net oil imports to be less than 33% of TPER, and for total oil requirements to be below 40% of TPER by 1995.

Quantitative targets were not set for solid fuels and gas. The objective was to make sure that the region had open access to the world market and that imports were from secure and diversified sources. There was no target for indigenous coal and gas production or for their share in TPER.

Electricity generation was considered to be the most promising area. The Council believed that it would grow faster than total energy demand. The proportion of electricity generated from oil and gas was to be reduced to 15%. Nuclear power was to make a substantial contribution by 1995 but no figure was given.

Finally there was a goal to 'achieve even greater energy efficiency in all sectors and act to highlight specific energy-saving possibilities'. And that 'the efficiency of final energy demand should be improved by at least 20% by 1995.'[3]

'Horizontal'. These sectoral objectives were given a theoretical background in what were called 'horizontal' objectives, which would apply to all fuels and would make it easier to achieve the targets. Energy security was the goal. Energy policy in the Community was to be open, flexible and diversified enough to cope with any problem. Greater security of supply was to be achieved by:

- developing indigenous resources;
- diversifying sources of supply and between different forms of energy;
- promoting flexibility in energy networks such as the European gas grid;

promoting efficient use of energy.

Other horizontal objectives aimed at opening up barriers to trade in energy, greater regard for the impact on the environment, special attention to the energy balances of less favoured regions, promotion of technological innovation and the development of Community external relations in the energy sector.

The IEA

All Western European countries except France are members of the International Energy Agency. Formed in November 1974 in response to the 1973-4 oil crisis, and including members from outside as well as within Europe, the IEA's immediate task was to deal with oil supply disruption. Some thought was also given even at that stage to the long term. The IEA has taken a somewhat different line from the EC in setting out its objectives. It has put forward three aims which were to be the basis of all future objectives:

improved energy security for all its members;

a balanced energy economy;

less dependence on oil.

In 1980 the IEA members decided that, as their countries were so diverse in terms of wealth, politics and energy profiles, the agency would not set numerical targets, but would concentrate on broad policy. In 1983, a meeting of the Governing Board concluded that, although much had been done to achieve energy objectives, it was not enough. Dependence on imported oil was still too high; coal and nuclear power were not making their expected contribution; some members were in danger of becoming heavily dependent on certain gas exporters; the outlook for investment in the efficient use of energy and for the development of indigenous energy resources was less than satisfactory.

The Board noted in particular that existing contracts would be insufficient to cover gas demand by the mid-1990s. Steps should be taken in filling the gap to ensure that no one producer could exercise monopoly power over OECD and IEA countries. Undue dependence on any one source of gas imports would be avoided and future supplies would be obtained from secure sources, with emphasis on indigenous OECD sources. These indigenous resources, particularly in North America and the North Sea, would be developed at economic cost. Although there was no agreement, formal or informal, on a particular level of dependence on a single source that would constitute 'undue dependence', it is widely assumed that anything over one third would give cause for concern in this context.

At a ministerial meeting in 1985 the IEA members surveyed their achievements over 10 years and came to the conclusion that energy security had been greatly improved, thanks largely to the effects of the high oil price. They agreed, however, that, although energy conditions had become easier, it would be imprudent to ignore possible tightening energy markets in the 1990s. They believed their policy objectives could be attained by: a freer energy market; conservation; restructuring of refinery capacity; a larger role for electricity; increased use of coal and nuclear power in electricity generation; a larger role for gas, with limits on non-OECD energy supplies; regard for the environment; collaboration over research, development and demonstration; and oil emergency preparedness.

Energy security in the future

The influence the objectives of the Community and the IEA have had on European member states is debatable. If those who maintain that the achievements in the past were brought about solely by response to the market and that high energy prices are right, we should now presumably expect those improvements to be reversed with declining prices. On the other hand, while it is unlikely that the benefits came about solely because of the activities of the member governments of the EC and the IEA, some responsibility must lie with them to avoid the full rigour of the market effect. Consumers, however, may take more notice of events than of the pronouncements of either the EC or the IEA. Now that there is cheaper oil and consequent lower prices for other fuels, consumers' perceptions of immediate interests will tend to diverge from the security policy interests of nations. The Community objectives for 1995 were the first to be put forward without the impetus of an energy crisis and in the hope of averting such a crisis. It is the theme of this paper that the public ought to be willing to continue to bear the resulting costs, by recognising the continuing risks; and that it is the task of government, as in the case of military defence, to make consumers and tax payers aware of this necessity.

Oil

Oil production in Western Europe has been significant only since the late 1970s (see Table 3.4). Development in the North Sea was accelerated by the oil price rises of 1973 and 1979-80. North Sea production not only generated government revenue, company profits and jobs, but also reduced Europe's dependence on OPEC, and particularly the Middle East. From minimal levels in 1975, production reached 3.9 million barrels per day (mbd) in January 1987, thereby providing a significant proportion of OECD Europe's oil demand, which in 1986 stood at 12.3 mbd. Total world non-OPEC production (not including the Centrally Planned Economies) grew from 17 mbd in 1973 to 26 mbd in 1986.

At the same time as non-OPEC production grew, a number of factors were working to reduce demand. The price rises meant that fuels such as coal and gas, and electricity generation by nuclear power, became increasingly competitive. Massive investments were made to develop these alternatives. Furthermore, the higher cost of energy drove consumers towards increasing energy efficiency, whether it be fewer units of energy required to produce a unit of GDP or fewer gallons of fuel to travel a given distance, and towards energy conservation, whether it be turning the lights out or turning the heat down in winter. In the period 1973-86, consumption of oil in the non-communist world fell from 47.4 mbd to 46.4 mbd, and OECD Europe's share of this total fell from 14.9 mbd to 12.3 mbd.

With world demand for oil falling and supply capacity rising, the market became increasingly competitive. OPEC producers found that they were losing market share to non-OPEC countries. Indeed, the OPEC members, despite their low cost and plentiful reserves, became producers of last resort, whilst the non-OPEC countries, with their relatively high cost and scarce reserves, met core demand.

Up to 1985 the stability of the international oil market rested largely on the ability and willingness of Saudi Arabia to restrict its production. However, when its exports fell to 2.4 mbd in the third quarter of 1985, the Saudi leadership felt that they had not only sacrificed too much revenue but also done enough to maintain what, to most observers, was a false price stability in the market. The Saudis increased their production to 4.2 mbd in the last quarter of 1985 and in so doing precipitated a collapse in the price. Spot prices fell rapidly (see Table 3.5) and in 1986 the international oil market entered into a new phase: the period of 'low price' oil (which in this study is defined as oil priced at under $15 per barrel).

Before examining the impact of 'low price' oil on oil exploration and production activities in the North Sea, we shall consider the importance of oil in meeting energy requirements in Europe.

Oil and European energy balances. The share of oil in Total Primary Energy Requirements (TPER) in OECD Europe declined from 59.9% in 1973 to 45.6% in 1984, and at the same time the share of net oil imports in TPER fell from 61.0% to 31.8% (see Table 3.6; the corresponding EC-12 figures are shown in Table 3.7). The growth of North Sea oil production accounts for most of the sharp drop in the share of net oil imports in TPER.

The high price of oil relative to competing fuels accounted for oil's declining share of TPER. The movement away from oil, particularly imported oil, to other fuels was endorsed and encouraged by both the EC and the IEA because it not only improved the balance in the primary energy mix but also enhanced energy security. In forecasts made prior to the 1986 oil price collapse, both bodies projected that the share of oil in TPER would decline further in the period to 2000 (see Tables 3.8 and 3.9). The same forecasts, however, anticipated a rise in net oil imports between 1990 and 2000 to reflect the expected decline in European oil production.

Indeed, despite the low prices, the Council of the European Communities adopted in 1986 policy objectives for oil stating that its 'consumption should be kept to around 40% of energy consumption and net oil imports thus maintained at less than one-third of total energy consumption in the Community in 1995'. The Council envisaged that net oil imports would be kept 'within reasonable proportions' both by encouraging switching out of oil into other energy sources and by promoting exploration and production within the Community.

If prices remain below the 1985 levels (roughly $28 a barrel) such objectives will be difficult to achieve, not least because of the growth in demand for oil and the lack of incentive to switch out of it. In 1986, for example, oil consumption within OECD Europe grew by 3.4% compared to 1985, rising from a level of 11.6 mbd in 1985 to 12.0 mbd in 1986. This growth reversed several years of declining consumption, which had fallen or remained constant in every year since 1979.

Assuming prices remained at $15 till 1990, it was predicted by the EC[4] that the EC-10's demand for oil would reach 438-466 million tonnes (i.e. 8.8-9.4 mbd) in 1990 compared to a level of 441 mt (8.9 mbd) projected for 1990 in the Energie 2000 study. Net imports were expected to be between 344 and 373 mt (6.9-7.5 mbd) as opposed to 330 mt (6.6 mbd) projected in the Energie 2000 study (see Table 3.9).

Low oil prices and the North Sea. Low prices will also have an impact on the supply side although it will tend to lag behind the demand side. 1985 was a good year for those involved in the North Sea. Production in the Norwegian and UK sectors had reached 3.6 mbd, its highest level yet. Several large developments were initiated and oil and gas exploration work reached near record levels: 93 exploration wells and 64 appraisal wells in the UK sector, and 29 exploration wells and 21 appraisal wells in the Norwegian sector. The drop in oil prices in fact occurred as North Sea oil production was near its peak: 1985 and 1986 were expected to be the years of peak production in the UK Continental Shelf (UKCS), with Norway's in about 1990.

i) Production. In 1986, production in the North Sea was around 3.8 mbd. There was no indication that the fall in oil prices had exerted any downward pressure on production, due to the fact that the production of oil (particularly offshore oil) is capital-intensive. A high proportion of the costs are incurred before production begins, actual operating costs are small in comparison, probably between $5 and $10 per barrel. As a result, low oil prices have little impact on production in the short run. Producers will continue to produce as long as they cover their operating costs and liability to royalties and taxes at the prevailing prices[5], tax of course declining with price so that the burden of declining prices falls mainly on Treasuries rather than on the owners of fields that are already in production.

Indeed, it is only if producers have particularly pessimistic expectations about future prices that they will discontinue production, because the alternatives of shutting-in or abandoning fields are not particularly attractive. Shutting-in production in a given field means that it yields no revenues, while at the same time a skeleton staff is retained to carry out essential maintenance activities. Before production is started up again, further expenditures will be incurred. Abandonment is far more complicated: aside from forgone revenue, heavy abandonment costs are incurred. A 1984 estimate suggested that the removal of structures in place in the UKCS would cost about £6 billion[6].

ii) Exploration and development. The 1986 fall in oil prices, however, had a severe impact on the level of exploration and development activity in the North Sea. Taking drilling activity as an example, it was reported as early as February 1986 that UK operators foresaw a reduction of 14% in their drilling rig requirements for the summer compared to projections made in November 1985. The fall became more pronounced in the second half of the year. In December 1986, only 20 exploration and appraisal wells were being drilled in the UKCS as opposed to 49 in December 1985; in the Norwegian sector, the corresponding numbers were 4 and 12[7]. However, the level of development drilling, which is not so price sensitive, was not adversely affected.

All companies were faced with a reduction in cash flow from their production, resulting both from the falling dollar price of oil and the strengthening of the pound and krone against the dollar. Small independent companies with little production or no downstream activities were worst hit. Budget stringency led to cutbacks in new investment. Exploration, for example, looked particularly risky, not only because of the long lead times between exploration and eventual production, but also the great uncertainty (and pessimism) about future price levels.

Most North Sea oil producers announced reductions in their exploration budgets in 1986, often by as much as 50%. Development activity was also affected by the fall in oil prices. However, initial statements made about the effect of falling oil prices on the viability of certain projects have now been replaced by cost-cutting exercises by the same companies (for example, Shell announced in 1986 that they were shelving the $3.75 million Gannet-Kittiwake project. In April 1987 Esso, Shell's partner on the project, announced that it would develop the project, but with a much reduced budget). What constitutes an acceptable rate of return clearly varies between fields and between companies depending on their tax position, but the chief executive of Lasmo (London and Scottish Marine Oil) gave a good indication of what price producers needed to expect before undertaking a development, when he said[8]:

> There are no North Sea development prospects which make a tolerable return on capital at $18 a barrel.

A study by the Grampian Regional Council[9] on the central and northern North Sea showed how 'low price' oil might affect development activity over the longer term. Considering the possibility of the oil price remaining at or below $15 until the end of 1987, rising to $21 by 1990, and then remaining constant in real terms till 2000, it forecast that 41 fields would be developed between 1987 and 2001, a drop of 15 compared to its 1985 forecast. For the period 1975-2001, it forecast that 84 fields would be developed compared with its 1985 forecast of 94 fields.

In the light of such considerations, it is inevitable that 'low price' oil will reduce both the future level of production in the North Sea and also the level of available reserves faster than previously expected. Only a depreciation of the pound and the krone against the dollar and/or changes in government policies towards oil production, particularly in the domain of taxes, work to offset the negative impact of 'low price' oil on new investment. The March 1987 UK Budget proposals gave some help to operators in the North Sea in the form of concessions against Petroleum Revenue Tax (10% of new field development and also research and development expenditure on a new field if, after three years, it was not already allowed). Many companies were disappointed that concessions did not go further. Wood Mackenzie did, however, estimate that the new tax allowances would help most projects by about 2% and accelerate the development of a number of fields.

<u>Future production</u>. i) <u>UK</u>. As suggested earlier, North Sea production is unlikely to be affected by low prices in the short run, unless there is a collapse in prices, say, to a level below $5 per barrel. After a few years, if new developments are not initiated, the expected decline will be more severe than would otherwise be the case for two reasons. First, certain development projects will have been postponed or even cancelled, thereby delaying the introduction of new production as production in older fields starts to decline. Secondly, declining production in existing fields will lead to a reduction in cash flow, which will affect the ability of companies to invest. In addition, with lower oil prices, there will be less incentive for many producers to extend the life of existing fields or to undertake enhanced oil recovery (EOR). In April 1987 a conference held on the decommissioning and removal of North Sea structures considered the possibility of tax concessions to help companies with abandonment costs, thereby encouraging production in fields nearing the end of their life.

Table 3.10 illustrates potential production profiles in the UKCS under different price assumptions, in comparison with those projected by the IEA before the price collapse and assuming no change in the tax regime. The production profiles, based on work by brokers James Capel and Wood MacKenzie, demonstrate the importance of the level of oil prices for the future rate of development and production.

The level of UK and Norwegian oil reserves will also be affected by 'low price' oil. Even before the oil price collapse, production had begun to outstrip additions to reserves; in 1985, for example, production in the UK was 127.5 mt while the level of initial proven and probable reserves was increased by 60 mt, which had the net effect of reducing the level of total remaining proven and probable reserves from 1300 mt (at end 1984) to 1230 mt (at end 1985[10]). This decline will be accelerated as long as the low oil price both reduces the ability and incentive for companies to undertake exploration and leads to pressures for the early abandonment of fields. Finally, the level of reserves will decline because it will no longer be economically viable to develop some of the reserves discovered prior to the decline of the oil price.

ii) Norway. A similar picture can be expected to emerge in Norway. Production will probably reach the conservative levels projected in the profile submitted to the IEA prior to the oil price collapse, ie. 1.1 mbd in 1990 and 0.4 mbd in 2000. These levels reflected existing production trends in operating fields and expected production in fields committed to development. The number of additional fields which are developed and brought on stream before 2000 will determine the extent to which production exceeds 0.4 mbd in that year. Wood MacKenzie's production profiles for Norway under differing price scenarios are shown in Table 3.11.

The Norwegian Government will probably attempt to maintain and encourage oil exploration and production even at low oil prices. Oil accounted for nearly 20% of Gross National Product and government revenues in 1985, while providing over 63,000 jobs, and is therefore of critical importance to Norway's economy. Despite the Norwegian Government's interest in maintaining activity, the majority of future development projects will look unattractive as long as 'low price' oil prevails. New field development costs in Norway are about $20 a barrel before tax and royalty, so the Government may be forced into making radical revisions to its tax regime.

The future of North Sea oil. As we move into the 1990s, and particularly if 'low price' oil persists, both the Norwegian and the UK Governments will have to make difficult choices between maintaining the levels of North Sea tax revenues and forgoing such revenues to maintain activity beyond the ability of the oil companies themselves to cut their costs and thereby protect domestic supply and oil-related jobs. Whatever fiscal action is taken and whatever technological and cost advances are made, however, it is unlikely that the contribution of the North Sea to European oil requirements will exceed half of the present level by the year 2000, for purely geological reasons (gas is a different matter dealt with below). A detailed study on the scope for modifications to the North Sea tax regime is attached at Appendix A.

Oil from the Gulf. It follows from the above that Europe will continue to be heavily dependent on imports for a large proportion of its oil supplies, and that any further success in switching to other primary fuels, in the development of alternative energies, or in efficiency of use will at best do no more by the year 2000 than offset the decline in North Sea oil production. If that decline and the long lead times for nuclear and for new technologies are aggravated by under-investment at home, or if the trend to lower oil consumption is reversed by the operation of the international market through lower oil prices, dependence on imports will increase. Production costs in the main producing areas of the Middle East are at least $10 a barrel less than the cost of developing new sources of oil within Europe. This means that, in the absence of government policy, European oil producers will always be at the mercy of their Middle East competitors.

Nor is there a possibility of importing oil from a diversity of non-Middle East sources. This is because more than half of the world's proved oil reserves, a higher proportion of probable reserves, and about the same proportion of spare productive capacity in being, lie in the Gulf region of the Middle East, that is to say, Iran, Iraq, Kuwait, Saudi Arabia and the other members of the Gulf Co-operation Council (see Table 3.12). In 1986, 40% of Europe's oil imports came from that region (see Table 3.13) and this proportion is likely to rise, since alternative sources are liable to be commercially or politically pre-empted by the US or Japan, and their output tends to be relatively small and in many cases in decline. Indeed Japan is already competing and the US (as the American chapter of this book shows) will increasingly compete with Europe for supplies from the Gulf. Given the political instability of that area therefore, to say nothing of any potential external threat, it is essential for the European countries not only to concert their own policies towards Middle East oil supplies, but also, as far as possible, to agree such policies with Japan and the United States. Unfortunately, as the history of the last ten years shows, efforts in this direction have been by no means successful, not least because of conflicting internal political pressures in many European countries and in the United States in the context of the Palestine problem.

In addition to issues of absolute physical insecurity of supply, this situation can only lead to the threat not simply of gradually rising prices, but of sudden economically disrupting price explosions, as short - to medium term demand - rises to match existing installed production capacity - itself dwindling due war damage and lack of maintenance.

European relations with the Gulf

It is therefore worthwhile to trace briefly the history of European policies towards the Gulf, and of the so-called Euro-Arab dialogue, as a basis on which to evaluate present attitudes. One must begin with the caveat that, in this area more than any other, the disparities between the policies of individual European countries referred to at the start of this chapter have so far outweighed attempts to co-operate. As far as policies towards revolutionary Iran are concerned, no constructive alternative to a policy of 'wait and see' has seemed possible, either individually or collectively. American attempts to go it alone have appeared to many Europeans not only misguided, but also a betrayal of the joint attempt to refuse to do deals with terrorism or with the export of Shi'a fundamentalism. Nor has there appeared to be any opening for mediation between Iran and Iraq. In relations with the Arabs, Britain, seeing itself self-sufficient in energy, has tended to give priority in its policy to trade and the provision of financial services, not excluding trade in arms, with the emphasis on Saudi Arabia and the Emirates. France has been at least a near competitor, building in the process a close relationship with Iraq, whilst still trying to maintain the personal ties with Syria and Lebanon which stem from its historic links with that area. Italy has sought to build a special Mediterranean entente. The other members of the Community have leaned more consistently towards a joint Community policy, which the UK, France and Italy have been willing to back only to the extent that it did not cut across their immediate individual interests, and especially in the case of the UK and Germany, to the extent that it did not involve a major breach with Washington. The difference of emphasis between Washington and the European capitals, with the former seeing the region primarily in the light of its alliance with Israel and its desire to contain the Soviet Union, and the latter somewhat more sympathetic to internal Arab concerns, runs right through the developments of the last decade.

Relations 1973-86. The 1973 embargo on oil exports to certain countries, initiated by the Arabs at the time of the war between Israel and Egypt, was directed at the United States and Britain, which were seen as the principal supporters of Israel, and at the Netherlands, where an injudicious ministerial statement provided a pretext to hit at Europe's main refining and distributing centre at Rotterdam. The European governments sought by diplomatic channels and public statements to dissociate themselves from American support for Israel, and in November 1973 condemned Israeli occupation of the West Bank and announced that they were planning to negotiate trade agreements with non-EC Mediterranean countries. In return, some Arab governments softened their boycott measures, and in some cases entered into direct oil deals with governments of importing countries, notably France and the UK - deals which did not in fact turn out to be particularly advantageous to the buyers.

Having demonstrated their new-found power, the Middle Eastern exporters put themselves at the head of the movement for a so-called 'New International Economic Order' on behalf of the developing world. France, with support from the rest of the Community, then convened the Conference for International and Economic Co-operation (alias the North-South dialogue) which it was hoped would solve the problems of both exporters and importers. This ran from December 1975 to June 1977, when it collapsed because of an inability to find common ground on any topic. The oil exporters refused to discuss matters of oil supply and prices in the Energy Commission set up under joint US and Saudi chairmanship, while the Western governments refused to make concessions to the Third World countries on trade and finance.

The so-called 'Euro-Arab dialogue' itself had been set up following the rather bizarre incident of the arrival of four Arab ministers uninvited in Copenhagen in December 1973, where an EC Foreign Ministers meeting was in session. This led to the issue of a declaration calling for negotiations with oil producing countries. Despite objections from the US, who preferred to keep dealings with the Arabs in its own hands and objected to Europe developing an independent approach, plans were made for the establishment of joint working groups from the EC and the Arab League and an eventual full Euro-Arab ministerial conference. Working groups met in Paris and elsewhere at technical level during 1974 and 1975 and achieved nothing. The desire of the Arabs to widen the talks at a political level foundered on a lack of agreement between the Arab participants as well as the refusal of the European side to discuss political matters. Attempts to make progress at a ministerial level were abandoned following the Camp David agreement between Egypt and Israel in 1979 and the rejection of that agreement by the other Arab states.

There is no evidence that either the Euro-Arab dialogue in any form or the constant bilateral contacts between individual countries had improved Europe's security of supply by the time the next oil crisis struck, with the Iranian Revolution in 1979-80. Statements of sympathy and moderation notwithstanding, Saudi Arabia actually cut its exports by one million barrels per day at the height of the Iranian crisis. No Arab government showed any reluctance to take advantage of the steep rise in prices which the revolution provoked; nor any inclination to respond to European overtures by offering favourable prices such as they offered for a time to some developing and Islamic countries. Nonetheless, the Community sought to respond to the situation by some political step and in June 1980 the EC Foreign Ministers issued the Venice Declaration (see Appendix B) in which they recognised the Palestinians' right to self-determination and the role of the PLO as their representative, and underlined the call for Israeli evacuation of the West Bank. This was as far as the Community was prepared to go on political issues.

Nevertheless the Venice Declaration was useful and it is still relevant, and talks have continued on such matters as European investment in the West Bank. The main effort, however, has shifted partly to the process of 'Political Co-operation' under the Single European Act, and partly to the officials of the Commission itself, in the context of talks about a possible Free Trade Area agreement with the Gulf Co-operation Council. Unfortunately there seems to be a lack of concerted approach between the two bodies, with the former concentrating on political and diplomatic matters, and the latter stalled on the reluctance of European governments to open their markets to unlimited imports of chemical and other products.

Future relations. It is possible, however, to argue that there has been some improvement in the prospects for security of oil supply from the Middle East in recent years. The collapse of the oil price in 1986 demonstrated to OPEC members the consequences of being too greedy, and the impossibility of retaining both high price and market share for more than a limited period. Organised exchanges with Middle Eastern countries of factual information and economic analysis by both the IEA and the Commission have lessened the likelihood of unintentional damage by one side to the other. There is also a growing community of interest, stemming not only from Arab investment in Europe, but also from direct downstream integration into European oil markets, such as that of the Kuwait National Petroleum Company. Gulf Co-operation Council members are still seeking increased tariff-free entry for their oil and chemical products into Europe, and if this results in a free trade area agreement, Iraq and Iran might eventually also become parties to it. Such a development would not of itself guarantee continued access at reasonable prices to Gulf oil. Still less would it procure any preferential rights for the European Community as compared with Japan or the United States. But it would further the notion of interdependence between the Gulf and the OECD countries and facilitate the orderly development of their oil and gas resources.

The fact has to be faced, however, that despite all efforts to develop alternative supplies, and whatever success may be achieved in improving relations with the Arab states and with Iran, Europe's principal source of oil is an unstable area. Europe is therefore particularly concerned to maintain in good repair the mechanisms for handling any future oil crisis. Within the Community, more could be done to improve the emergency stock situation, both in terms of the number of days held (now in some cases below the EC and IEA requirement of 90 days) and in terms of ready availability for release. In general, reserves are held in the facilities of - and at the expense of - commercial companies and are not readily available for release in the early stages of a crisis when they might be most effective in checking a major rise in prices.

Europe, however, can do little on its own to counter an international oil crisis, being especially weakened by the absence of Norway from the Community and by the absence of France from the International Energy Agency. It is to this latter body, which groups together the world's major oil importers, that European governments must mainly look to take the necessary measures to offset the initial supply effects, and the sudden price rises, that a major crisis within or in relations with the Gulf countries could cause. It is a major European interest that Japan and particularly the United States remain committed members of that organisation because, without their participation, crisis management will not be possible.

Natural gas

Reserves. Estimates of commercial gas reserves in Western Europe have traditionally erred on the conservative side. Partly this reflects policies which were not primarily concerned with encouraging exploration, and partly it indicates advances in technology which have allowed identification of, and development prospects for, resources located in deeper water.

The volume of available reserves, both domestic and imported, depends on the cost of extraction and transport, and the ability of supplies to compete against other fuels in end-use markets. This latter issue is of increasing importance, given heightened inter-fuel competition in the 1980s. At present, gas is produced in large quantities in the Dutch, UK (southern and northern basins) and Norwegian sectors of the North Sea; and imported from Algeria and the USSR (plus a small quantity from Libya). In the future, there will be gas produced from the central basin of the UK North Sea and also from the northern Norwegian shelf. Gas may be imported from Middle East and African countries in liquefied form or eventually by pipeline. The viability of both indigenous and import developments will depend on the cost of production and transportation of the individual source.

As far as the three important West European gas producing countries are concerned, the Norwegian proven resource base indicates a reserve life of around 80 years compared with the UK at 13 and the Netherlands at 23 years (see Table 3.14). These strategic perceptions should take precedence over short-term market conditions. Nevertheless, the latter may exert considerable influence on short-term development decisions which, on projects with long lead times, such as the Troll development, will have a major influence on the security situation in the 1990s.

Demand. In the 1980s, previous concern resulting from perceptions of spiralling gas demand has turned into fears about over-supply and a 'gas glut'. After two decades of uninterrupted growth, gas demand declined between 1979 and 1983, but then rose by 5.4% and 9.7% in the two succeeding years, with demand in OECD Europe reaching 239 BCM in 1985.

The projections of the 1960s and 1970s which assumed gas demand in Europe of over 400 BCM by 2000 have been dramatically scaled down in the 1980s, with some forecasts anticipating no growth whatsoever. IEA projections present alternative scenarios of gas demand at high and low oil prices; the EC estimates (which are lower because only the ten members are included) show almost no growth during the 1990s (see Table 3.15).

These estimates are a basis for looking in more detail at the individual sectors. In most countries, the largest market is the residential/commercial sector where gas commands a premium price. In Continental Europe competition is mainly against heating oil and electricity and although pricing policy will affect demand levels, the situation has not yet reached the pitch of competitiveness found in the industrial sector. In countries such as Germany and France, there is substantial scope for increasing gas penetration in the residential market. The future progress of conservation, particularly in new residential and commercial buildings, will have an important bearing on whether European gas demand continues to expand in the period up to 2000.

The industrial sector is the main battleground of inter-fuel competition between gas and coal and fuel-oil. Gas is essential for certain industrial processes but for steam-raising and space-heating fuel-switching, especially with falling oil prices, could pose considerable threats to expansion of demand. During the 1970s, at the urging of the EC, phasing natural gas out of power generation became an objective in all West European countries. In the mid-1980s, that process has been reversed in Italy and the Netherlands (due to local circumstances). In all other countries, it would require both a shift in price competitiveness and a radical change in policy concerning coal-fired and nuclear power generation for natural gas to do better than hold its present market share in this sector. It is possible that environmental problems associated with coal and nuclear power could give rise to a reappraisal of the role of gas in power generation. On the other hand, if natural gas fails to maintain competitiveness in the industrial and power generation sector, this could have an adverse effect on security of supply considerations, since interruptible contracts are concentrated in this sector.

<u>Supply</u>. As mentioned above, earlier perceptions of a 'supply gap' have been largely overtaken by lower

demand projections and increased availability from indigenous sources.

The gas contracts signed in the 1960s, following the discovery of the Groningen field in the Netherlands, enabled the spread of natural gas as a major fuel source for Continental European countries. However, in the period since the first oil crisis, there have been two abrupt reversals in Dutch gas export policy. The first occurred in the mid-1970s when, as a result of concern about insufficient reserves and rising demand, Gasunie joined the Continental consortium importing gas from the Norwegian Ekofisk field. The second took place in the mid-1980s when upward revisions of reserves and faltering domestic demand led Gasunie to extend its export contracts to all Continental importers for another decade, which takes them into the first decade of the next century. While the earlier Dutch depletion policy, which restricted exports, has been abandoned, there is a need for some caution in order to avoid repetition of the mistakes of the post-1973 period.

Two of the three operating Norwegian contracts will expire in the early 1990s and, with the failure (in early 1985) of the negotiations to sell gas from the Sleipner field to the UK, much depended on a speedy and successful conclusion of the negotiations for the development of the Troll-Sleipner gas development. With the agreement, reached in 1986, for the sale of 18 BCM of gas per year from the first phase of the Troll-Sleipner fields, commencing in the late 1990s, Norway has ensured its future as a major gas exporter over the next several decades.[11]

Imports from outside the OECD area are confined mainly to Algeria and the USSR. Both have contracts for gas running through to 2000 and beyond, and both have the reserves and the spare capacity in their facilities to increase exports still further: Algeria by means of its under-utilised LNG facilities and by expansion of the Trans-Mediterranean pipeline, and the USSR in existing pipelines as a result of lower than expected volumes in sales contracts.

The events of the past two years, with the Dutch extensions of contracts and agreement for the start of the first phase of the Troll gas field in the mid to late 1990s, have raised the possibility that Continental European utilities will not need to contract for any new gas (other than extensions of existing contracts) in this century.

Gas exporters. In addition to those exporters already mentioned there are also a number of potential projects which would further diversify European sources of natural gas. However, neither the LNG projects involving countries such as Qatar, Nigeria, Canada and Cameroon, nor the much-discussed possibility of a gas pipeline from the Middle East, are likely to make an impact on the European market before 2000, particularly in a world of lower oil prices (see Table 3.16). Libya will continue to be a marginal exporter to Western Europe, but apart from the limited context of Spanish supply, this will not be significant for Europe's security as a whole.

Thus European gas imports up to 2000 will be concentrated on four exporters: two European (Norway and the Netherlands) and two non-European (the USSR and Algeria). The Netherlands exports to all the major Continental gas consumers, but its market is concentrated in Northern Europe. Norway's exports are divided between the UK and the Continent but, as mentioned above, the British Government's decision not to contract for Sleipner gas, and the agreement on exports from the Troll development, may mean that Norway's major (and perhaps only) gas export market in the late 1990s will be Continental Europe.

Algeria's major customers are Southern European countries: Italy, France and Spain. The USSR, with 40% of world gas reserves, has its present export market concentrated in Northern and Central Europe but by the late 1980s the country will have the potential to reach most European countries with the addition of a comparatively short pipeline extension.

Gas security

i) Origins. The problem of gas security first entered the public consciousness in the early 1980s, and centred on Soviet supplies to Western Europe and American anxiety that this might make Europe vulnerable to Soviet political pressures. The Reagan Administration was anxious to persuade Europe not to import Soviet gas, and imposed sanctions first on US companies exporting pipeline components and then on European subsidiaries of those corporations. Subsequent disagreements between members of the Atlantic Alliance gave rise to a difficult period in transatlantic relations.

With the immediate question of Soviet deliveries having been shelved, the emphasis changed with studies from both the EC and the IEA which showed that, in the period up to 1990, Europe would be able to withstand an interruption of supplies from any source for at least six months and probably up to a year. The eventual outcome was an agreement between IEA Governments to lay stress on developing sources of gas in IEA countries (and specifically the Troll field), and 'to avoid undue dependence' on a single exporter, by limiting to approximately 30% (or one third) of total supply the contribution of any one source.[12]

ii) Reliability of supply. For all West European utilities which import natural gas, dependence on exporters, both within and outside Europe, has to be based on contractual trust, as well as confidence in the logistics of producing and transporting gas. The following gives some idea of exporter reliability.

Very little publicity has been devoted to the problems of reliability of supply associated with Norwegian gas deliveries. These have taken a number of different forms. First, there was a downgrading of reserves in the Ekofisk and Frigg fields after production and exports had begun, which has meant that the life of exports from these fields has been shortened. Second, in the case of Ekofisk, production problems stemming from seabed subsidence have led to a drastic reduction in export volumes, for a prolonged period. Third, and potentially most serious, there is the risk of loss of Norwegian gas supplies as a result of strikes on the rigs. The most recent of these disputes occurred in April 1986 and shut down the entire Frigg field - both UK and Norwegian sectors - depriving all Norwegian customers of their gas deliveries. As a result, British Gas also lost 40% of its gas supplies for almost a week.

In the event of disruptions to Continental European supply, the ability to use the excess deliverability of Groningen gas as emergency supply means that Dutch gas acts as the 'supplier of last resort' for Continental European utilities. Importers are required to pay higher prices for the privilege of using this facility (and there was a question in the early 1980s about Dutch willingness to supply those customers who were slow to adapt to changing market conditions). Dutch gas exports have become an extremely important revenue earner for the country, which suggests continuity and reliability of supply.

Given the amount of discussion about the security aspect of Soviet gas supplies, there is little hard evidence that the USSR is an unreliable exporter. Interruptions occur during severe winter conditions as a result of lack of storage capacity and peaking facilities in the USSR and Eastern Europe. No political motives have been involved. Disruption for political reasons remains a possibility, but is heavily counterbalanced by the Soviet need to earn foreign currency. Arguments about the security aspects of Soviet gas supplies have not been solved, but in the mid-1980s the amount of publicity which they are attracting has fallen considerably. Some countries (Austria 76%, Finland 100%) are and will continue to be heavily dependent on the USSR for gas supplies.

In comparison to other exporters, Algeria has a bad record as far as reliability is concerned. Since 1980, there has been difficulty over the Algerian demand for gas prices to be related to crude oil, and subsequently the exporter failed to live up to contractual commitments in respect of starting-up and/or maintaining deliveries. Although there were indications in 1986 that the Algerians were beginning to conform to other exporting countries, it will take some time and exemplary behaviour in its conduct of contractual and supply relations before Algeria is considered a reliable supplier by its customers.

Gas supply security remains an important issue and one which requires careful definition. For utilities, the term security is more immediately related to the logistical and contractual reliability of a source. For governments, security of supply has a more directly political connotation and is highly dependent upon the source of supply, particularly as regards imports. Each country regards indigenous production as the most secure, with some consensus among European governments that supplies from other European countries are more 'desirable'. Their utilities may take a different view about which imported supplies are the most 'reliable'. While it is commonplace to assert that a country should avoid undue dependence on any one source of supply, in practice there has been little public and governmental concern about over-reliance on any source of supply other than the USSR.

iii) Measures to ensure security. The answer for each importing country must be individual. The merits of avoiding undue dependence on any one supplier are obvious. The problem is one of balancing perceptions of the reliability of individual suppliers with competitiveness of their supplies, while at the same time avoiding over-dependence. The arrangement of the Continental gas grid goes a long way towards protecting the Continent against interruption from a single source of supply, and the situation in the mid-1980s did not present any serious problems (see Table 3.17).

Pipeline ownership is spread among companies from different countries so there is no question of one country controlling gas flow to another. European storage capacity is currently around 25 BCM and this is planned to reach 33 BCM by 1990.[13] Compared to a consumption rate of 200-250 BCM, storage in itself may not be sufficient, but Europe is able to draw on offshore fields and pipeline flexibility to supplement this. However, it will be important to maintain spare capacity in the system in order to promote flexibility for both storage and source switching.

In addition, each country has contingency plans for dealing with disruptions: demand reduction (cutting interruptible contracts); indigenous surge production; import flexibility; storage; and finally some government contingency planning.

iv) UK gas security. This needs to be considered separately, as the UK is not connected to the Continental gas grid.

Three-quarters of UK gas is produced from domestic fields, thus one of the main security issues is whether this should be extended to total self-sufficiency or whether gas should be imported and from which sources. In rejecting the import of Sleipner gas, the British Government has arrived at a policy of near-total self-sufficiency in the period after 1992-3. If security of supply is a major issue in the long term, there may be a case for ensuring that a significant proportion of supply continues to be taken from an external source in order to prolong the life of the UK resource base. There are a number of possible sources of gas, but the most likely source of imports still appears to be Norway, with eventual UK participation in the Troll/Sleipner development.

The construction of a pipeline link between the UK and the Continent has been proposed in order to assist supply security. While this would undoubtedly help the Continent, there would not be an immediate benefit for the UK (given the gas storage facilities which have been built), unless there is the genuine possibility of importing gas from a variety of sources, including the USSR, the Netherlands and Algeria. The UK relies on onshore liquefied natural gas storage (of domestic supplies) as well as offshore storage in depleted reservoirs. The development of the Morecambe field in the Irish Sea as a peak-load facility with an eventual capacity of 1.2 bcf/d provides a very substantial additional security buffer. Nevertheless, in the context of a base-load import arriving from or via Continental Europe, the ability to reverse the flow, using gas from UK fields, would be a notable advantage for Continental European gas security.

v) Is there a case for a security premium? If security of supply is important to a government or a utility, then logically it should be taken into consideration when contracts are negotiated. In the 1980s, government subsidies paid to gas importers have been for diplomatic reasons. The French and Italian government subsidies, which operated for a brief period at the beginning of the Algerian contracts renegotiated in the early 1980s, were particularly unfortunate in that they seemed to be awarding a premium to the most unreliable supplier.

Importing utilities have consistently rejected the notion of a security premium, unless connected to the provision of additional flexibility of deliveries, particularly in emergency situations. If a case could have been made for a security premium, it would have been principally applicable to the Troll development, where lower oil prices endangered the conclusion of a satisfactory agreement. The fact that the price of Troll/Sleipner gas is (we are given to understand) totally market-related, and the seller is responsible for ensuring sufficient storage capacity to cope with interruptions in deliveries, indicates that the case for a price premium on political/security grounds has been decisively rejected.

Electricity generation

Since 1974 many European governments, encouraged by the IEA and the European Commission, have promoted an increase in electricity's share of the final energy market, mainly in order to reduce dependence on oil, particularly imported oil. Between 1975 and 1984, electricity's share of total final consumption of energy increased from 12.2% to 15.9% in OECD Europe. Final consumption of electricity grew by 34.7%, whereas total final consumption of energy only increased by 3.5% for the period.

Turning to the source of electricity generation, oil's share in generation in OECD Europe fell. As the share of oil diminished so that of nuclear power increased, reflecting a commitment to nuclear power as a clean, viable and secure source of electricity generation. In France this commitment was particularly strong; the share of nuclear power in electricity generation grew from 9.9% in 1975 to approximately 70% in 1986. The share of solid fuels in electricity generation in OECD Europe remained relatively stable, while those of hydropower and gas fell (see Table 3.18).

It is difficult to make generalisations about electricity demand in Europe as a whole. Demand is determined by economic growth, electricity pricing, and efficiency in electricity use. However, within these broad areas, other factors play an important part. The amount of industrial restructuring within each European country's economy and the growth of information technology and service industries can alter demand growth. In addition, the ability of electricity to compete against other fuels in certain markets, such as domestic space and water heating, can also affect demand. Table 3.19 shows OECD Europe's growth in electricity demand between 1985 and 2000 as projected by the IEA; Table 3.20 shows the corresponding figures for the EC-10 as projected by the EC. The figures are placed within ranges to reflect the uncertainty attached to such projections.

The task of providing the capacity to satisfy this demand is made more complex by the need to have surplus capacity above that needed to satisfy peak demand both daily and seasonally. Reserve capacity is required for circumstances in which power stations are unavailable due to maintenance, breakdowns and also bad weather.

IEA figures showing projected growth in generating capacity for all OECD European countries between 1984 and 2000 are set out in Table 3.21. These projections take account both of the need to meet expected growth in demand and to replace lost capacity through decommissioning of obsolete plant.

In most countries, coal-fired and/or nuclear power stations will provide base load, oil- and gas-fired stations will meet peak demand and provide reserve capacity. Hydropower will remain an important source of electricity generation, constituting total installed capacity in Norway and retaining significant shares of capacity in other countries, including Italy and Spain. (See Tables 3.28 and 3.29 for country projected generation capacity by fuel and the respective share of fuels).

<u>Nuclear power</u>. Since its beginnings, the development of nuclear power in Europe has been the subject of controversy. This has centred on the issues of nuclear waste and the safety of nuclear plants, on the one hand, and relative economics, on the other. In 1986, the accident at the Chernobyl nuclear power plant complex in the USSR shook public, and indeed professional, confidence in nuclear power. In this section, we assess whether Chernobyl will have any effect on nuclear

power programmes in Europe, and the contribution that nuclear power makes to European energy security.

Certain countries had taken 'non-nuclear' energy policy decisions before Chernobyl, which the latter can only have reinforced. The Austrians, for example, decided in 1978 to mothball the Zwentendorf nuclear power station following a referendum. By September 1986, they had decided to dismantle it. In Sweden, a decision was made in 1980 to complete the nuclear construction programme but that all twelve reactors, with a generating capacity of 9.5 Gigawatts (GW), would be shut down by 31 December 2010. Some Swedish officials and energy experts now expect this process to be accelerated. In 1984, the Spanish Government imposed a moratorium on the construction of five reactors (totalling 4.9 GW capacity). Figures in the 1983 National Energy Plan had indicated that excessive nuclear plant was under construction in view of the projected growth in electricity. In Denmark, the Parliament voted in 1985 to pursue an energy policy which excluded nuclear power as an option - a decision now unlikely to be reversed in the foreseeable future.

At the opposite end of the scale, France and Belgium seem totally committed to nuclear power, Chernobyl having had no noticeable impact on their level of commitment despite some adverse comment from the media and public. In the period to 2000, demand saturation is the factor most likely to have a negative impact on the French nuclear programme. In their plans for new nuclear capacity, the Belgians have avoided potential siting problems by making a 25% investment in the construction of two Pressurised Water Reactors across the border in France at Chooz. In addition, they are planning to construct a PWR at an existing site (Doel near Antwerp) for connection to the grid in 1996. There is no sign that these decisions will be reversed.

Regardless of Chernobyl or other considerations, it does appear that most, if not all, nuclear power stations under construction will be completed. It is hard to justify the abandonment of a nuclear project once the vast capital outlays have been made. A decision to order no new power stations now will have no effect on the proportion of nuclear power before 1995, because of lead times and the number of stations that are at present under construction. However, this does not mean that there will not be opposition to nuclear power on other grounds. The possibility of Austrian-type decisions (see above) should not, however, be ruled out. Table 3.22 sets out nuclear capacity and units under construction in OECD Europe as of 30 November 1986.

With the exceptions of France and Belgium, a greater degree of uncertainty surrounds the nuclear power plants which were still in the planning phase when Chernobyl occurred (see Table 3.23). In other European countries, heightened public concern forced nuclear power to the forefront of political debate, particularly if general elections were approaching or if important decisions on nuclear plant were imminent. Some of the planned plant was already in jeopardy; for example, in Italy local environmental opposition had long threatened to limit any expansion of the nuclear programme.

The following countries are engaged in active debate about nuclear power. Their present and immediately succeeding governments will take decisions which will be crucial in determining the role of nuclear power in electricity generation in Europe after the key date of 1995.

Germany. Within a month of Chernobyl, the Greens had seen their standing in the polls rise to 9%. At their May Congress in Hanover, they demanded the closure of all nuclear plants and made this a condition of their support for the Social Democrat Party (SPD). Following its Congress in August, the SPD committed itself to phasing out all nuclear power within ten years. However, Chancellor Kohl came out strongly in favour of Germany's nuclear programme. Nuclear power proved to be a central and divisive issue in the run-up to the federal elections in January 1987, with the pro-nuclear conservative Christian Democrat (CDU) and Christian Social (CSU) parties ranged against the SPD and the Greens. Despite the CDU's victory, it seemed inevitable that the issue of nuclear power would remain controversial.

United Kingdom. At the 1986 Labour Party conference, the National Executive's proposal to stop new nuclear construction and to phase out nuclear power over a number of decades received overwhelming support, thereby becoming incorporated in the Party's programme from which the manifesto is drawn. The SDP/Liberal Alliance, despite internal differences, supported a moratorium of five to ten years on any new stations. The Conservative Party alone remained unconditionally committed to nuclear power, with the Prime Minister willing to stand behind the past performance and safety record of the nuclear industry. Her then Energy Secretary, Peter Walker, suggested in a speech in June 1986 that it would be 'irresponsible' not to pursue a nuclear programme. By March 1987 the Layfield Report on the Sizewell B project had been published and its recommendation to approve the building of one PWR there had received the backing of the government. The Conservative victory in the June 1987 election ensured that construction of the PWR would go ahead.

Italy. Both the Socialists and the Radicals moved against nuclear power in the wake of Chernobyl. Funds for experimental reactor projects were suspended. In view of the rising anti-nuclear mood, ENEL, the state utility, decided to abandon siting procedures for two nuclear power plants in Lombardy and Puglia. ENEL did decide, however, to continue with the construction of two 1000 MW PWRs at Montalto di Castro and to begin at an unspecified date the construction of two 950 MW PWRs at Trino Vercellese, where site preparation had begun in 1986. The future of these nuclear power stations depends on the formation of a government committed to a nuclear future.

Netherlands. The pro-nuclear Centre-Right coalition under Ruud Lubbers made the first political U-turn on nuclear power in the aftermath of Chernobyl. It had gained parliamentary approval for construction of two 1000 MW stations in 1985. However, a mere fourteen days before the general election in May 1986 it decided to freeze all nuclear construction plans until more information on the accident became available. As part of the evaluation process, it invited a team from the IAEA to assess the safety of the nuclear plants at Borssele (452 MWe PWR) and Dodewaard (55 MWe PWR).

Power station lead times. Uncertainty in these countries may lead to delays in decision-making about the type of future electricity generating capacity. In some countries, where there is sufficient spare capacity in reserve, such decisions can be put back. However, in others, if nuclear power is to be a chosen option, decisions cannot be delayed for long because of the lengthy lead times involved in nuclear plant construction and the high costs that this entails. The average lead time for the 27 nuclear units which were completed in IEA Europe in the period 1980-84 was 11.1 years[14]. In the aftermath of Chernobyl, the environmental, regulatory and safety factors which caused these long lead times in IEA Europe have been reinforced; and indeed the costs increased because of time and additional safety measures. If governments believe that a proportion of nuclear power is vital to a country's security, they may have to provide the additional funds.

A perceived inability to meet demand, say, 5-7 years ahead would probably lead to the construction of plant with the shortest lead times (oil, gas and coal). However, whether a 'non-nuclear' policy was pursued actively or by default, one based on the construction of such plants would itself raise a range of environmental, political and security of supply concerns both within and between countries. The need for new plant could be partially offset by a variety of demand- and supply-side measures including: improvements in the efficiency of electricity use and load management; reduction of spare capacity requirements; upgrading plant; life extension of existing plant; purchasing electricity from industrial autoproducers; and lastly, increasing international trade in electricity.

Electricity trade. Electricity trade is good for European energy security because it increases the diversity of sources of electricity within Europe, freeing certain countries from regional dependence on one particular method of electricity generation. The scope for increasing intra-European trade in electricity is considerable. There are two blocs, the Union for the Co-ordination of Production and Transport of Electricity (UCPTE)[15] and an association of Nordic electricity producers (Nordel)[16], involved in the production and transmission of electricity. However, trade in electricity within these blocs and between them and third parties accounted for less than 10% of their electricity consumption in 1983. The IEA has recognised that expansion of trade within Europe would be beneficial, because it 'would reduce consumption of oil, would reduce costs by optimising systems over a wider area and would improve security of supply'[17]. The future development of electricity trade is likely, however, to be constrained more by public and political attitudes to importing electricity rather than by the ability of utilities to export at competitive prices.

France is the country with the greatest potential for exporting electricity. It has already exported significant quantities to both Italy and the Netherlands. In the latter part of 1986, it had the capacity to export 2000 MW to Britain via the Anglo-French cable which is also designed to accommodate a flow in the opposite direction. The French themselves expect to be exporting 30-50 TWh a year in the 1990s. A 1982 UNIPEDE study estimated that maximum potential electricity exchanges between OECD European countries (Yugoslavia included) would reach 35,950 MW in 1992-3 on the basis of existing and planned interconnections. If, however, there were substantial additions to the grid beyond those expected, the figure could be as high as 52,900 MW[18].

Alternative methods of electricity generation. If future electricity supply is not to come from nuclear power, there are a considerable number of alternatives. Tables 3.28 and 3.29 show that there are many viable options to choose from, but some at present have limited application. The case for renewable forms of energy is not examined here as large-scale use is not possible within the time scale of this study.

Hydro-electric power generates a large proportion of the electricity produced in countries such as Austria, Norway, Sweden, and Switzerland. Most countries have exploited this to its fullest extent. The few major schemes still left undeveloped in Europe have environmental problems attached, so that expansion in demand could not be met by this source.

Limits exist preventing the increased use of oil and gas. According to the European Community's 1995 objectives, oil and gas are only supposed to produce 15% of total electricity generated. If reducing oil dependence is the crux of the security issue, then perhaps this objective should address oil only. This will be especially important as, if oil prices stay low, some European countries may be tempted to burn more oil in electricity generation. There is no need to build new oil-fired power stations because existing dual-fired capacity can be switched to oil, or, as in the UK, oil-fired power stations which at present make up 26% of total generating capacity and are only used for peak load or are mothballed could be switched to base load - as they were during the coal strike in 1985. Table 3.24 shows European oil-firing capacity.

Increased oil and gas burning is also prevented by two Community Directives issued in 1975.[19] Restrictions were introduced to prevent the 'wasteful' use of premium fuels and in order to reduce dependence on oil and gas imports - the most important aim of the 1974 Community energy objectives and of objectives issued since then. However, with the development of highly efficient gas turbines and combined cycle units that are cheap and quick to build this argument may now seem wrong. In addition, gas can be acquired from a reasonably diverse number of sources. Therefore in the interests of security, gas burning should be an option for electricity generation - as is indeed being considered in Sweden as an alternative to nuclear power.

Coal. At present, however, the main alternative to nuclear power is coal. Coal enjoys many advantages over other primary fuels; it is an abundant resource, spread widely throughout the world. European coal self-sufficiency has declined from 86% in 1973 to 70% in 1985 - a level that is likely to be maintained for the rest of the century. This fall in European self-sufficiency is largely offset by expansion of coal production elsewhere in the OECD, e.g. in Australia and the USA, where costs are lower and domestic production has been able to satisfy the internal growth in demand that has taken place as well as exports to Japan and Western Europe. Apart from a limited amount from the lowest-cost mines, European indigenous production can only compete against imports if it is subsidised by national governments, or if imports are restricted by legislation or other forms of government pressure on electricity utilities.

Throughout 1986 the price of imported coal was exceptionally competitive due to the dollar/sterling and dollar/deutschemark exchange rates. But even if a strong dollar returns, exporters in Australia, South Africa and even the US will be able to land coal in Europe at prices below average European costs.

The UK and West Germany are the largest West European domestic coal producers. In both countries coal is linked to electricity generation by a series of subsidies and quotas.

In West Germany the 'Jahrhundertvertrag' specifies the minimum domestic coal take for electricity. This is to be 173 mt for 1986-90, and 187.5 mt for 1991-5, subsidised by a 4.5% charge on all prices to consumers. This permits coal producers to sell 11 mt of domestic coal at a price competitive with the current price of imports and 22 mt at a price competitive with the current price of heavy fuel oil. Coal has dominated electricity production but newer capacity is mainly planned to be nuclear. By 1990 coal electricity generation capacity is due to increase from 43.1 GW to 43.9 GW, and nuclear from 14.8 GW to 22.6 GW. If the plan to increase nuclear power is slowed down, it will not be difficult to cover the gap in capacity from domestic coal - at increased subsidy. New coal-fired plant or retrofitted old plant may mean higher-cost electricity because of increasing concern about the effect of emissions. For example, in 1985 one of the largest utilities, RWE of Essen, announced that in addition to ordinary tariff increases there would be a 5% per annum 'environmental surcharge' to deal with acid rain.

In the UK, there has been an agreement since 1979 between British Coal and the Central Electricity Generating Board covering the volume and price of coal in such a way as to limit the amount of imports. The agreement between the two nationalised industries was last revised in June 1986 in the light of lower oil prices. The terms were as follows: British Coal provides 50 mt at a price that covers its production cost, a further 10 mt at a price competitive with imported coal, and a further 12 mt at a price competitive with heavy fuel oil. The greater part of electricity is generated by coal and is likely to remain so. Even if the CEGB's full construction proposal went ahead, nuclear's share of electricity generated would only amount to 16.5% by 1990.

If additional nuclear capacity is not to be built and/or existing nuclear capacity is phased out before its useful life is ended, then it is possible that the life of old coal-fired capacity may be prolonged. This would satisfy short-term demand but pose greater environmental problems.

European imports. Increased coal use in electricity generation will mean increased coal imports from countries outside Europe. The share of OECD European coal imports in total coal supply is projected to be approximately 35% by 1990 and 39% by 2000. Given that imported coal is expected to be cheaper than domestically produced coal, any increase in coal-fired capacity is likely to increase the level of import dependence. This raises questions about the reliability of the exporters and their capacity to fulfill demands made of them. In 1986 world coal trade across frontiers was growing slowly, but while there is a surplus of supply, prices will not rise rapidly. It is a buyers' market and any problem with a single exporter could soon be overcome.

Tables 3.26 and 3.27 give European steam and coking coal imports. An idea of the level of reliability of exporters can be gauged in the following list.

South Africa exports 25% of its production of 168 mt and has a port capacity of 40 million tonnes per annum at Richards Bay. There are plans to expand this to 80 mt p.a., but with falling coal prices this could be delayed. The problems of relying on South African coal are of a different nature. Early in 1986 South African coal was banned by the French government coal-importing agency and also by the Danish Parliament. In September 1986 the European Community members considered applying a boycott to all South African coal imports, although they were unable to reach a unanimous decision. Moreover, it is possible that political instability and/or labour unrest within South Africa could disrupt exports to Europe.

US coal production in 1985 was 800 million tonnes, of which only 10% was exported. American coal export costs are high, largely due to internal transportation by rail to the coast, although this has been partially overcome by use of river transport and there is increased interest in the use of coal slurry pipelines. In 1985, US port capacity was measured as 180 mt/year of which only 82 mt/year was utilised. There is therefore a large surplus capacity which could meet a surge in export demand. America's reliability is affected by strikes which caused the price to rise in 1984 and also by uncertainty over the level of internal demand. Currency fluctuations also affect the competitiveness of US coal in European markets.

Australia exports 70% of its coal, and produced 127.1 million tonnes in 1985. It overtook the US as the world's largest exporter, largely because of a favourable US/Australian dollar exchange rate. Previous bottlenecks hampering exports have been removed and Australia now has sufficient port and transport capacity to handle any increase in demand. Again, like the US, there are labour problems. In January 1987 unions were warning that there would be a year of conflict in the industry unless their demands were met. Internal transport costs are high because of the large government revenue taken from freight; and sea freight rates favour the Japanese as against the European market.

Polish coal production has largely recovered from the industrial and political unrest of 1980-1 and production had returned to 191.6 million tonnes in 1985. However, total exports dropped from 43.1 mt in 1984 to 36 mt in 1985 (to OECD Europe from 22.7 mt in 1984 to 18.9 mt in 1985). There is less coal available for export as more is needed for the domestic market. The lack of investment in the coal industry has meant that there have been no increases in productivity. In addition, Polish coal is required to meet the shortage in Eastern European energy demand, and exports to the West will probably decline.

Europe thus has a wide choice of major sources of coal and the number will increase as new producers begin to export. Investment already committed in Colombia is expected to lead to an export capability of

15 million tonnes which could rise to 60 mt by the year 2000. Other possibilities include Botswana and Indonesia where coal reserves are large but the necessary infrastructure is unlikely to be developed at present prices.

The main uncertainties surrounding future coal trade lie in the demand and supply prospects for India and China. Production in 1985 was 150 and 847 million tonnes respectively. India is a net importer at present. Both countries have plans to expand coal production in the future to meet an increased demand level by 2000. If they fail to reach their targets their need for imported coal could affect the European market.

Given the surplus of export capacity, European imports are not likely to be affected by problems in a single exporting country. Even if two or three separate problems coincide, as they did in 1982 with political unrest in Poland and industrial troubles in the US and Australia, the effect is likely to be more one of price than of absolute shortage of supply. The expected level of dependence on diverse imports therefore does not involve insecurity.

Environmental problems associated with burning coal are more likely to have a serious effect. Although the scientific details of the 'acid-rain' phenomenon are still not fully understood, it is now generally accepted that emissions of sulphur dioxide (SO_2) and nitrogen oxide (NOx) do cause damage to the environment, not only in the country of emission but probably also in the countries to which these substances can be carried by the wind. The technology to remove these emissions is known and can be costed, but at present it imposes an extra cost on coal-fired power station building. The UK in particular has been criticised by other European countries for refusing to adhere to the 1985 Protocol adopted by the Economic Commission for Europe's Convention on Long Range Transboundary Air Pollution, to cut total emissions of sulphur dioxide by 30% (compared with total emissions in 1980) by 1993. In 1986, however, the UK Government went some way towards recognising a responsibility to reduce pollution of Scandinavian forests and lakes with a decision to fit 3 existing power stations with desulphurisation equipment at a cost of £600m. Many environmentalists and politicians consider that the UK has not gone far enough. Other countries in Europe have certainly done more. West Germany, for example, has been fitting flue gas desulphurisation into all new large power stations since 1974 and has recently started modifying existing stations.

In addition, there is concern about the so-called 'greenhouse effect' in which a build-up of carbon dioxide from burning all fossil fuels is thought to modify the earth's atmosphere in a way which could affect the climate. Further research is required to establish the extent of this danger and the steps which would be necessary to counteract it.

No fuel is without environmental problems of one sort or another, nor can the political acceptability of one fuel over another be separated from the problem. The only way of sidestepping these issues is to ensure a diversified fuel mix in electricity generation (not including oil) and to make sure that the sources of that fuel are also diversified.

Conclusion

Europe's most vulnerable feature is its dependence on imports for a large proportion of its energy, not only of oil but also of gas, coal and, potentially, uranium. In the case of the last three, this vulnerability is mitigated by the number and diversity of possible external sources of supply. In the case of oil, diversification of sources will become increasingly difficult as sources outside the Gulf are progressively depleted, or pre-empted for exports to other regions, or for internal consumption. Nor does the enmity between Iran and the Arabs offer the Europeans any grounds for complacency: indeed it simply exacerbates the instability of the Gulf region.

The European nations therefore have the strongest possible grounds for pursuing concerted energy policies; internally, in order to improve the efficiency of energy use, to open up the internal market, and limit their dependence on imports; externally, in order to deal with both united suppliers and competing buyers, from a position of strength. While much has been achieved, particularly in respect of internal efficiency and switching out of oil, a common external policy has so far eluded the European nations. Even those that are members of the European Community find it difficult to reconcile differing economic philosophies or to pursue either coherent and effective research and development programmes for the long run, or coherent stock-holding policies for emergencies. Externally, the members of the Community have repeatedly failed to adopt effective common responses to events that affect oil supplies from the Gulf. It is hardly surprising therefore that the US Administration tends to go its own way, without much regard for European susceptibilities, fatal though these divisions may prove to be for the energy security of the OECD.

Given increasing public opposition to nuclear power, because of fears over safety, and to coal on environmental grounds, natural gas development presents the most promising resource from an energy security point of view, particularly where it can be produced from within the borders of Europe.

Appendix A by Prof. A. Kemp, Department of Economics, Aberdeen University.

Summary of the Fiscal Systems Applied to Petroleum Exploitation in the UK and Norway in the Context of Energy Security.

In a petroleum producing province the fiscal and regulatory regimes applied to the exploitation of the resource can influence the level of energy security in various ways. The majority of schemes conventionally employed can affect the pace of exploration, development and production of the resource. Incremental investments in existing fields can be influenced, as can the timing of field abandonment. Conventional fiscal devices create a wedge between pre-tax and post-tax returns. The extent to which this happens is a function both of the level and structure of the fiscal system. Governments can legitimately aim to extract the economic rents from petroleum exploitation. Conventional fiscal devices are not well-directed at this target and so the possibilities of distortions emerging are produced.

In the UK the fiscal system applied to new exploration and development activities in the Central and Northern North Sea incorporates the special Petroleum Revenue Tax and normal company corporation tax. Royalties are abolished for new fields. The system is thus profit-related. The difference between pre-tax and post-tax discounted returns is fairly modest and with the introduction of the new cross-field allowance in the 1987 Finance Act this difference is further reduced, especially on small fields. Only on larger fields where a considerable amount of PRT is payable is the difference between pre-tax and post-tax returns significant. The main factor retarding the pace of new field developments is the fall in oil prices and the uncertainties regarding future price levels. Progress in reducing new field development costs will make a significant contribution to accelerating the pace of new field development. In this respect the allowance of general R and D costs as a deduction for PRT should make a useful contribution.

Energy security is also facilitated by ensuring that maximum economic recovery is obtained from the fields already in production. This means that incremental investments such as satellite projects or enhanced recovery schemes should not be inhibited. For PRT purposes no 'uplift' is available on investment expenditures taking place after field payback has been achieved. Royalties are payable on the extra production and so the rate of relief for the expenditure is considerably less than the marginal rate of tax payable on the extra revenues. The difference between pre-tax and post-tax returns is thus noticeable and there is a danger that some incremental projects could be inhibited. There is a case for introducing a fiscal incentive here either in the form of an extra PRT allowance on post-payback expenditures or in the form of a lower rate of tax on incremental revenues by devices such as royalty reliefs.

Energy security can be enhanced to a modest degree by ensuring that the premature abandonment of fields does not take place. The royalty is not based on profits (though relief for some relevant expenditures is allowed) and so the possibilities of premature abandonment do exist. The government does have the discretionary ability to remit royalties to ensure that such distortions do not arise. There is uncertainty surrounding the circumstances of the introduction of such reliefs and government guidelines regarding their introduction, preferably in the form of a formula, would represent an improvement to the efficiency of the system and ensure that overall field recovery was optimised.

In the Southern North Sea the fiscal system applied to new fields still incorporates a royalty at 12½% and a smaller volume allowance for PRT. The difference between pre-tax and post-tax returns is thus greater than in Central and Northern waters. The lower development costs in this part of the UKCS are used to justify the higher tax levels. Activity levels in the Southern sector have not fallen by as much as in Northern waters in 1986 and new field developments are still proceeding at a respectable pace. This is consistent with the view that the fiscal system is not deterring new developments.

On the other hand, there is evidence that new developments are taking place in more difficult and high-cost reservoirs. Development costs are higher because the reservoirs have lower permeability and thus entail extra drilling costs and sometimes additional platforms. The indications are that increasingly new developments will be at higher unit cost. The chances of the fiscal system inhibiting developments are thus likely to increase. In these circumstances, and in the absence of significant increases in gas prices, fiscal reliefs may well become necessary. In that event royalty reliefs would represent the most obvious way to improve the efficiency of the system by making it more profit-related. Because royalties are deductible for both PRT and corporation tax the abolition of royalties would to a considerable extent be recouped by these taxes.

In Norway there is also a distinction between 'old' and 'new' fields for fiscal purposes. On 'old' fields there is a royalty, income tax and Special Tax. Expenditures on incremental projects are not eligible for the Special Allowance for Special Tax nor the new production allowance, and royalty is still payable on incremental production. The acceleration in availability of depreciation provisions may not compensate for the other adverse factors noted above. It is quite possible that the fiscal system can inhibit incremental projects on 'old' fields. Acceleration of relief for the necessary investment and/or royalty reliefs on the incremental revenues would represent efficient forms of relief to facilitate such projects.

The same situation as exists in the UK prevails in Norway with regard to the premature abandonment of fields. Royalty reliefs can ensure that overall recovery is optimised.

Regarding the pace of new field development, the abolition of royalties, the acceleration of the availability of depreciation provisions and the abolition of carried interest on the state's participation interest have considerably improved incentives compared to the old scheme. Discounted tax takes on a number of new field situations are now tolerable to investors. It remains the case, however, that at development costs of $6 per barrel and above tax takes can become sufficiently high to cause disincentives. Some high-cost fields will be uneconomic on a pre-tax basis, but if a further stimulus to development were required fiscal concessions could provide such an impetus.

Appendix B

European Community, Venice Declaration, 13 June, 1980

1. The heads of state and government and ministers of foreign affairs held a comprehensive exchange of views on all aspects of the present situation in the Middle East, including the state of negotiations resulting from the agreements signed between Egypt and Israel in March 1979. They agreed that growing tensions affecting this region constitute a serious danger and render a comprehensive solution to the Israeli-Arab conflict more necessary and pressing than ever.

2. The nine member states of the European Community consider that the traditional ties and common interests which link Europe to the Middle East oblige them to play a special role and now require them to work in a more concrete way towards peace.

3. In this regard, the nine countries of the Community base themselves on (UN) Security Council resolutions 242 and 338 and the positions which they have expressed on several occasions, notably in their declarations of 29 June 1977, 19 September 1978, 26 March and 18 June 1979, as well as in the speech made on their behalf on 25 September 1979 by the Irish Minister of Foreign Affairs at the 34th UN General Assembly.

4. On the bases thus set out, the time has come to promote the recognition and implementation of the two principles universally accepted by the international community: the right to existence and to security of all the states in the region, including Israel, and justice for all the peoples, which implies the recognition of the legitimate rights of the Palestinian people.

5. All of the countries in the area are entitled to live in peace within secure, recognized and guaranteed borders. The necessary guarantees for a peace settlement should be provided by the UN by a decision of the Security Council and, if necessary, on the basis of other mutually agreed procedures. The nine declare that they are prepared to participate within the framework of a comprehensive settlement in a system of concrete and binding international guarantees, including (guarantees) on the ground.

6. A just solution must finally be found to the Palestinian problem, which is not simply one of refugees. The Palestinian people, which is conscious of existing as such, must be placed in a position, by an appropriate process defined within the framework of the comprehensive peace settlement, to exercise fully its right to self-determination.

7. The achievement of these objectives requires the involvement and support of all the parties concerned in the peace settlement which the nine are endeavouring to promote in keeping with the principles formulated in the declaration referred to above. These principles apply to all the parties concerned, and thus to the Palestinian people, and to the PLO, which will have to be associated with the negotiations.

8. The nine recognize the special importance of the role played by the question of Jerusalem for all the parties concerned. The nine stress that they will not accept any unilateral initiative designed to change the status of Jerusalem and that any agreement on the city's status should guarantee freedom of access for everyone to the holy places.

9. The nine stress the need for Israel to put an end to the territorial occupation which it has maintained since the conflict of 1967, as it has done for part of Sinai. They are deeply convinced that the Israeli settlements constitute a serious obstacle to the peace process in the Middle East. The nine consider that these settlements, as well as modifications in population and property in the occupied Arab territories, are illegal under international law.

10. Concerned as they are to put an end to violence, the nine consider that only the renunciation of force or the threatened use of force by all the parties can create a climate of confidence in the area, and constitute a basic element for a comprehensive settlement of the conflict in the Middle East.

11. The nine have decided to make the necessary contacts with all the parties concerned. The objective of these contacts would be to ascertain the position of the various parties with respect to the principles set out

in this declaration and in the light of the results of this consultation process to determine the form which such an initiative on their part could take.

Notes

[1] Council resolution of 16 September 1986 concerning new Community energy policy objectives for 1995 and convergence of the policies of Member States (86/C 241/01). Published in the Official Journal of the European Communities, Vol. 29, 25 September 1986, C 241/3.

[2] EC, Energie 2000, Paris: Economica, 1986.

[3] Council resolution of 16 September 1986, op.cit.

[4] 'How much oil will the European Community need in 1990 if oil prices stay low?', Energy in Europe, No. 5, September 1986, pp.10-15.

[5] Operating costs of the various North Sea fields depend largely on their size; generally, the larger the size of the field the lower its operating costs. The UK Department of Energy gives figures for the average costs of production in the UKCS in its 1986 Brown Book. The overall average cost is \$9 per barrel in 1985 dollars for fields already in production; for fields which started production before 1980 the average cost of production is \$8, and for those which started in 1980-85 the average cost is \$12. These costs include taxes, and assume a real return capital of 10% (Development of the Oil and Gas Resources of the United Kingdom 1986, The Brown Book, Department of Energy, London: HMSO, 1986, pp.58-9). Average costs are of the same order in the Norwegian sector. These are the costs which were relevant to investment decisions affecting fields which came on stream up to the end of 1985.

[6] The Times, 25 November 1986, p.4.

[7] Figures taken from Wood MacKenzie's North Sea Service (personal communication with Gareth Davies, Oil Analyst, Wood MacKenzie).

[8] Financial Times, 13 March 1986, p.11.

[9] Future Oil and Gas Prospects - 1986 Update, Grampian Regional Council, Department of Physical Planning, June 1986.

[10] Brown Book, op. cit., pp.7 and 18.

[11] A number of details remain to be settled in the final framework of the Troll (Sleipner) Phase 1 agreement. The plateau volume of 18 BCM assumes that Gaz de France does not take up its option for an additional 2 BCM per year.

[12] Although the wording of the communiqué referred to 'avoiding undue dependence upon' a single source of supply, this was immediately interpreted as referring to dependence for more than one third of supplies on the USSR. IEA, Energy Policies and Programmes of the IEA Countries, 1983 Review. Paris: OECD/IEA, 1984, Appendix A, Annex 1, pp.72-3.

[13] IEA, Natural Gas Prospects, Paris: 1986, pp.112-3. This also has figures on the expansion of maximum daily working capacity.

[14] Electricity in IEA Countries - Issues and Outlook, OECD/IEA, Paris: OECD/IEA,1985, p.77. Lead time is defined here as the length of time between the date when the order for a unit was placed and the date when the unit was commissioned.

[15] UCPTE comprises the utilities of Austria, Belgium, France, Germany, Italy, Luxembourg, the Netherlands and Switzerland, with four associated countries - Greece, Portugal, Spain and Yugoslavia.

[16] Nordel comprises the utilities of Denmark, Finland, Iceland, Norway and Sweden.

[17] Electricity in IEA Countries - Issues and Outlook, op. cit., p.101.

[18] Ibid., pp.87-93.

[19] Council Directive 13 February 1975 on the restriction of the use of natural gas in power stations. Council Directive 14 April 1975 concerning the restriction of use of petroleum products in power stations. Official Journal of the European Communities. 9 July 1975, Vol. 18 No. L178, pp.24-6.

Table 3.1 Aims and achievements in EC energy objectives

Aims in 1974	Achieved in 1980	Achieved in 1985
Imports in energy mix down to 40-50%	Imports made up 54%	Imports made up 43%
Electricity to make up 35% of total energy	Electricity made up 13%	
Coal production 180 mtoe with diverse imports	Coal production 183 mtoe imports 47 mtoe 15% S.Africa 16% Poland 34% USA 10% Australia	Coal production 138 mtoe imports 55 mtoe 20% S.Africa 15% Poland 31% USA 16% Australia
Gas production 175-225 mtoe Imports 95-115 mtoe	Gas production 129 mtoe imports 41 mtoe 19% USSR 47% Netherlands 28% Norway 5% Algeria	Gas production 144 mtoe imports 113 mtoe 26% USSR 33% Netherlands 23% Norway 18% Algeria
Oil production 18 mtoe imports 420-540 mtoe	Oil production 91 mtoe imports 438 mtoe	Oil production 148 mtoe imports 288 mtoe
Aims in 1980		**Achieved in 1985**
Oil 40% of TPER		Oil 44% of TPER
70-75% of electricity generated from solids + nuclear		solids + nuclear = 65% of electricity generation

Table 3.2 The energy situation in the EC in 1985

Total primary energy consumption	944.2 mtoe
oil	415.5
gas	181.2
nuclear	116.4
coal	218.2
electricity demand	1,343.4 Twh
Domestic production	
solid fuel	137.9 mtoe
oil	147.6
gas	125.7
nuclear	116.4
hydro	12.1
Net imports	
coal	55.3 mtoe
oil	287.8
gas	59.4
Net imports as % of primary energy consumption	
coal	25.3%
oil	65.6
gas	32.8
Electricity generation	
hydro	140.2 Twh
nuclear	429.5
thermal	778.4
Thermal input as % of total thermal generation	
hard coal	54%
lignite	15.8
petroleum products	18.4
gas	11.8

Table 3.3 The percentage of total oil imports taken from the Gulf* and from the Gulf + other Arab states in 1985

	Gulf states	Gulf + other Arab states
France	31	36
Germany	10	31
Italy	33	56
UK	19	28
EC-10	25	40

* The Gulf states are Iran, Iraq, Kuwait, Qatar, Saudi Arabia, the UAE and Oman.

Source: OECD, Oil and Gas Statistics, 4th Quarter 1985.

Table 3.4 Oil production in the UK and Norway (mbd)

	1975	1976	1977	1978	1979	1980	1981	1982	1983	1984	1985	1986
UK	0.03	0.24	0.77	1.10	1.60	1.65	1.84	2.13	2.36	2.58	2.64	2.67
Norway	0.19	0.28	0.28	0.35	0.39	0.53	0.51	0.53	0.66	0.76	0.84	0.91

Source: BP Statistical Review of World Energy, June 1984-7.

Table 3.5 Assessed product values and spot crude prices (US $/barrel)

	Sept. 1985	Jan. 1986	Sept. 1986	Jan. 1987
Dubai				
Spot Price	26.41	22.77	13.20	17.15
Product	28.58	23.86	14.50	18.41
Arabian Light				
Spot Price	27.58	20.95	N/A	N/A
Product	28.02	23.39	14.16	18.12
Brent				
Spot Price	27.60	21.89	13.40	18.50
Product	30.27	25.56	15.73	20.05

Product values are for Northwest Europe and are calculated on the basis of yields of a catalytic cracking refinery in the area.

Source: IEA, Oil Market Report.

Table 3.6 OECD Europe - TPER, oil requirements and net oil imports (in million tonnes of oil equivalent - mtoe)

	1970	1973	1978	1980	1984
(A) TPER	1,022.72	1,181.16	1,226.24	1,237.03	1,209.99
(B) Oil requirements	592.91	707.27	679.04	644.00	551.53
(C) Net oil imports	624.14	737.25	616.33	564.38	384.22
B as a % of A	58.0	59.9	55.4	52.1	45.6
C as a % of A	61.0	62.4	50.3	45.6	31.8

Source: OECD/IEA, Energy Balances of OECD Countries 1983/1984, Paris: 1986.

Table 3.7 <u>EC-12 - TPER, oil requirements and net oil imports</u> (mtoe)

	1970	1973	1978	1980	1984
(A) TPER	887.94	1,018.31	1,047.35	1,052.59	1,017.38
(B) Oil requirements	515.59	616.89	589.10	557.75	479.20
(C) Net oil imports	547.41	653.60	546.57	500.54	350.25
B as a % of A	58.1	60.6	56.2	53.0	47.1
C as a % of A	61.6	64.2	52.2	47.6	34.4

Source: *Ibid.*

Table 3.8 <u>IEA projected TPER, oil requirements, and net oil imports for IEA Europe</u> (mtoe)

	1990	1995	2000
(A) TPER	1,083	1,139	1,209
(B) Oil requirements	457	447	444
(C) Net oil imports	302.2	317.7	343.8
B as a % of A	42.2	39.2	36.7
C as a % of A	27.9	27.9	28.4

Source: *Energy Policies and Programmes of IEA Countries*, *op. cit.*

Table 3.9 <u>EC projected TPER, oil requirements, and net oil imports for EC-10</u> (mtoe)

	1990(i)	2000(i)	1990(ii) (oil at $15/barrel)
(A) TPER	1,034	1,136	1,005-1,040
(B) Oil requirements	441	439	438- 466
(C) Net oil imports	330	331	344- 373
B as a % of A	42.6	38.6	44.2
C as a % of A	31.9	29.1	35.1

Source:

(i) *Energie 2000*, *op. cit.*

(ii) 'How much oil will the European Community need in 1990 if oil prices stay low?', *Energy in Europe*, No. 5, September 1986.

Table 3.10 UKCS oil production profiles (mbd)

	IEA(i)	Wood MacKenzie(ii)		James Capel(iii)	
		$15	$23	$10	$23
1988		2.27	2.27	2.3	2.3
1990	2.0	1.80	1.87	1.7	1.9
1992		1.35	1.61	1.0	1.7
1994		0.91	1.50	0.7	1.3
1996		0.62	1.25	0.4	0.9
1998		0.41	1.00	0.3	0.6
2000	1.6	0.24	0.73	0.2	0.4

Sources:

(i) OECD/IEA, Energy Policies and Programmes of IEA Countries - 1985 Review, Paris: OECD/IEA, 1986, p.73. A conversion factor of 49.8 has been used to convert from mtoe to mbd.

(ii) Figures taken from Wood MacKenzies's North Sea Service (personal communication with Alan Sinclair, Oil Analyst, Wood MacKenzie). Prices are assumed to be constant until 1989, rising by 5% per annum thereafter. An exchange rate of £1 = $1.50 is assumed.

(iii) A North Sea Shutdown? - Never!, James Capel Research, 4 February 1986. Prices are assumed to be constant until the end of 1987, rising by 4% per annum until the end of 1990, and then by 5% per annum thereafter. An exchange rate of £1=$1.35 is assumed in the $23 case and one of £1 = $1.20 in the $10 case. In both cases, costs are inflated at 5% per annum from the beginning of 1987.

Table 3.11 Norway: oil production profiles (mbd)

	IEA(i)	Wood MacKenzie(ii)	
		$15	$23
1988		0.96	1.1
1990	1.1	1.20	1.25
1992		1.25	1.26
1994		1.03	1.12
1996		0.70	0.90
1998		0.53	0.82
2000	0.4	0.35	0.66

Sources: (i) and (ii) as for Table 3.10.
Prices are assumed to be constant until 1989, rising by 5% p.a. thereafter. An exchange rate of 7.4 Kroner = $1 is assumed.

Table 3.12 World proved reserves of oil (at end 1986) and reserves/production (R/P) ratios (based on 1986 production levels)

	Thousand million barrels	Share of total(%)	R/P Ratio
Middle East	402.0	57.3	85.5
- Saudi Arabia	166.6	23.7	90.3
Kuwait	91.9	13.1	Over 100 years
Iran	48.8	6.9	71.1
Iraq	47.1	6.7	74.7
Abu Dhabi	31.0	4.4	80.6
OECD Europe	18.2	2.6	12.2
- UK	5.3	0.3	5.5
Norway	10.5	1.5	31.2
North America	40.4	5.7	9.0
- USA	32.5	4.6	8.5
Canada	7.9	1.1	12.3
Others			
- USSR	59.0	8.4	13.1
Mexico	54.7	7.8	56.3
Venezuela	25.0	3.6	38.7
Libya	21.3	3.0	55.1
China	18.4	2.6	18.5
Nigeria	16.0	2.3	30.2
Total World	703.1	100	32.5
of which OPEC	477.7	67.9	68.7

Note: Proved reserves are 'those quantities which geological and engineering information indicate with reasonable certainty can be recovered in the future from known reservoirs under existing economic and operating conditions'.

Source: BP Statistical Review of World Energy, June 1987, p.2.

Table 3.13 <u>OECD Europe's oil imports by source in 1986</u>

	(million tonnes)	%
Middle East(a)	174.5	40.0
North Africa(b)	88.7	20.4
USSR	64.3	14.8
West Africa(c)	52.7	12.1
Latin America(d)	30.9	7.1
Eastern Europe	13.2	3.1
Others	11.1	2.5
Total Imports	435.4	100

Notes:

(a) Arabian Peninsula, Iran, Iraq, Syria.

(b) Territories on the north coast of Africa from Egypt to Western Sahara.

(c) Territories on the west coast of Africa from Mauritania to Angola, including Cape Verde Islands.

(d) Mexico, Caribbean (including Puerto Rico but excluding Cuba), Central and South America.

Source: <u>BP Statistical Review of World Energy</u>, June 1987, p.18.

Table 3.14 West European gas reserves[(a)]

	Reserves at 1/1/86 (billion cubic metres)	R/P Ratio[(b)] (years)
Western Europe	5,409	27
Netherlands	1,855	23
Norway	2,228	81
United Kingdom	648	13
Italy	255	18
Federal Republic of Germany	192	11

(a) countries in OECD Europe with more than 100 BCM of reserves.

(b) reserves to production ratio = reserves at 1 January 1986 divided by production in 1985.

Source: Cedigaz, Le Gaz Naturel Dans Le Monde en 1985, Institut Français de Pétrole, 1986, Tables 2 and 3, pp.5-9.

Table 3.15 West European gas demand projections (billion cubic metres)

	1985	1990	2000
IEA (OECD Europe)	(actual)		
high demand/low oil price	(239)	224	248
low demand/high oil price	(239)	244	280
EC (European 12)	(231)	213	220

Sources: IEA, Natural Gas Prospects, Paris: IEA/OECD, 1986, p.59.
Energie 2000, Brussels: 1986, p.13.

Table 3.16 Western Europe: possible LNG import projects*

Country	Under consideration since	1986 status	Likely lead time (years)	Likely annual volume
Nigeria	1964	Government changes in the country have led to uncertainty. New consortium of importers (Shell/AGIP/ELF) set up in late 1985.	7–10	4.2 BCM (scaled down down from 16 BCM)
Cameroon	1980/1	Uncertain	5	4–5 BCM
Canada:				
Arctic Pilot(a)	1980	Suspended	5–7	2–4 BCM
King Christian	1982	Suspended	5–7	5 BCM
Qatar(b)	1980/81	Under consideration, partners expected to have lined up customers by 1986.	5–7	8.5 BCM but potential is enormous
Trinidad(c)	1982	?	?	less than 5 BCM

(a) To Western Europe; project for LNG to Nova Scotia and/or Quebec since early 1970s.

(b) LNG project with Japan may take precedence, although reserves are ample for trade with both markets.

(c) Trade with US is likely to take precedence; would preclude trade with Western Europe.

* In August 1986, none of these projects had a firm starting date.

Table 3.17 West European dependence on natural gas supplies by source, 1985 (billion cubic metres)

	Domestic production	Netherlands	USSR	Norway	Algeria	Libya	Federal Republic of Germany	Denmark	Domestic Consumption
Federal Republic of Germany	17.21	25.40	12.44	5.97				0.35	60.02
Netherlands	80.64			1.77					37.35
Italy	14.25	5.03	5.96		8.40	0.28			33.92
France	5.35	8.30	6.77	2.67	7.86				30.95
Belgium & Luxembourg		5.43		1.73	2.40				9.56
Austria	1.16		4.15						5.31
Switzerland		0.90					1.35		2.25
Spain	0.27				1.67	0.76			2.70
UK	42.95			13.55					56.50
Finland			0.98						0.98
Sweden								0.08	0.08
Yugoslavia	2.33		3.58						5.91

Source: Cedigaz, Le Gaz Naturel Dans Le Monde en 1985, Institut Français de Pétrole, 1986, Tables 16 and 17, pp.46-7.

Table 3.18 Electricity generation 1975-84 in OECD Europe

	1975	1984	
Total final energy consumption	844.7	874.5	mtoe
Total final electricity consumption	103	138.8	mtoe
Total generating capacity	369.6	490.3	GW
Total electricity production	1419	1905	TWh
Fuel mix in electricity generation %			
oil	23.3	12.4	
nuclear	7.8	25.6	
coal	31.6	31.7	
hydro	26.6	24	
gas	10.6	6.3	

Table 3.19 Electricity demand in OECD Europe (TWh)

1985	1990	2000
1,989	2,196-2,305	2,676-3,098

Source: Electricity and Nuclear Energy in OECD Countries, OECD/IEA, internal document, 7 October 1986, p.10.

Table 3.20 Electricity demand in EC-10 (TWh)

1985	1990	1995
1,322-1,336	1,482-1,556	1,642-1,785

Source: Programmes and Prospects for the Electricity Sector, (1984-1990 and 1990-1995), UNIPEDE, March 1986, p.8.

Table 3.21 European generating capacity by fuel (GW)

	Coal	Oil	Gas	Nuclear	Hydro/Geo	Total
end 1984 operating						
	145	86.4	40.9	76.8	137.7	488.3
Planned	32	0.5	2.3	45.7	23.5	104.9
Decomm.	-23.3	-8.7	-3.6	-0.4	-0.3	-36.6
end 1990 operating						
	154.7	78.1	39.6	122.1	160.9	556.6
Planned	59.2	3	5.6	55.9	36.1	159.9
Decomm	-22	-18.6	-13.4	-9.9	-1.9	-65.8
end 2000 operating						
	192	64.7	31.8	173.5	195.5	658.9

Source: OECD/IEA, Coal Information 1986, Paris: OECD/IEA, 1986, p.255.

Table 3.22 Nuclear capacity and units under construction in OECD Europe (30 November 1985)

	Capacity (GW)	Units
France	19.7	16
Germany	5.2	5
Italy	2.0	3
Spain	1.9	2
UK	2.5	4
Total	31.3	30

Source: World Nuclear Industry Handbook 1987, Nuclear Engineering International, 1986, pp.135-49. (The table takes account of the connection to the grid of Brokdorf in Germany and Cattenom 1 in France).

Table 3.23 Planned nuclear capacity and units in OECD Europe (28 April 1986)

	Capacity (GW)	Units
Belgium	1.4	1
Finland	*	2
France	11	8
Germany	6.4	5
Italy	9.5	10
Netherlands	*	2
Switzerland	2.1	2
Turkey	2.8	3
UK	2.5	2

* (Capacity not yet known; the Dutch Parliament had, however, given approval for the construction of two 1000 MW PWRs in 1985)

N.B. What constitutes 'planned nuclear capacity' is open to wide interpretation depending both on the country concerned and the source of information.

Source: Ibid.

Table 3.24 Multi-firing capacity in selected European countries 1985 (GW)

	coal/oil	oil/gas	coal/oil/gas	Total installed capacity
Belgium	1.5	0.0	3.4	12.3
Denmark	6.4	0.0	0.0	8.0
France	8.8	0.0	1.4	84.6
Germany	0.1	0.0	11.9	89.8
Italy	0.2	9.4	6.1	54.0
Netherlands	0.0	7.9	2.2	15.0
UK	2.0	0.0	0.0	66.9

Source: IEA Coal Research estimates. UNIPEDE, *op.cit.*, Appendix 2.

Table 3.25 Coal in Europe 1985 (mt)

	Production	Net imports	Electricity use
France	16.1	18	15.6
Germany	119.3	-3.2	77.3
Italy	0.7	19.8	9.7
Spain	19.7	7.1	18.6
UK	76.5	8.8	62.9

Source: Coal Information 1986, op. cit. See tables 5,6, and 13 in the relevant country sections.

Table 3.26 1985 Steam coal imports (thousand tonnes)

	France	Italy	Spain	Germany	UK	Total Europe*
South Africa	4,698	6,724	2,243	3,196	723	24,619
USA	558	3,600	855	1,072	498	16,439
Australia	718	180	408	720	2,469	10,972
Poland	818	1,100	388	2,709	258	13,879

Table 3.27 1985 Coking coal imports (thousand tonnes)

	France	Italy	Spain	Germany	UK	Total Europe*
South Africa	-----	----	----	------	----	57
USA	3,314	5,250	2,401	26	2,647	22,627
Australia	1,949	2,021	996	4	2,921	9,712
Poland	185	914	637	82	1,129	4,995

* The countries named are by no means the only importers in Europe, as the total OECD Europe figures show. Other major importers include Belgium, Denmark, and the Netherlands.

Source: Ibid. See Table 7 in the relevant country sections.

Table 3.28 Projected electricity generating capacity by fuel and by country (GWe)

	Coal		Oil		Gas		Nuclear		Hydro	
	1984	2000	1984	2000	1984	2000	1984	2000	1984	2000
Austria	3.7	5.8	0.3	0.2	0.8	0.8	0	0	10	15
Belgium	5.1	5	0.6	0.5	1.8	1.7	3.5	6.7	1.3	1.3
Denmark	6.2	6.8	1.8	1.2	0	0	0	0	0	0
Finland	3.9	6.5	2.2	1.3	0.4	0.7	2.3	3.6	2.5	2.6
France	18.2	20.8	10.9	5.4	1.2	0.6	32.9	78	21.4	26
Germany	43.1	46.9	12.7	6.9	12.6	8.4	14.8	24.3	6.6	6
Italy	8.2	23.3	18	14.3	8.6	8	1.3	12.1	17.8	20.8
Netherlands	2.3	4	0.2	0.1	12	6.7	0.5	4.1	0	0
Norway	0	0	0.2	0.2	0	0	0	0	22.8	30.7
Spain	9.3	14.3	7.2	1.9	1.9	1.5	4.7	7.5	13.2	20.4
Sweden	0.5	0.8	6.8	5.4	0	0	7.4	9	15.4	16.5
Switzerland	0	0	0.7	1.2	0	0	2.9	3.8	11.5	12
UK	38.6	35.4	17.5	20.3	0	0	6.6	17.6	4.2	4.2

Table 3.29 Fuel mix in electricity production (%)

	Coal		Oil		Gas		Nuclear		Hydro	
	1984	2000	1984	2000	1984	2000	1984	2000	1984	2000
Austria	11	14	7	4	12	5	0	0	70	77
Belgium	34	35	8	5	5	1	51	58	2	5
Denmark	96	87	4	4	0	0	0	0	0	9
Finland	25	27	3	1	2	1	41	49	29	22
France	16	6	3	1	1	1	59	79	21	14
Germany	61	52	2	2	8	7	23	34	5	4
Italy	15	50	41	10	14	6	4	16	26	18
Netherlands	27	34	5	6	62	29	6	32	0	0
Norway	0	0	0	0	0	0	0	0	100	100
Spain	42	40	10	2	2	1	19	31	28	25
Sweden	2	4	2	1	0	0	41	44	55	51
Switzerland	1	2	1	1	1	1	36	42	62	53
U.K.	45	56	32	3	1	0	19	39	2	3

4 US Energy Security to 2000

CHARLES K. EBINGER

4 US Energy Security to 2000

When historians reflect on the latter half of the twentieth century, three years - 1973, 1979 and 1986 - will be seen as landmarks that transformed the world economic and political system. While the significance of the first two dates is obvious, in 1986 the United States and much of the rest of the industrialized world forgot the energy lessons of the 1970s. With gasoline and home heating fuel prices at the lower levels in thirteen years and with an Administration addicted to the wisdom of the marketplace, consumers and their governments have been lulled into complacency. Likewise, in 1986, the Chernobyl nuclear power accident in the Soviet Union once again raised doubts about the further expansion of this vital energy source.

This cavalier attitude has begun to unravel the efforts of three Presidents - Nixon, Ford and Carter - to ensure the nation's long-term energy security. The goal of the now defunct Synthetic Fuels Corporation to produce 2 million barrels a day (mbd) of alternative fuels by 1990 is only a distant memory. The solar industry is reeling with the loss of its federal and state tax credits. Conservation credits have expired and General Motors and Ford have led the charge to roll back auto fuel efficiency standards. The President and the Congress have recently enacted a new law rescinding the 55 mile per hour speed limit on rural interstate highways. Raising the speed limit to 65 miles per hour could, according to auto industry studies, increase consumption by 5-8%.

In the energy debates of the 1970s, there was almost no dissenting voice to the proposition that rising levels of US oil import dependence were a threat to national security and economic prosperity. Rather, as William Fisher of the University of Texas reminded a Senate hearing, debate focused on the 'means to curb and reduce levels of imports'.[1] Today the nature of the national security debate is fundamentally different and centers not on whether imports will rise and domestic oil production will fall but rather whether such developments pose a threat grave enough to merit government intervention.[2]

Those who argue that market forces will solve the problem do a grave disservice to the nature of the national security threat posed to the country as oil import volumes continue to soar. As Dr James Schlesinger, a CSIS Counselor, has recently warned:[3]

> The same falling oil price that provides consumer benefits and provides a macroeconomic stimulus while easing inflation and interest rates also implies serious problems for domestic oil supply and national security .... We are today sowing the seeds of the next energy crisis.

The events of 1986 have set the United States back on the path toward reliance on imported crude oil and petroleum products and away from further development of its own resources. If the US remains on this path, the question is not whether it will have another energy crisis. The question is simply when it will occur.

Consider these developments, all of which threaten the energy security of the nation:

- In 1986, the US suffered the largest annual oil production decline in its history - nearly 800,000 b.d. When final figures are in later in April, this figure may even hit 1.1 - 1.2 mbd.[4]. The reason for this is that while the Energy Information Administration states that oil production stabilized in the last quarter of 1986, producers and service contractors dispute this view and argue that production continued to fall. In 1987, oil production may fall by another 500,000 to 600,000 bd if oil prices hover in the $14-20/b range.

- US oil imports in 1986 (6 mbd) were up nearly 1 mbd from 1985 levels.

- In the first week of 1987, net oil import dependence was 39.4%, the same level prevailing at the time of the 1973 OAPEC oil embargo.

- The oil service sector has been devastated. From a high of nearly 4000 rigs in July 1981, the oil rig count plummeted to just below 700 in July 1986 before rebounding to 964 at year's end. As the US Government conducted its high-level inter-agency assessment: Energy Security: A Report to the President of the United States[5], on the impact of the collapse of the oil price on US national security, scores of mud companies, helicopter firms, drill bit operators, and pipeline manufacturing concerns have, in the words of Bennett Johnston, Chairman of the Senate Energy and National Resources Committee, been 'dismantled bit by bit and piece by piece'.[6]

- In response to the collapse in oil prices, seismic activity in 1986 was down nearly 50% from 1985 levels and today approaches only about one-third the level of the early 1980s.

- During 1986, reserve additions fell by nearly 1.5 billion barrels, simply as a result of the fall-off in drilling.

- The oil price collapse has led to a plummeting in graduate enrollments in technical disciplines vital for the future of the US petroleum industry.

- Based on oil prices between $14 and $20/b over the next several years, the US may be importing nearly 50% of its oil needs before the next President is inaugurated. In volumetric terms, by 1990, the US may be importing 8-9 mbd; by 1995 oil imports may reach 9-11 mbd accounting for 60-70% of domestic consumption. Most of this oil will increasingly come from the Persian Gulf which will pose major challenges for US foreign policy.

- Even at today's prices of $18/b, each 1 mbd of crude oil or petroleum product import dependence adds $6.5 billion to the nation's oil import bill. If oil imports rise to 9 mbd by 1990 and oil prices escalate to $22/b the nation's oil import bill would soar to $73 billion.

- Although oil output from Alaska rose slightly in 1986, by 1988 the supergiant Prudhoe Bay field will peak. If oil prices remain less than $20/b until 1990, thus constraining the development of new Alaskan capacity, US production in Alaska could fall by 400,000 bd.

While the upstream segment of the oil market has received the predominant attention as a national security issue, the problems confronting the US refinery industry are no less perilous. Indeed, unless this fact is recognized, clearly it is possible that national energy policies may be adopted to deal with upstream problems that may exacerbate problems in the downstream market. For example, were an oil import fee to be enacted in isolation, the impact of such action would be to increase costs to US refiners. Since oil refiners in other nations would not be covered by the fee, they would incur lower feedstock costs and thus would be in a position to gain market share in the US at the expense of domestic refiners.

With some US refiners already at a competitive disadvantage vis-à-vis their foreign competition owing to higher environmental costs in the US, less favorable taxation policies and, in some cases, with their competitors enjoying subsidized crude feedstocks or other economic benefits, it is imperative that policies not be enacted to address upstream policies if they penalize the downstream sector. For this reason, if an oil import fee were enacted, there should be a differential fee enacted for petroleum products to ensure that the country does not simply exchange rising crude oil import dependence for rising dependence on imported petroleum products. However, at this time, the political prospects for an oil import fee seem at best remote.

Even before the collapse in oil prices that commenced in January 1986, CSIS testified before the House Armed Services Committee on behalf of the Independent Refiners Coalition that the adequacy of US refining capacity was nearing the point at which national security interests might be threatened if the US had to mobilize its economic and military forces to meet a crisis.[7]

If those concerns were valid in December 1985, they may become even more serious over the next several years, especially if US economic growth leads to rising demand for light petroleum products, especially gasoline.

In 1986, the National Petroleum Council, after an extensive review of the US refining industry, stated: 'the US refining industry is operating near or at capacity to produce light petroleum products'.[8] The NPC noted that the US refining industry can sustain a production rate of 6.8 mbd of gasoline and can produce 7.4 mbd for short periods of time. With US gasoline consumption in excess of 7 mbd since April 1986 and occasionally peaking at 7.5 mbd, and with US available domestic refining capacity at about 15 mbd, there is virtually no excess of spare refining capacity.[9] Consequently, any additional rise in gasoline demand will have to be met by imports, unless additional conversion capacity is developed to yield larger volumes of light petroleum products.

The problems confronting domestic producers and refiners do not necessarily run in parallel. As noted, as a result of OPEC's pricing actions, nearly 1 mbd of US domestic production was closed in 1986. At the same time, lower oil prices have increased demand, necessitating higher refinery utilization rates which have strained refinery capacity. If oil prices remain low, US refiners will have to build new capacity to meet demand or else see their market share further eroded by product imports. US refineries, however, are caught in a bind because their costs arising from environmental regulations (pollution abatement, lead phasedown), and higher feedstock costs, make it difficult for them to invest in new capacity which might be undercut by their foreign competitors. One thing remains certain, however; if new domestic refining capacity is not built, US imports will increase, which will have adverse economic effects in peacetime and threaten US security if the nation had to mobilize for a military contingency. While refined products could be purchased elsewhere when markets are glutted, when the international oil market tightens in a few years, this could become a more serious problem.

The problems confronting the US petroleum sector arise from the unique role that oil plays in the US economy. As a large nation with a well integrated highway and marketing network, the US has a much larger demand for transportation fuels than any other OECD nation. Transportation accounts for nearly 27% of primary energy consumption, but nearly 63% of total oil consumption.[10] The generation of electricity, the commercial/residential market and the industrial sector account for 3%, 9%, and 25% respectively of US oil consumption. It is this overwhelming dependence of the transport sector on liquid fuels that in 1987 remains the central problem confronting the nation's energy security.

Oil use is pervasive in the economy. As one of the leading agricultural producers in the world, the United States utilizes large volumes of refined petroleum products to run machines necessary for the planting, harvesting and marketing of its huge agricultural production.

Moreover, in addition to being the world's largest consumer of energy, the US is also the world's second largest producer of oil. However, oil reserves, while officially still listed as 28 billion barrels, are now probably closer to 26.5 billion barrels owing to the fall in the US reserve/production ratio that occurred in 1986.

As the newly-released Energy Security: A Report to the President report notes, the US has no shortage of energy. What it lacks is energy that can be produced at today's prices with existing technology. In terms of available resources, the US is a profusely rich energy nation.[11]

- 300 billion barrels of oil remains in the ground after primary production.

- US shale oil resources equal 4 trillion barrels of oil equivalent of which about 10% could be produced with current technology if cost and environmental problems could be overcome.

- Proven US coal reserves equal nearly 500 billion tons which could be converted to liquid fuels if oil prices were substantially higher than they are today.

Despite these prodigious resources, the US will not be able to rely on any of them over the next ten to fifteen years to reduce either foreign oil import dependence or to alleviate vulnerability to oil supply disruptions and economic price manipulation. Furthermore, even if economic and environmental constraints could be overcome, the long lead times necessary to develop these alternatives to oil suggest that they will do little or nothing to reduce rising US oil import dependence on the Persian Gulf during the rest of this century.[12]

While the United States is the world's largest oil consumer accounting for nearly 25% of world oil demand, since 1979 it has contributed nearly 60% of the net reduction in world oil demand. No region of the world has been more extensively explored for crude oil and natural gas. As of 1986, about 80% of all the wells ever drilled worldwide - 2.9 million - have been drilled in the US.[13]

As an old producing province, the United States has seen a remarkable drop in the productivity of its wells. With crude oil production averaging about 8.7 mbd over the last five years, the US is drawing down reserves at a rate of 3.2 billion barrels per year. With a discovery rate of about 8 barrels per foot drilled, nearly 375 million feet of drilling are needed simply to keep the reserve/production ratio steady. With the finding rate for new oil in decline, oil producers have to engage in more drilling simply to keep reserve/production ratios steady.[14]

The collapse in oil prices sent shock waves through the US petroleum sector. With the oil rig count down to 765 it appears that, in 1987, the US will drill only about 41,650 wells (oil, gas, dry), only slightly above the 1986 level.[15] In contrast, between 1981 and 1985, about 80,000 wells per year were drilled. With flush production (first year) accounting for about 1.5 mbd of US domestic production, there can be little doubt that sustained low oil prices will lead to a fall-off in US production down the road.

While there remains considerable scope for new large oil additions either through enhanced oil recovery or through a large strike in the Arctic or off the US continental shelf, exploration and development activity will not occur quickly in the absence of the resolution of major environmental disputes (Arctic National Wildlife Refuge) or at least the expectation that future oil prices will justify such activities.

In short, the US confronts the reality that, whereas the average oil well in the US produces 14 barrels per day, the average well in the Middle East produces over 3,200.[16] Likewise with US finding and development costs far in excess of those prevailing elsewhere in the world, it appears unlikely that the US will be successful in keeping production from falling precipitously and imports from skyrocketing. Finally, with oil prices drastically down from late 1985 levels, it is clear that US oil demand will continue to rise, though perhaps at rates less than the 400,000 bd increase (2.7%) that occurred in 1986.

It is the deteriorating reserve and production position of the United States and its major OECD allies that makes the nations of Western Europe, Japan, Canada and the United States vulnerable to political pressures emanating from the Middle East and North Africa.

In 1986, the United States imported about 33% of its oil supplies, of which about one half came from OPEC. According to the Joint Economic Committee of the Congress, US oil imports will rise by 1 mbd per year through 1989, with OPEC oil accounting for nearly one-half of US imports by 1988.[17] What is most significant is that increasingly these oil imports will come from the Arab members of OPEC.

To deal with the deteriorating condition of the US oil industry, a variety of proposals have been promulgated ranging from imposition of a variable or fixed oil import fee to enactment of quotas, establishment of a price floor and a whole host of changes in regulatory and tax policy.[18]

While each of the varied proposals has its merits and demerits in regard to the costs/benefits unleashed on the oil industry and the broader US macroeconomy, it should be noted that, costs aside (which are large), a $10/b import fee would add perhaps 500,000 bd of new production by 1995. Total imports might fall by 1.5 mbd with the additional 1 mbd accruing from lower oil consumption in response to higher oil prices. Oil imports might, with a fee, be held to 7.5-9.5 mbd by 1995.

In contrast to an oil import fee, the tax proposals put forward to Energy Secretary Herrington in his letter of transmittal of Energy Security: A Report to the President of the United States would increase domestic production by about 420,000 bd by 1992.[19] For those unfamiliar with US tax law it is important to note that the proposals are not cumulative.(see Table 4.1)

What these numbers suggest is that while each of the above proposals and the others suggested (oil-indexed bonds, decontrol of old gas) might give some relief to domestic oil and natural gas producers, they will do little to reverse the declining fortunes of the oil industry in the near future.

Natural gas

Still another issue that threatens US national security is the devastation that has been unleashed on independent natural gas producers by the collapse in oil prices. While abundant natural gas supplies may well exist at crude oil equivalent prices of $25/b, too little attention has been paid to the implications for natural gas supplies of oil prices remaining at levels less than $20/b over the next several years.

Despite the existence of the natural gas bubble, at the end of 1985, US dry natural gas reserves stood at 193.4 trillion cubic feet (including 33.8 TCF of Alaskan gas) down 18% from 1984.[20] Bleak as these figures are, especially when one considers that crude oil prices in 1985 averaged $26/b, they mask the fact that new discoveries fell by 60%.

While the potential for large discoveries, especially offshore, remains considerable, with gas well drilling down dramatically in 1986, natural gas reserves will continue to plummet, dropping estimated annual deliverability to as little as 15.36 TCF by early 1988.[21] This development would have momentous implications not only for the natural gas industry but also for the electric power industry where many market forecasters foresee a large increase in demand for natural gas to offset shortfalls from coal and nuclear power arising from environmental, financial and regulatory constraints.

Estimates of US natural gas deliverability differ widely depending on sources. Whereas the American Gas Association estimates that deliverability was flat between 1981 (20.5 TCF) and 1985 (20.2 TCF), AGA believes that in 1986 deliverability fell to 19.3 TCF. In sharp contrast to AGA, Texas Oil and Gas, which has conducted a detailed study of peak natural gas production since 1972, estimates that deliverability has declined from 20.1 TCF in 1981 to 18.2 TCF in 1985 and 17.6 TCF in 1986.[22]

Numerous industry studies demonstrate that roughly 50% of US natural gas production comes from wells drilled during the past five years. From conversations with officials in Texas Oil and Gas and the Texas Railroad Commission, it appears that new natural gas well completions produce approximately 15% of total supply in their first full year (e.g. 1983 completions account for 15% of 1984 gas supply). Consequently, this means that flush production from 1985 vintage gas wells provided at least 15% of the non-associated gas produced in 1986 or approximately 2.1 TCF (13.8 TCF x .15 = 2.1).

In 1986, natural gas drilling plummeted by 42% from 1985 levels, presaging that flush production of non-associated gas in 1987 will decline by .87 TCF (2.07 x .42 = .87). In 1985, associated natural gas production was about 2.8 TCF. Since crude oil production cascaded between February and December 1986, it appears that associated natural gas production from old wells was down about 13.3%. Production from new wells dropped by nearly 50%. These figures, when combined, suggest that associated natural gas production in 1986 fell by about .4 - .5 TCF with an additional drop of around .36 TCF in 1987 anticipated in response to a further fall in US crude oil production and continued depressed levels of new well completions in comparison to the 1981-5 era.[23]

Consequently, it appears that the combined loss of associated and non-associated natural gas deliverability will be about 1.23 TCF (.87 + .36) in comparison to a drop of about .71 TCF in 1986.[24]

The projected high and low impacts of these losses on total deliverability are demonstrated in Table 4.2 produced by AGA and Texas Oil and Gas.

As demonstrated in Table 4.3, the so-called US natural gas bubble may evaporate far sooner than anticipated even with some upturn in the number of producing wells.

While, in the short run, sagging US natural gas production could be offset by rising imports from Canada (1.5 TCF by 1988-90) and Mexico (given a change in Mexican policy), for the next several years Canada will only be able to expand exports during the spring and summer, since in the winter Canadian domestic natural gas demand uses up its pipeline transmission capacity, thus precluding large export volumes.

On the basis of current projections, by 1990 or 1991, even without revocation of the Fuel Use Act and even if electric load growth as forecast by the US Department of Energy averages only 2% per year, natural gas demand by electric utilities and co-generation will exceed the historic high level of nearly 4 TCF used by the electrical power industry in 1970-71.

This demand could perhaps be readily met by drawing down the gas bubble, and by developing new supplies. However, if, as seems likely, electricity demand grows at an average annual rate in excess of 2%, gas drilling remains constrained owing to sustained low oil prices ($20/b or less) over the next several years, and additional shortfalls in coal and nuclear power occur, constraints on gas supplies could become severe and tear asunder many forecasts predicated on new construction of gas-fired generating units, be they gas turbines, combined cycle plants, co-generation or solar plants requiring supplementary natural gas.[25]

If these circumstances occurred, by 1995, gas deliveries would be sufficient only if (i) gas were diverted from other sectors, (ii) imports rose faster than forecast, (iii) gas could be delivered to electric utilities and co-generators at the rate of 6-7 TCF per year, and (iv) gas demand were reduced by switching to residual fuel oil and diesel, potentially increasing fuel oil demand by utilities by 1-5 mbd by 1995.[26] All this incremental oil demand would be met by imports.

While natural gas presently accounts for about 24% of total US primary energy consumption, its future contributions to US energy supplies will be largely determined by (i) the relative costs of alternative fuels, (ii) major revisions in US regulatory policy affecting natural gas production, transportation and end use.

In 1985, natural gas consumption by end-use sector was as follows:[27]

Utilities	3.0 TCF	(19%)
Industrial	5.9 TCF	(37%)
Residential	4.4 TCF	(28%)
Commercial	2.4 TCF	(15%)

In addition to these existing markets, future natural gas market penetration (assuming that appropriate market conditions and regulatory environments exist) could occur in space cooling, natural gas vehicles, methanol powered vehicles and gasoline from natural gas. However, all these markets will potentially only contribute about 3-5% of total energy supply by 2000. Nonetheless, a decision to promote alternative transportation fuels today, of which NGVs and methanol vehicles could play a part, could begin to have a sizeable market impact after 2000.

Currently, the regulatory environment affecting all aspects of natural gas production, transportation and marketing is undergoing profound changes. While the full complexity of these changes are beyond the scope of this study, their resolution is extremely important for two critical reasons. First, if all natural gas currently under price controls were decontrolled, natural gas production could be increased as reserve additions rise by 19-42.5 TCF.[28] Second, in a decontrolled price environment greater competition among fuel sources would exist as consumers were free to weigh the relative costs/benefits of various fuels based on economic, environmental and other criteria.

Nonetheless, until these changes are fully implemented (and there is no certainty they will be) the availability of natural gas could come under severe strain especially if oil prices remain at levels under $20/b over the next several years.

Electric power

The electric utility industry is the largest single energy consuming sector of the US economy. 50% of all US non-transportation energy is consumed during the production of electricity. Because electricity can be generated from a plethora of energy sources, it can be readily tailored to meet the energy requirements of different regions of the nation possessing highly differentiated resource endowments. At the time of the 1973-74 OAPEC oil embargo, the utility sector consumed nearly 2 mbd of oil, today it consumes only about 400,000 bd with some fluctuations occurring owing to the relative price fluctuations of oil vis-à-vis alternative fuels. Of paramount importance is the fact that since 1980 it has been the addition of large volumes of non-oil fired electricity capacity (especially coal and nuclear power) that has allowed the utility industry to reduce its consumption of oil by an amount equal to one-third the total decline in US oil imports. Furthermore, unlike demand for oil and natural gas, electricity demand has risen nearly in tandem with GNP since the oil price shocks of 1973-74.[29]

As in the case of natural gas, there is tremendous debate as to the future of the US electric power industry. Whereas many critics of the industry have highlighted the consequences for the American consumer and utility companies of overestimating future electric power demand and constructing surplus power plants, from a national security standpoint concern has recently arisen over the consequence of:

. electric demand growing more rapidly than forecast;

- the inability of utilities to meet higher than anticipated demand with new non-oil-fired power owing to long lead times and regulatory, environmental, political and financial constraints.

- Growing concerns about the availability, competition and pricing of non-utility sources of electric power generation (Purpa plants) and the effect that regulatory promotion of this new source of power is having on the competitive position of more conventional sources of electricity generation.

- Growing financial problems posed to some utilities by the reluctance of regulatory authorities to allow utilities to pass on costs to consumers arising from 'surplus capacity' ordered in the 1960s and 1970s when perceptions about electricity growth rates were far more bullish.

- Concern that uncertainty over the future of electricity demand and the regulatory environment is forcing utilities to avoid building new capital-intensive projects with protracted lead times (nuclear, coal, wind, solar, geothermal) and relying instead on lower cost options such as demand management, co-generation, and refurbishing of existing plants even though the capital-intensive plants may over the longer term offer not only better economics but also greater electric generation supply security.

Of particular concern is the planned dramatic escalation in the number of co-generation plants utilizing natural gas which in a low oil price scenario may not be available in requisite volumes. Of equal concern is the prospect that utilities may 'de-mothball' existing oil-fired capacity (75,000 MW) which, while expensive to operate, entails little capital cost. Any oil-fired capacity that is reactivated will have to rely on oil imports. Clearly a decision by local utility companies to build large amounts of new oil- and natural gas-fired capacity should not be allowed to occur in isolation from broader national and international energy trends, since a rise in the utilization of these fuels by the US electric power industry could place major price pressures on the international market in the 1990s. Likewise, from a national energy policy perspective, the wisdom of allowing oil or natural gas imports to rise because of the lack of societal courage to resolve the bottlenecks to coal, nuclear power and other electricity options raises serious national security concerns.

For the foreseeable future, electricity generation will play a critical role in the US energy balance for several reasons. It accounts for about 15% of primary energy consumption; as noted, since 1973 it has been the only energy source to grow roughly in concert with GNP; it is the fastest growing energy; because electricity can be generated from many diverse fuel sources, it allows the development of a highly diversified supply system which can reduce the nation's vulnerability to disruption of any single fuel source.

Based on current trends, future demand for electricity will be closely tied to the level of economic growth. If the growth of the US and world economy accelerates in response to low oil prices and at the same time major changes in the financial and regulatory systems that have burdened many utilities and led to their current aversion to major new construction programs do not occur, there is a strong possibility that oil- and natural gas-fired capacity, currently idled or used to meet peak load demand, may be utilized to meet base load demand. The reason for this is that if electricity demand grows faster than anticipated there is little time between now and 1994 to put into place major amounts of new capital-intensive non-oil capacity. The situation is exacerbated by the fact that plummeting oil prices are threatening the entire range of 'alternative' energy sources that were developed in response to high energy prices. If low oil prices persist for some time, even some conservation and co-generation projects will appear less attractive to many utilities. In a low price oil scenario, some 'new' oil units might have to be built quickly to meet new demand and to replace existing generation plants that will be retired over the next six or seven years.

The demand for electricity would have to increase only by 3% per year (compared to current projections of 2.5%) to require an additional 700,000 bd in US oil imports by 1994. Between 1983 and 1985 electricity demand rose an average 3.2% per annum, while growth slowed to 1.8% in 1986. To date, this demand has been met overwhelmingly by surplus coal, nuclear power capacity and demand maintenance programs.

If power demand grows faster than anticipated, the 75,000 MW of readily available oil-fired capacity could prove to be an attractive generation alternative once the last group of nuclear and coal plants under construction or planned are completed, if demand exceeds the capability of existing non-oil units.

While this development need not occur were massive changes in regulatory policy affecting coal and nuclear power to be made quickly, there is little to no likelihood this will occur quickly, especially given growing concern in the United States over the danger of acid rain, rising anti-nuclear opposition and a low oil price environment.[30]

Because surplus oil and natural gas capacity already exists and pressing it into greater service will entail relatively few regulatory obstacles, no long construction 'lead times', and few financing difficulties since the plants are amortized, there will be little public opposition as long as oil prices remain low and regulatory authorities continue to pre-approve fuel adjustment price increases.[31]

From Figure 4.1 the complexity of the electric power sector is readily apparent. Clearly, what finally happens to those coal and nuclear power plant units under construction will have a profound impact on the need for currently idled oil- and gas-fired electric capacity, especially in a high electricity growth scenario.

While foreigners constantly cite the negative impact of US regulatory policies on nuclear power plant development, in reality there is currently as much uncertainty about how many of the coal plants under construction (less than 50% complete) will be built as there is in the nuclear sector.

What emerges from the analysis is the fact that, despite the very profound need for new base load coal and nuclear power plants in a high growth scenario, the

United States has already forgone the nuclear option. By the early 1990s, all those plants currently under construction will have been completed (perhaps not licensed). At this time, nuclear power will account for about 19% of total electricity demand. If the nuclear option is to grow further this century, new plants will have to be ordered in the next several years. Consequently, it remains up to Western Europe, Canada and Japan to decide if nuclear power is to reduce OECD dependence on imported oil during the remainder of the century. It is time that Western Europe and Japan recognized this fact and realized that they will on the basis of current trends be the dominant actors in international nuclear commerce.

The one fact that might change this over time would be a major US policy initiative to develop a smaller-scale reactor (300-400 MW) which could offer many advantages (size, reduced lead times for construction, safety, environmental). However, the realities of the NRC licensing process make it difficult to see such a reactor being deployed on a commercial scale until after the year 2000. While streamlining of the regulatory process affecting existing Light Water Reactors should be pursued if nuclear energy is to regain its competitive position, it appears unlikely this will happen soon.

The depressed state of the US nuclear power industry projected after 1990 mandates a growing US dependence on coal to meet its electricity needs. Between 1991 and 1995, some 36 coal-fired plants (21.6 GW) are scheduled to be completed. If electricity demand grows faster than anticipated, additional coal plants will be needed. However, as in the case of nuclear, there are serious environmental, regulatory, institutional and financial constraints on the coal sector and unless they are resolved, renewed pressure, at least in the short run, to build oil- and gas-fired plants or combined cycle plants will occur, with grave implications for US national security. While the potential for clean-burning coal technologies to penetrate the commercial market remains possible, this will not occur unless oil prices rise to levels near $30/b. Even then it will take many years for these technologies to penetrate the market on a sizeable scale.

On the basis of existing trends, there is rising concern that the current electricity regulatory environment is allowing the electricity supply system to evolve in a manner that will not only be economically inefficient but also ensure dependence on insecure supplies of natural gas and imported oil. One of the problems that plagues effective national electricity planning is that most of the decisions that will affect the nation's electricity future are made on a decentralized basis and involve decision makers with highly diverse interests - electricity producers, consumers, state or municipal regulatory authorities, and personnel of the Federal Energy Regulatory Commission (FERC) if wholesale electricity rates are involved.

In addition, decisions can be influenced by the shareholders of investor-owned utilities; by the nation's major financial institutions which make judgements concerning the utilities' stocks and bond prices as well as comparative assessments of these firms as investments in relation to other industries; by the US Treasury which by loaning resources to many publicly-owned utilities at below market rate financing creates powerful constituencies; and by other entities (Rural Electric Co-operatives, Tennessee Valley Authority, Bonneville Power etc.) all of which have special interests which may or may not be commensurate with either the national interest or effective national energy planning.[32] Furthermore, all facilities that produce and distribute electric power are subject to environmental and safety regulation at the federal, state and sometimes local level.

Two of the difficulties in assessing the future electricity needs of the nation are (i) determining the rate of electricity growth and (ii) planning which energy source or other alternative strategy should be pursued to meet this growth. One of the chief problems confronted by electricity planners is that, while on a national basis weather-adjusted electricity demand growth continues to rise nearly in concert with GNP, on a regional basis variations can be profound, ranging from 50% of GNP between 1982 and 1985 in the Mountain Census Region to 1.7 times GNP in the East North Central Census Region.[33]

The problem is exacerbated by the fact that while the basic forecast in DOE's new report: Energy Security: A Report to the President of the United States predicts that electricity demand growth will average 2% per annum between 1985 and 2000 and that the average plant will have its life extended to 50 years, a change in either variable could lead to profound shortages in the electricity supply system.[34] In this regard, it should be noted that even in DOE's base forecast an additional 100 GW of new electric capacity will be needed (beyond all plants currently under construction) to maintain reliable project supplies. In a report completed by CSIS in April 1987 for the US Department of Energy[35], if oil prices remain at levels less than $20/b until 1990, electricity demand is forecast to grow at a rate (2.7%) substantially in excess of that projected in the Energy Security report, leading to a surge in oil imports by 1995. Even if oil prices rise to $24-$25/b, CSIS and its principal consultants, Science Concepts, predict that oil imports could rise by significant amounts by 1995 to fuel the electric power sector. A key finding of the CSIS/Science Concepts report is that at any rate of electric growth in excess of 2.3% per annum, oil use for electricity will increase, the magnitude being determined largely by how many of the power plants currently under construction are not completed on schedule.

It is important to note that current construction plans will only be adequate under two conditions. First, if all plants are completed on schedule and second, if the load growth is less than 2.3% per annum.

As CSIS notes in its report:

> The failure to complete nuclear and coal-fired power plants will not lead to a shortage of electrical energy in the short run because there is ample excess generating capacity to meet increased load requirements. That excess capacity, however, is largely fueled by natural gas and residual fuel oil. Thus as generating capacity requirements expand beyond peak requirements in 1985 of 470,000 megawatts, available fossil fuel generating capacity will come on line, expanding the nation's requirements for oil and gas for electricity generation. Since the lead times for constructing

coal or nuclear power stations, or the anticipated newer technologies of coal conversion/combined cycle, exceed the time frame of this study (2000), the only recourse will be the use of existing capacity and new gas and oil-fired turbines and combined cycle units which can be brought on line quickly. The future increase in the need for oil is especially deceptive because it is not likely to become obvious until 1990 or 1991 when there will be too little time to build generating capacity based on fuels other than oil or gas.

In the months ahead continued uncertainty over both relative energy prices among competing fuels for electric power generation and other alternatives (load management, plant life extensions and conservation) will continue to bedevil forecasters of future electricity supply/demand. As noted above and in Table 4.4 drawn from Energy Security: A Report to the President of the United States, each energy 'alternative' has its potential benefits and pitfalls.[36] What is certain, however, is the fact that on the basis of current trends for oil and gas prices, there is acute danger that oil demand and imports to fuel the electric power sector could rise dramatically over the next three to five years.

Energy efficiency and renewables

Since 1973, the US has saved nearly 14 mbdoe as a result of improvements in energy productivity and efficiency.[37] As a result, despite a rising population, the US economy uses no more energy today than it did in 1973. Since 1979, the broader OECD group of nations have reduced their energy, and especially oil, consumption by a combination of enhanced energy efficiency and the accelerated development of nuclear power, coal, natural gas, and hydropower. As a group, these nations now use 20% less energy than in 1973.[38]

While many nations are more fuel-efficient than the United States, the US has reduced its energy use proportionately more than any other nation. Nevertheless public and private studies demonstrate that further advances with resulting savings of 5-12 mbd by 2000 could occur if energy efficiency were given a higher national priority.[39] To accomplish this will require a dedicated national commitment across successive presidential administrations. Surprisingly, if a way could be found to install the most energy-efficient appliances currently on the market during the next decade, total residential energy consumption (oil, gas, and electricity) could be reduced by 33% from project levels.[40] However, this is unlikely to occur in the absence of some market regulatory stimulus, since many of these technologies' current purchase costs are substantially higher than less fuel-efficient alternatives. While the life cycle operating costs of these energy-efficient appliances are drastically below those of their cheaper-to-purchase competitors, consumers seem to give overwhelming consideration to purchase costs over operating costs.

Similarly, renewable energy sources for electricity (windpower, solar cells, geothermal energy, hydro), heat (passive solar designs, solar hot water systems, industrial collectors) and biofuels (solid, liquids and gaseous fuels from wood, other agricultural products and municipal wastes) offer real potential as future energy sources, though their contribution will remain limited in the short to medium term owing to financial, regulatory, environmental and institutional constraints.[41]

From a national security perspective, biofuels are of particular interest since they can be converted to liquid fuels and used to replace oil in automobiles, trucks and airlines.[42] The problem, however, is that while conservation and renewable energy sources offer enormous potential, under current market conditions they can not easily compete with cheaper conventional fuels in the absence of federal price supports. Nevertheless, from a national security standpoint they offer the nation a partial solution to reducing national dependence on imported oil, especially in the transportation sector.[43]

US energy security at the crossroads

The prospect of skyrocketing increases in oil imports (both crude oil and petroleum products) and plummeting domestic oil production would be devastating enough given the implications for the US trade balance.

However, of far greater consequence, from a geopolitical perspective, is the certainty that these imports will increasingly come from the Middle East and North Africa. It is this fact, more than any other, that mandates the national need for nuclear power and all other electric options that will keep cheap imported oil from recapturing a large share of the US electric power market.

Despite these trends, however, there is an illusion pervading the nation that extends to the media, the boardrooms of major corporations and even to high levels of the legislative and executive branches of government, that the energy crisis is behind us and that the nation has solved the energy problems of the last decade.

The fact that so many people believe that the energy crisis is over is vexing in light of the fact that history has repeatedly demonstrated that excessive dependence upon oil imports threatens the broad range of US national security interests defined by both legislative enactment (Section 232 of the Trade Expansion Act of 1962) and executive findings by the Treasury Department in 1975 and 1979.[44] The official documents of the US Government clearly demonstrate that some members of Congress and at least three US Presidents - two Republicans and one Democrat - have recognized that the overall threat of energy dependence on foreign sources of crude oil and petroleum products arises not only from the occasional burdens placed upon military preparedness encountered during supply disruptions but also from the threat posed to both the domestic and international economy, even when supplies are available, through price manipulation by OPEC producers. Clearly, the first line of defence against such economic manipulation must be continued support for a vigorous domestic energy program encouraging energy production as well as enhanced energy efficiency.

The links between energy and national security are multifarious. International competition for oil, especially in times of real or perceived crisis, strains foreign policy flexibility and political and diplomatic alliances as nations move unilaterally rather than in concert to secure access to vital energy supplies.

Reliance on insecure oil supplies impinges on the military security of the United States and its allies in several other areas. Safeguarding major oil producing states against external and perhaps even internal subversion requires difficult strategic choices. The military must have the bases and operational mobility it needs to move rapidly to protect against the threat of sabotage of the energy logistics systems inside the major energy-exporting nations and on the high seas. The military must also position adequate fuel supplies for the defense of Europe, Japan and the United States, as well as to support allied interests in other conflict arenas. The West's ability to support sufficient military forces to guard oil supplies in an era of fiscal austerity is also a source of profound allied squabbling and necessitates a greater amount of burden sharing and a re-examination of whose strategic interests are most at stake in volatile areas such as the Persian Gulf. With Japan dependent for nearly 67% of its imports on oil from the Middle East and OPEC and Europe 74% dependent, it is clear that the economic threat posed to the domestic energy industries of these regions by the collapsing prices of the 1980s, is as great as the rising prices of the last decade. Likewise, with Japan dependent on the Middle East (defined to include Arab exporters of North Africa) for 58% of its oil imports (2.6 mbd out of 4.5 mbd) and Europe for 59% (4.6 mbd out of 7.9 mbd), it can no longer be credibly argued that the US should shoulder the defense burden required to ensure access to the Persian Gulf and North African oil which is more vital to its allies than to itself.

The security of the United States and its allies is also threatened by large oil import bills which pose grave problems not only for Western Europe, Japan and the United States but also for the aspiring nations of the Third World. In this latter case, the prospect for more equitable income distribution, as well as these nations' political and economic stability, are directly linked to the price of oil. While low oil prices have provided partial relief to some of these nations, a reversal of import substitution policies in the energy sector could pose yet another shock to their economies and to the stability of the international banking system were oil prices to rise dramatically once again in the 1990s. Even for major oil producing nations, such as Mexico, the collapse in oil prices in 1986 sent oil export revenue plummeting by 57% from $14.8 billion in 1985 to $6.3 billion in 1986.

To demonstrate how rapidly changes can occur in the economic dimension of the energy 'crisis', one has only to look at the historic record of US oil import bills.

	Imports(mbd)	Cost($bn)
1973	6.3	8
1979	8.4	60
1980	7.0	79
1985	5.1	54
1986	6.0	35
1990	9.1 (est.)	
	at $24/b	81
	at $18/b	59

Energy and national security are linked in another way: political, economic and environmental policy conflicts over the relative priority given to energy development, conservation, and government-sponsored energy R & D engender uncertainties over future economic conditions and the supply and cost of energy, thus constraining investment and the prospects for enhancing industrial productivity. To the extent that the 'regulatory' climate emanating out of Washington, the state capitals or local public utility commissions constrains fuel switching or hinders efforts at greater fuel efficiency, the nation's reliance on foreign oil will resurrect its ugly head and US national security and that of its trading partners will be impaired. Likewise, to the extent that the Chernobyl nuclear tragedy leads to a slow-down or curtailment of nuclear power in any OECD nation, the security of all our nations will be lessened.

The challenge posed to the United States is stark. Over the last fourteen years, US dependence on imported oil has been dramatically reduced by arresting the decline in domestic production through the oil industry's investment of $335 billion in exploration and development, including $36 billion in lease bonuses paid to the Federal Government for offshore drilling rights. Billions more have been invested in the development of coal and nuclear power plants, the natural gas industry and in abortive attempts at synthetic fuel development. Further investments have been poured into enhanced energy efficiency in the US commercial, residential and industrial sectors.

Unfortunately, the deliberate manipulation of world oil prices by several OPEC members has reduced the value of these investments in the petroleum sector to a level which is inadequate to provide the required cash flow and the incentive to maintain adequate levels of domestic activity. In 1959, nearly 30% of oil and natural gas revenue generated at the wellhead was ploughed back into new oil exploration. By 1971, this had fallen to 13%, in July/August of 1986 it had plummeted to 7%. Given these figures, it is clear the US is once again headed for excessive dependence upon insecure imports.

The national security threat implicit in these statistics and those for Western Europe and Japan cited earlier can only become worse as the exporters' price manipulation denies the required investment in worldwide energy production, fuel switching, conservation, research and development and frontier petroleum operations from the North Sea to the Beaufort Sea. Inevitably, protracted policy debates in Washington between the legislative and executive branches will mandate that the growing shortfall in free world oil supplies will be met not by domestically available fuels such as nuclear power and coal, but by greater dependence on OPEC oil especially from the Middle East oil producers. This fate is already increasingly inescapable under a low oil price scenario because oil consumers will turn first to installed but currently unutilized production capacity, over 95% of which is located in OPEC countries and at least 85% in the Middle East. When the output of currently unutilized productive capacity is absorbed, non-communist consumers will turn next to the development of proven but currently underdeveloped global reserves, over 76% of which are located in OPEC (476 billion barrels out of a free world total of 623 billion) and 69% in the Middle East (433 billion barrels). These developments will be especially troublesome in the electric power arena where the ready availability of inexpensive oil-fired capacity will make up shortfalls arising from excessive regulatory and environmental constraints on coal and nuclear power. While Soviet natural gas supplies will provide Western

Europe with some alternative energy policy options to dependence on Middle Eastern oil, reliance on Soviet energy will not improve Western energy security.

The policy choices before the United States, Western Europe, Japan and Canada are stark. Either we move forward in concert to develop our domestic energy alternatives while taking measures to secure access to vital energy supplies, or we remain at the mercy of more parochial interests, both at home and abroad, and thus lose control of our economic, political and strategic destiny.

The collapse in world oil prices

In January 1986, as a result of cheating by its OPEC brethren, Saudi Arabia supported by Kuwait and the United Arab Emirates made a political decision to regain control of the world oil market by forcing oil prices down to a level where interfuel substitution (coal, gas, nuclear etc.) would be slowed or curtailed; where fiscal incentives for conservation would be reduced owing to longer payback periods; where new energy R & D would be cut back; where new high-cost oil exploration in Alaska, the Outer Continental Shelf, the North Sea and other high-cost areas would be slowed; where oil demand over time would increase, thus alleviating pressure on OPEC while increasing global dependence on the volatile Middle East region; and where high-cost non-OPEC producers would have to absorb a lesser share of the world market, either through collaboration with OPEC or through an open price war.

Before January 1986, the US Administration believed so strongly in the wisdom of the marketplace that it had systematically rejected cries from independent refiners and producers who argued that events in the energy marketplace were creating conditions dangerous to US national security. While some in the Administration perceived the dangers posed to banks with large energy portfolios, on balance the Administration continued to believe that the benefits of low oil prices far outweighed the costs of government intervention to bolster oil prices.

While banks have for decades financed the vast bulk of the energy industry's capital needs for oil and gas drilling and exploration, even before the January 1986 oil price collapse there were serious industry-wide concerns that created an aura of apprehension about energy financing. These concerns focused on the prospect that either a major regional bank with large energy exposure or a major debt-laden Latin American nation dependent on oil revenue might default, triggering massive defaults leading to the collapse or the dangerous tottering of the international financial system. With the collapse in oil prices, those concerns intensified.

The collapse in oil prices led to drastic cuts in exploration and drilling expenditures by the major oil companies. However, it was the small independent producers so dependent on cash flow to finance continued new exploration and development who were devastated by the oil price collapse.

While the impact of the price collapse on oil and natural gas producers and service contractors was visibly apparent, far less attention was riveted on the impact of nose-diving oil prices on alternative energy development. In retrospect, this is especially curious since it was fuels utilized for the generation of electricity (nuclear - 4.3 mbd, coal - 5 mbd, hydro - 2.3 mbd) minus oil that between 1972 and 1984 contributed 11.6 mbdoe, an amount equal to one-half of the 23 mbdoe in new free world energy supplies produced during this period.[45]

By February 1986, a confluence of events - the oil price collapse, growing economic difficulties in the oil producing states, the crossing of the Shatt-al-Arab into Iraqi territory by Iranian forces placing them close to the Kuwaiti frontier, and growing Iranian verbal attacks blaming Saudi Arabia and Kuwait for the price collapse in the world oil market - began to generate concern in Washington.

Nevertheless, both the legislative and executive branches of government remained divided over whether low oil prices posed a serious enough threat to merit government intervention in the marketplace. While some in the Administration argued that energy security could best be protected by relying on conservation and greater use of coal and nuclear power, left unaddressed as oil prices sank below $15/b were the questions of how new supplies of coal, nuclear and other alternative fuels, which cost more than $12-$13/b and which had been instrumental in breaking OPEC's stranglehold, would be developed at extremely low oil prices and how the US would avoid increasing dependence on oil imports. To deal with the growing crisis, President Reagan in September 1986 announced the formation of a high-level inter-agency group, chaired by Deputy Energy Secretary, William Martin, to study the impact of the oil price collapse on US national security. As the report was under way, the Administration was besieged by growing calls for government intervention to stem the destruction of the domestic oil and natural gas industry. In March 1987, the report was released.[46]

The Middle East: The need for policy reassessment

In the aftermath of the 1973-74 Arab oil embargo, US energy policy was based on two assumptions: namely, that over time the United States could reduce its import dependence by developing alternative energy resources, and that through arms and technology sales to Iran and Saudi Arabia it could create strategic relationships that would reduce the risks of new oil supply disruptions. While great success was achieved on the first policy as evidenced by the drop in US oil imports from 8.8 mbd in 1977 to 5.1 mbd in 1985, these achievements are now being eroded owing to the collapse in oil prices. While forecasters vary widely in their assessments, a review of thirty-one recent forecasts projects US oil imports ranging from 7 to 9 mbd and between 9 and 11.5 mbd in 1990 and 1995 respectively.[47] Obviously, each of these forecasts is based on widely different assumptions about oil pricing and the health of the US and the global economy. Nonetheless, what seems clear is that US oil import dependence will rise dramatically and that increasingly this dependence will be on the Persian Gulf.

The second assumption has been shattered by the fall of the Shah of Iran in 1979, the revocation of the US security treaty with Teheran, the advent and spread of the Ayatollah Khomeini's Islamic revolution, the ongoing Iran-Iraq war, the rejection of the Camp David peace agreement by Saudi Arabia and most of the Arab world, the advent of international terrorism directed by Libya, Syria, and Iran, the Israeli invasion of Lebanon, and a growing desperation on the part of moderate Palestinians and several of the Arab Gulf states who increasingly believe that the United States has abandoned the peace process.

Washington's reluctance to lead and direct the peace process is of deep concern to moderate Arab states who do not agree with Washington's view that access to Gulf oil is a separate issue from resolution of the Arab-Israeli dispute. It is ironic that in numerous conversations with political leaders throughout the region, the view has been constantly expressed that no issue, including the possibility of Soviet intervention in the Gulf, is seen as more potentially destabilizing to Jordan, Egypt, Saudi Arabia, Kuwait, the UAE, etc., than the failure to resolve the Palestinian problem.

The prospect of growing dependence on oil imports from the Gulf, combined with the recent revelations of the Tower Commission report, mandate more than ever before the need for a fundamental reassessment of US interests in the Middle East. US influence in the Middle East has been shattered by events since 1980. After serving as the honest broker in effecting the Egyptian-Israeli Peace Treaty, the United States is seen by moderate Arab spokesmen as having sunk into a morass that endangers not only its own interests but also those of its Arab friends. Even before the publication of the Tower Commission report, the direction of US policy in the Middle East was difficult for America's friends to understand. Viewed from the region, US acquiescence in the 1982 Israeli invasion of Lebanon, the shelling of Lebanese villages by the battleship <u>New Jersey</u> in the aftermath of the Marine tragedy in Beirut, the abandonment of the Arab-Israeli peace process, the muted US response to continued Israeli settlement expansion on the West Bank, and numerous statements by high-level US officials linking 'Muslims' and 'terrorists' have left the friends of the United States in the Arab world at best dismayed and at worst angered.

The fact that during this time the United States protested only weakly to Tel Aviv concerning the Pollard spy scandal or Israel's failure to comply with US anti-apartheid legislation vis-à-vis South Africa and has commenced discussions regarding elevating Israel to the status of a US 'ally' has sent a message to the Arab world that it has few friends in Washington. While businessmen may pay little attention to these political vagaries, they become overriding determinants of policy when juxtaposed to a Middle East policy in which the US, for better or worse, is seen as an 'ally' of Israel and, hence, in the view of Arab radicals and increasingly of Arab moderates, as an enemy.

It is against this backdrop that revelations of US arms sales to Iran and Israeli complicity in these transfers have devastated US influence in the region - the same region which will be increasingly vital as a source of crude oil and petroleum products for the United States, Western Europe, Japan and Canada.

The revelation of US assistance to revolutionary Iran has left the United States' Arab friends profoundly disturbed and in deep despair. For the United States not only to have traded arms with a known terrorist state (Iran) which is locked in a life and death struggle with an Arab state (Iraq), but also to have done so either in concert with or at the behest of the Arabs' worst enemy (Israel), is seen as devastating.

As Karen Eliot House wrote recently in The Wall Street Journal:[48]

> Those Arabs who by choice, or lack of it, have cast their lot with the West, speak with the bitterness of the betrayed .... Such genuine friends as Jordan's King Hussein and Egyptian leaders .... are humiliated at having vouched for American fidelity in the fight against Khomeinism only to discover that the US was secretly carrying on an affair with their enemy. As for the Iraqis, whose army is now bleeding, their bitterness and anger are palpable. 'The region feels shattered', says Iraqi Foreign Minister Tariq Aziz. .... Saudi Arabia, widely suspected by its Arab brethren of having knowledge of the secret arms sales through Saudi arms merchant Adnan Khashoggi, is simply too frightened to say anything.

US arms sales to Iran have left moderate Arab leaders throughout the region 'staring into the abyss'.[49] While it remains unclear what the Arab world's ultimate reaction will be, it is up to the United States to take initiatives that will begin to regain its trust. The demands by the Government of Israel that the US apologize for 'sucking the Israelis into the Iran affair' should be rejected publicly if Washington hopes to regain any credibility in the region.

Although in the short run it is difficult to perceive a direct link between Arab anger and threats to oil supplies, in the current political environment it will be increasingly difficult for moderate Arab leaders, both inside and outside the Gulf, to be seen as friendly to US interests. In this climate, one must query how the US-Saudi 'special relationship' will evolve. Will the conflicting policy signals emanating out of Washington weaken or strengthen Saudi oil production and pricing policies, and thus derivatively US national security interests?

With 60% of the world's proven oil reserves and 85% of the world's surplus oil productive capacity lying in states adjacent to the Gulf and in North Africa, access to the region's oil resources will remain vital for global economic security for the rest of this century and beyond. Even if the United States were able to keep its dependence on the region at low levels, which seems problematic at best, the continued threats posed to Western Europe and Japan mandate that Washington maintain an interest in the region for years to come.

However, if the area is to be stabilized, Western Europe and Japan must play a more active role both in supporting friendly regimes in the area through enhanced security and economic assistance and in putting diplomatic and economic pressure on states supporting international terrorism.

Conclusion

From the above analysis, it is apparent that the energy situation confronting the United States is deteriorating to the point where falling domestic oil and natural gas production, combined with the prospect of skyrocketing demand for oil and natural gas in the electric power sector, will lead to a doubling of oil import levels from 5 mbd in 1985 to 9-11 mbd within a decade. These developments need not happen but may well occur either as a result of protracted national debate over the proper direction of US energy policy or as the result of the enactment of piecemeal energy policies.

In the spring of 1987, three energy reports reflecting highly diverse views as to the proper policy mix to insure the nation's energy security were released.[50] Each merits serious examination. However, the United States does not need more energy reports! What it needs is the enactment of policies that will insure the continuation of a viable domestic energy industry, while at the same time preserving access to Middle East oil both for the US and its major allies.

With rising US oil import dependence a virtual certainty over the next decade, the United States should begin to enact the following measures:

- Restore nuclear power as a vital energy source for the future energy security of the nation by: (i) streamlining the federal and state licensing process; (ii) reforming the regulatory system to allow construction work in progress to be put into the rate base; (iii) resolving the institutional inertia surrounding enactment of a nuclear waste disposal policy; (iv) resolving jurisdictional conflicts among federal, state and local authorities for nuclear safety.

- Remove federal and state taxation policies that discourage investment in oil and natural gas production and other fuels.

- Establish a cost/benefit impact statement for all existing and new environmental laws.

- Provide greater federal research expenditures on alternative transportation fuels (natural gas vehicles, ethanol, methanol, LPG, fuel cells, electric, etc.).

- Improve federal fuel efficiency standards by 3-5 miles per gallon every five years.

- Encourage greater conservation measures in the residential, commercial and especially transportation sectors.

- Establish greater price competition in the generation of electricity by removing regulatory obstacles that currently favour electricity options which rely on sources of energy that may be insecure in the future.

- Support enhanced R & D on clean-burning coal technologies.

- Work within the context of the IEA to co-ordinate stock build and drawdown strategies.

The above recommendations are not meant to be inclusive but rather are considered by the CSIS Energy and Resources Program to provide the cornerstone of an effective national energy policy.

Notes

[1] See statement of William L. Fisher, Director, Bureau of Economic Geology, and Leonidas T. Barrow, Chair of Mineral Resources, the University of Texas at Austin, on Production Impacts of Low Oil Prices before US Senate Finance Committee, Subcommittee on Energy and Agricultural Taxation, Washington, D.C., 30 January 1987, p.11.

[2] Ibid.

[3] See statement of Dr James Schlesinger before US Senate Committee on Energy and Natural Resources, Washington, D.C., 22 January 1987.

[4] I am indebted to Bob Spears of Spears Associates, Tulsa, Oklahoma, for calling these figures to my attention.

[5] Energy Security: A Report to the President of the United States, US Department of Energy, Washington, D.C., March 1987.

[6] See statement by Senator Bennett Johnston, Chairman US Senate Committee on Energy and Natural Resources, at Domestic Oil and Gas Industry Conference, Lafayette, Louisiana, 9 February 1987.

[7] See statement of Dr Charles K. Ebinger before the Readiness Subcommittee, House Armed Services Committee, US House of Representatives, Washington, D.C., 5 December 1985.

[8] *U.S. Petroleum Refining: A Report of the National Petroleum Council*, NPC, Washington, D.C., 1986.

[9] *Ibid.*

[10] *Energy Security: A Report to the President, op. cit.* pp.100-1.

[11] *Ibid.* p.51.

[12] Charles K. Ebinger, *U.S. Energy Security to 2000.* Paper presented to the Royal Institute of International Affairs, London, 28 October 1986.

[13] *Energy Security: A Report to the President, op. cit.*, p.53.

[14] Data provided by Spears and Associates, Tulsa, Oklahoma.

[15] *Ibid.*

[16] Christopher Flavin, Denis Hayes and Jim MacKenzie, *The Oil Rollercoaster: A Call to Action*, Fund for Renewable Energy and the Environment, Washington, D.C., April 1987.

[17] 'Letter report' from Joint Economic Committee economist George R. Tyler to Senator Lloyd M. Bentsen, 20 May 1986.

[18] *Energy Security: A Report to the President, op. cit.* pp.72-83.

[19] See letter of transmittal by Secretary of Energy, John Herrington, to the President of the United States. US Department of Energy Library.

[20] Figures provided by Energy Information Administration, USG. Washington, D.C.

[21] Figures provided by Texas Oil and Gas Corporation, Office of Strategic Planning, Dallas, Texas.

[22] Figures provided by the American Gas Association and Texas Oil and Gas Corporation.

[23] Industry Outlook and Forecast, March 1987, Howard Weil Labouisse and Friedrichs, Inc., New Orleans, Louisiana; Spears and Associates, Tulsa, Oklahoma.

[24] Ibid.

[25] A Return to the Age of Oil? An Analysis of the Role of the Electric Supply System in Future U.S. Oil Demand, Science Concepts, Washington, D.C., 1986.

[26] Ibid.

[27] Energy Security: A Report to the President, op. cit. p.118.

[28] Estimates provided by Office of Technology Assessment, US Congress; Shell Oil, USA, Corporate Planning Department, Houston, Texas; Energy Information Administration.

[29] A Return to the Age of Oil, op. cit.

[30] Ibid.

[31] Ibid.

[32] Energy Security: A Report to the President, op. cit. pp.154-160.

[33] Ibid. p.136.

[34] Ibid. p.137.

[35] Commercial Nuclear Power and the National Interest. Report prepared by Georgetown Center for Strategic and International Studies for the US Department of Energy, April 1987.

[36] Energy Security: A Report to the President, op. cit. p.142.

[37] Ibid. p.94.

[38] The Oil Rollercoaster, op. cit., p.14.

[39] Ibid.; see also Energy Efficiency Appliances, American Council for an Energy Efficient Economy, Washington, D.C., 1983; Energy Security, A Report to the President, op. cit., p.94.

[40] The Oil Rollercoaster, op. cit., p.14.

[41] Energy Security, A Report to the President, op. cit. pp.197-210; Ethanol: National Security Implications, A Report of the Georgetown University Center for Strategic and International Studies, Washington, D.C., Significant Issues Series, Vol. 5, No. 7, 1983.

[42] The Oil Rollercoaster, op. cit., p.15.

[43] Ethanol: National Security Implications, op. cit.;see also Natural Gas Vehicles: A National Security Perspective, A Report of the Georgetown University Center for Strategic and International Studies, Washington, D.C., Significant Issues Series, Vol. 6, No. 16, 1984.

[44] US Department of Treasury, 'Report of Investigation of the Effects of Petroleum and Petroleum Product Imports on the National Security', 40 Federal Register 4457 (30 January 1975); US Department of Treasury, 'Report of Investigation of the Effects of Oil Imports on National Security', 44 Federal Register 18818 (29 March 1979); The Trade Expansion Act of 1962, section 239, as amended (Title 19, US Code).

[45] A Return to the Age of Oil, op. cit.

[46] Energy Security, A Report to the President, op. cit.

[47] Charles K. Ebinger, Did OPEC Kill Oil?. Paper delivered to seminar on the Political Economy of World Oil, July 1986.

[48] Karen Elliot House, 'Our Disillusioned Arab Friends', _The Wall Street Journal_, 21 January 1987.

[49] _Ibid_.

[50] _Energy Security, A Report to the President, op. cit.; The Oil Rollercoaster, op. cit.; A Call for Action_, United States Energy Association, Washington, D.C., April 1987.

Table 4.1 Estimated effect of DOE tax proposals on US oil and gas production (mbd)

	Increased production	
	oil	oil and gas
Repeal of 'Transfer Rule' - percentage depletion	30	55
Rise in net-income limitation - percentage depletion	32	58
Faster recovery geological and geophysical costs	110	200
5% Exploration and development tax credit		
All explo. & dev. spending	180	325
Geological & geophysical only	44	80
Higher depletion for independents (27.5%)	154	280
Higher depletion on new production	200	370

Figures derived from Energy Security: A Report to the President, op. cit. pp.74-83.

Table 4.2 Losses in natural gas deliverability

	Estimated Deliverability TCF (AGA)	Estimated Deliverability TCF (TXO)
1985 Deliverability	20.2	18.2
Minus 1986 loss	- .71	- .71
Minus 1986 loss	-1.2	-1.23
Seasonal excess required to serve winter markets	- .90	- .90
Est. annual deliverability 1.1.88	17.36	15.36
US production 1986*	15.70	15.70
Anticipated US production with normal weather and minimum fuel switching	16.2-16.8	16.2-16.8

* In 1986 natural gas demand was less than normal owing to warm weather -.2 TCF and fuel switching -.35 TCF.

Table 4.3 <u>Gas production capacity</u>

Non-associated production capacity per gas well(a) MCF	Number of producing gas wells	Non-associated production capability in BCF	Associated dissolved production in BCF(b)	Total BCF
66.37	235,000	15,597	2,957	18,554
66.39	235,000	14,662	2,597	17,259
58.65	238,000	13,959	2,434	16,393
55.13	243,000	13,396	2,357	15,754
51.82	250,990	13,006	2,357	15,363

a) The 1986-90 estimates are based on a 6% per year decline from the production capability after 1985.

b) These values are implied associated-dissolved production based on Spears and Associates estimates.

Figures provided by Spears and Associates, Tulsa Oklahoma and reprinted in <u>Industry Outlook and Forecast</u>, <u>op. cit</u>.

Table 4.4 Electricity supply options and uncertainties

Electricity supply options	Potential economical input to new supply by the year 2000	Reservations and other comments
Conservation and load management	EPRI's midrange estimate 45 GW(a)	Economic efficiency of utility programs subject to debate, and consumer behaviour is uncertain
Co-generation	20-50 GW(b)	Frequently oil-or-gas-fired under current regulation may displace more economic generation if all technologies are not allowed to compete fairly
Renewables and fuel cells	Uncertain, but technical and economic viability are improving	Some options unproven in commercial applications and real and perceived market risks
Canadian imports	5-10 GW(c)	Economically competitive, but overreliance as a result of constrained domestic alternatives could lead to an excessive dependence in certain regions
Enhanced transmission	Unknown, but probably large(d)	Siting of new lines controversial. Option will be less important as excess generation capacity now available for interregional transfers is eroded by demand growth. However, transmission needs could increase substantially depending on trends in generation technologies
Plant-life	Uncertainty, but probably significant	Total potential uncertain. Defers, but does not eliminate, future supply needs
Nuclear	Additional capacity (beyond 21 GW under construction) very uncertain	Simpler, certified/standardised light-water reactor designs could be developed in the early 1990s. Designs for advanced systems may become competitive after 2000
Conventional coal	As needed, if requirements are not met by more economic options. Coal is currently the mainstay of the industry	Cleaner coal-using technologies are under development and are likely to make a major contribution

Table 4.4 cont'd Electricity supply options and uncertainties

Electricity supply options	Potential economical input to new supply by the year 2000	Reservations and other comments
Gas-fired combustion turbines/combined cycle (w/potential conversion to coal/synfuels)	Depends on future oil/gas prices	Virtually unlimited capacity additions possible independent of economic consideration. Increasingly a a preferred option in utility supply plans due to short lead times and low capital requirements. However, future operating costs may be high and may raise oil/gas use for electricity generation, unless coal/synfuel conversion proves economically feasible.

NOTES:

a) Impact of Demand-Side Management on Future Customer Electric Demand, EPRI report EM-4815-SR (October 1986).

b) Electricity Outlook, EPRI, December 1985; forthcoming study from AES, Industrial Cogeneration, July 1985; Industrial Cogeneration Potential (1980-2000), Dun and Bradstreet (August 1984); Industrial and Commercial Cogeneration, OTA, Feb. 1983.

c) Canadian Power Imports, GAO, April 1986; US International Electricity Trade, EIA, Sept. 1986; Canadian Energy Supply and Demand 1985-2005, National Energy Board, October 1986.

d) ECAR/MAAC Interregional Power Transfer Analyses, ECAR/MAAC Coordinating Group, June 1985.

Figure 4.1 Sources of new electricity generating capacity

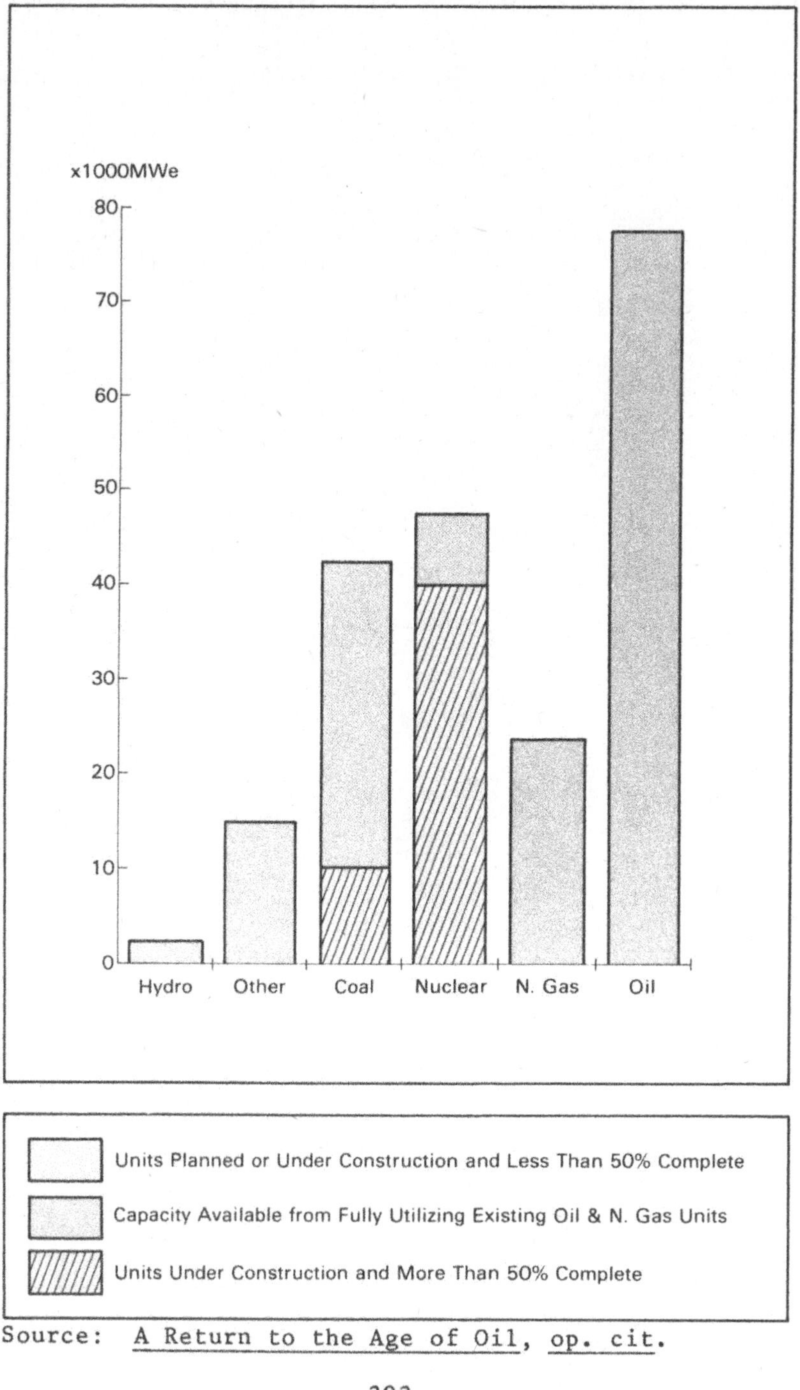

Source: A Return to the Age of Oil, op. cit.